PROLOGUE TO REVOLUTION

NOTE ON THE FRONTISPIECE

The Repeal was one of the most popular English cartoons of the period. The first version appeared in London on March 18, 1766, the day when the act repealing the Stamp Act received the King's signature. Sales were so large that it was pirated by several imitators, and hundreds of copies survive. The version given here was accompanied by the following explanation:

Over the Vault are placed two Skeleton Heads. Their elevation on Poles, and the dates of the two Rebellion Years, sufficiently shew what party they espoused, and in what cause they suffered an ignominious Exit.

The reverend Mr. Anti-Sejanus (who under that signature hackney'd his pen in support of the Stamps) leads the procession as officiating Priest, with the burial service and funeral sermon in his hands.

Next follow two eminent Pillars of the Law [Alexander Wedderburn and Sir Fletcher Norton], supporting two black flags, on which are delineated the Stamps with the White Rose and Thistle interwoved: an expressive design, supposed to have been originally contrived on the 10 of June [birthday of the Pretender]. The significative motto Semper Eadem is preserved, but the Price of the Stamp is changed to three farthings, an important sum taken from the Budget. The numbers 122 and 71 declare the minority which fought under these Banners [the numbers voting against repeal on the final reading in the Commons and on the second reading in the Lords respectively].

Next appears the honourable Mr. George Stamp [Grenville] full of Grief and dispair, carrying his favourite Childs Coffin, Miss Americ Stamp, who was born in 1765 and died hard in 1766.

Immediately after follows the chief Mourner Sejanus [Lord Bute].

Then his Grace of Spitalfields [the Duke of Bedford], and Lord Gawkee [Earl Temple].

After these Jemmy Twitcher [Lord Sandwich], with a Catch, by way of funeral anthem, and by his side his friend and partner Mr. Falconer Donaldson of Halifax [Lord Halifax].

The rear is brought up by two right reverend Fathers of the Church [probably the bishops of Bristol and Gloucester].

These few mourners are seperated from the joyful scene which appears on the River Thames, where three first rate ships are riding, Viz. the Conway, Rockingham and Grafton. Along the opposite Shore, stand open Warehouses for the several goods of different manufactoring towns from which Cargoes are now shipping for America. Among these is a large Case containing the Statue of Mr. Pitt, which is heaving on board a Boat No. 250. there is another boat taking in goods nearer the first Rates, which is No. 105. Those Numbers [the majorities in the Commons and Lords respectively] will ever be held in esteem by the true SONS of LIBERTY.

The Repeal is reproduced by courtesy of the John Carter Brown Library, Brown University. A description of the various states in which it is known can be found in F. G. Stephens and E. Hawkins, Catalogue of Prints and Drawings in the British Museum: Division I, Political and Personal Satires (London, 1883), IV, 468-73.

Prologue to Revolution

Sources and Documents on the
Stamp Act Crisis, 1764-1766

EDITED BY

EDMUND S. MORGAN

W · W · NORTON & COMPANY · INC ·
NEW YORK

DOCUMENTARY PROBLEMS IN EARLY AMERICAN HISTORY

The Great Awakening
Documents on the Revival of Religion, 1740–1745

Edited by Richard L. Bushman

The Glorious Revolution in America
Documents on the Colonial Crisis of 1689

Edited by Michael G. Hall, Lawrence H. Leder, and Michael G. Kammen

Massachusetts, Colony to Commonwealth
Documents on the Formation of Its Constitution, 1775–1780

Edited by Robert J. Taylor

Prologue to Revolution
Sources and Documents on the Stamp Act Crisis, 1764–1766

Edited by Edmund S. Morgan

This volume is published for the Institute of Early American History and Culture at Williamsburg, Virginia. The Institute of Early American History and Culture is sponsored jointly by the College of William and Mary and Colonial Williamsburg, Incorporated.

This edition first published 1973
by arrangement with The University of North Carolina Press

ISBN 0 393 09424 3

Published simultaneously in Canada
by George J. McLeod Limited, Toronto

PRINTED IN THE UNITED STATES OF AMERICA

1 2 3 4 5 6 7 8 9 0

CONTENTS

Chapter IV. THE AMERICAN PRESS

Chapter V. THE BRITISH PRESS

CONTENTS

INTRODUCTION

Aᴺʏᴏɴᴇ ᴡʜᴏ has taught history knows the alarming confidence with which students accept what they read. The printed word can lend credibility to any statement; and the statements in a textbook generally have the sanction not merely of print but also of moderation, a quality often mistaken for objectivity. Students coming to history, as they generally must, through the tidy, pre-digested, simplified moderation of a textbook, can form no conception of the welter of complexities and contradictions that may lie behind the simplest statement of fact.

To overcome the disadvantages of the textbook and bring the student closer to actuality, many teachers have resorted to another approach. They have focused on certain episodes or "problems" which either aroused controversy when they occurred or have aroused it among historians subsequently. The student is presented with contemporary statements of opposing or divergent points of view and must himself make sense out of them by rejecting, reconciling, and interpreting. In some cases he may be assisted, or further confused, by the divergent interpretative statements of historians.

The present volume is in part an application of this method. I have tried to furnish the materials from which a student can formulate his own interpretation of the first great controversy between Great Britain and her colonies. Although there are no supplementary statements by historians, I have offered in each section a number of questions for discussion that may lead the student to the issues over which historians have disagreed.

In these respects the book resembles other sourcebooks or books of problems. I hope, however, that it will have an additional usefulness. The scope is sufficiently limited so that it has been possible to give a much wider documentary coverage than is usual. Although some items are presented simply as representative of different points of view, in the case of certain crucial questions nearly all the relevant materials now extant are reproduced. In examining these questions, the student will have most of the information that has ever been available to historians and more than historians have generally made use of. He will thus be able to assess the answers given in his textbook or in more specialized works. On these questions he can become an expert.

When, for example, he reads a factual summary of what Patrick Henry and the House of Burgesses did about the Stamp Act, he will realize that however confident an author's assertions, there is much about the episode that cannot be known with any degree of certainty. When he reads about the colonists' objections to parliamentary taxation, he will have at hand all the resolutions adopted by the colonial assemblies as well as selections from the public press. It will be possible for him to know more about the colonists' objections than most of the authors who have hitherto written on the subject.

Such an intensive and inclusive examination of the sources will confront the student with the kind of historical problem that is ordinarily met only by scholars: not the problem of judging who was right in a controversy but the more basic problem of determining from the sources what the controversy actually was. What *were* the colonial objections to taxation? How do historians know? If the student has first considered this problem, he will approach the issues themselves with more understanding. What is more, he will approach his textbook and every other secondary work with more understanding. He may recognize that what the textbook says about the Stamp Act is right but not right in the way he had formerly supposed. Having seen some of the complexity beneath the simple statements, he will realize that a textbook necessarily operates at several removes from the facts, that what appear to be statements of fact are often interpretative generalizations.

Obviously it would be impossible for him to probe so far beneath the surface at every point. Even the briefer collections of source problems are no substitute for a continuous narrative and if used without a text are likely to leave the student with no sense of chronology. But if he can plunge into a close study at one or two points, he may emerge with an understanding of historical problems and historical method that no amount of secondary works can give him.

The Stamp Act crisis offers a number of advantages for close study. It was the time when Americans first formulated clearly and extensively their ideas about local and central authority in a representative government, a problem that has not ceased to occupy them ever since. Students encountering the problem in the form that Americans faced in 1765 will not fail to recognize the importance of the issues. Documents for studying the period are abundant enough so that one can form opinions about it with some degree of confidence. Yet on some matters (such as the composition of the Virginia Resolves or Grenville's offer to let the colonies tax themselves) the evidence is so scanty or so conflicting that it is difficult, if not impossible, to reconstruct precisely

what happened. In attempting to do so the student will be grappling with
real problems that historians have not yet fully solved.

I hope that scholars may find the volume useful for the same reasons as
their students. Most of the documents are not readily available elsewhere.
Several have not been printed before, and many more have not been reprinted
since their original publication in newspapers or pamphlets. I have tried,
so far as space permitted, to avoid chopping small segments of a document
out of context, and I have followed the text in the source indicated without
modernizing orthography or punctuation, though I have expanded manuscript
abbreviations.

Since this is a book of documents, I have furnished only brief introductions
to each section. The reader who wishes a more detailed interpretative account may consult Edmund S. and Helen M. Morgan, *The Stamp Act Crisis:
Prologue to Revolution* (Chapel Hill, 1953).

I am grateful to the following individuals and institutions for permission
to print documents in their possession: Mr. M. F. Bond, Clerk of the Records
of the House of Lords, for the letter of Francis Bernard to Lord Halifax,
August 15, 1765; Mr. Edward J. Cronin, Secretary of the Commonwealth of
Massachusetts for the letters of Thomas Hutchinson to Richard Jackson,
August 30, 1765, and to Thomas Pownall, March 8, 1766; Mr. James H.
Easterby and the South Carolina Archives Department for the South Caro-
lina Resolves, November 29, 1765; Mr. William A. Jackson and the Harvard
College Library for the letter of Francis Bernard to Richard Jackson, August
18, 1764; Mr. Paul North Rice and the New York Public Library for the
letter of Thomas Moffat to Joseph Harrison, October 16, 1765; Mr. Stephen
T. Riley and the Massachusetts Historical Society for the letter of Henry
Cruger, Jr., to Aaron Lopez, March 1, 1766; Mr. Fred Shelley and the Mary-
land Historical Society for the letters of Charles Garth to Ringgold, Murdoch,
and Tilghman, February 26 and March 5, 1766; Mr. R. W. Thomas and the
New Haven Colony Historical Society for the letter of Jared Ingersoll to
Thomas Fitch, February 11, 1765; and Mr. R. N. Williams 2nd and the
Historical Society of Pennsylvania for the letter of John Dickinson to William
Pitt, December 21, 1765. I am also indebted to Mr. Malcolm Freiberg and
Mr. David S. Lovejoy for assistance in checking against the original manu-
scripts the letters of Thomas Hutchinson and the Rhode Island Resolves,
September, 1765.

PROLOGUE TO REVOLUTION

CHAPTER I

THE SUGAR ACT

AT THE CLOSE of the Seven Years War in 1763, England was faced with a national debt that had nearly doubled in size as a result of wartime expenditures. Most of the expenditures had been made in America, and it had been decided to keep an army of ten thousand men there to see that the territory acquired from France (Canada and the eastern Mississippi Valley) stayed conquered. No one seems to have questioned the wisdom of this decision, which involved a considerable additional expense for the maintenance of the troops.

In order to pay the bills, England naturally looked to America, where the expenses were incurred. George Grenville in 1763 found that the American customs service was not collecting enough in duties even to cover the costs of operation. He immediately took steps to tighten up enforcement of the existing customs regulations, and in 1764 he secured passage of a new revenue act, usually called the Sugar Act. The act contained two kinds of provisions: alterations in colonial import duties (most notably in the duties on foreign molasses) and new regulations to make smuggling more difficult. It was much longer than the selection (No. 1) given here, but the provisions included are the ones that attracted the greatest attention among the colonists.

The colonists knew of the imminent passage of the act and sent protests both before and after its enactment. Formal protests were drawn up and endorsed by the assemblies of Massachusetts, Rhode Island, Connecticut, New York, Pennsylvania, Virginia, North Carolina, and South Carolina. These were delivered to the royal governor or to agents in London for relay to the proper British authorities. The New York petition to the House of Commons (No. 2) and the three Virginia petitions to the King, the House of Lords, and the House of Commons (No. 3) have been selected for inclusion as samples of the colonial position in 1764.

In reading these statements one should bear in mind that Grenville, at the time when he introduced the Sugar Act in Parliament, suggested the possibility of a future Stamp Act. In framing their protests to the Sugar Act, the colonists also included objections to the threatened stamp tax.

The English answer to the colonial objections was expressed most authoritatively by Thomas Whately, Secretary to the Treasury under Grenville. In a long pamphlet entitled *The Regulations lately Made concerning the Colonies and the Taxes Imposed upon them, Considered* (London, 1765), Whately maintained that the Sugar Act was a beneficial regulation of trade as well as a means of raising revenue. In the concluding passage (No. 4) he considered the question of Parliament's right to raise revenue from the colonies. At the time when it was printed the pamphlet was generally attributed to Grenville himself.

QUESTIONS

1. Did the Sugar Act itself indicate whether it was designed to regulate trade or to raise revenue or both?

2. Did the Sugar Act affect trial by jury?

3. On what grounds did the assemblies of New York and Virginia object to parliamentary taxation?

4. Did they object on grounds that would be applicable to other colonies?

5. Did they acknowledge the right of Parliament to levy external taxes?

6. Did they acknowledge the right of Parliament to regulate trade?

7. What did the Virginia Assembly mean by the phrase "internal Polity and Taxation"?

8. What did the New York Assembly mean by the words "internal Taxes, or Duties paid, for what we consume"?

9. Did Whately's defense of parliamentary taxation rest on basic assumptions different from those exhibited in the colonial objections?

1. The Sugar Act, April 5, 1764

[Danby Pickering, ed., *The Statutes at Large* (Cambridge, 1762-1869), XXVI, 33-51. The Act is designated as 4 George III, c. 15.]

WHEREAS *it is expedient that new provisions and regulations should be established for improving the revenue of this kingdom, and for extending and securing the navigation and commerce between* Great Britain *and your Majesty's dominions in* America, *which, by the peace, have been so happily enlarged: and whereas it is just and necessary, that a revenue be raised, in your Majesty's said domin-* ions in America, *for defraying the expences of defending, protecting, and securing the same; we, your Majesty's most dutiful and loyal subjects, the commons of* Great Britain, *in parliament assembled, being desirous to make some provision, in this present session of parliament, towards raising the said revenue in* America, *have resolved to give and grant unto your Majesty the several rates and duties herein aftermentioned;* and do most humbly beseech your Majesty that it may be enacted; and be it enacted by the King's most excellent majesty, by and with the advice and consent of the lords spiritual and temporal, and commons, in this present parliament assembled, and by the authority of the same, That from and after the twenty ninth day of *September,* one thousand seven hundred and sixty four, there shall be raised, levied, collected, and paid, unto his Majesty, his heirs and successors, for and upon all white or clayed sugars of the produce or manufacture of any colony or plantation in *America,* not under the dominion of his Majesty, his heirs and successors; for and upon indico, and coffee of foreign produce or manufacture; for and upon all wines (except *French* wine;) for and upon all wrought silks, bengals, and stuffs, mixed with silk or herba, of the manufacture of *Persia, China,* or *East India,* and all callico painted, dyed, printed, or stained there; and for and upon all foreign linen cloth called *Cambrick* and *French Lawns,* which shall be imported or brought into any colony or plantation in *America,* which now is, or hereafter may be, under the dominion of his Majesty, his heirs and successors, the several rates and duties following; that is to say,

For every hundred weight avoirdupois of such foreign white or clayed sugars, one pound, two shillings, over and above all other duites imposed by any former act of parliament.

For every pound weight avoirdupois of such foreign indico, six pence.

For every hundred weight avoirdupois of such foreign coffee, which shall be imported from any place, except *Great Britain,* two pounds, nineteen shillings, and nine pence.

For every ton of wine of the growth of the *Madeiras,* or of any other island or place from whence such wine may be lawfully imported, and which shall be so imported from such islands or places, the sum of seven pounds.

For every ton of *Portugal, Spanish,* or any other wine (except *French* wine) imported from *Great Britain,* the sum of ten shillings.

For every pound weight avoirdupois of wrought silks, bengals, and stuffs, mixed with silk or herba, of the manufacture of *Persia, China,* or *East India,* imported from *Great Britain,* two shillings.

For every piece of callico painted, dyed, printed, or stained, in *Persia, China,* or *East India,* imported from *Great Britain,* two shillings and six pence.

For every piece of foreign linen cloth, called *Cambrick,* imported from *Great Britain,* three shillings.

For every piece of *French* lawn imported from *Great Britain,* three shillings.

And after those rates for any greater or lesser quantity of such goods respectively.

II. And it is hereby further enacted by the authority aforesaid, That from and after the said twenty ninth day of *September,* one thousand seven hundred and sixty four, there shall also be raised, levied, collected, and paid, unto his Majesty, his heirs and successors, for and upon all coffee and pimento of the growth and produce of any *British* colony or plantation in *America,* which shall be there laden on board any *British* ship or vessel, to be carried out from thence to any other place whatsoever, except *Great Britain,* the several rates and duties following; that is to say,

III. For every hundred weight avoirdupois of such *British* coffee, seven shillings.

For every pound weight avoirdupois of such *British* pimento, one halfpenny.

And after those rates for any greater or lesser quantity of such goods respectively.

IV. And whereas an act was made in the sixth year of the reign of his late majesty King *George* the Second, intituled, *An act for the better securing and encouraging the trade of his Majesty's sugar colonies in* America, which was to continue in force for five years, to be computed from the twenty fourth day of *June,* one thousand seven hundred and thirty three, and to the end of the then next session of parliament, and which, by several subsequent acts made in the eleventh, the nineteenth, the twenty sixth, and twenty ninth, and the thirty first years of the reign of his said late Majesty, was, from time to time, continued; and, by an act made in the first year of the reign of his present Majesty, was further continued until the end of this present session of parliament; and although the said act hath been found in some degree useful, yet it is highly expedient that the same should be altered, enforced, and made more effectual; but, in consideration of the great distance of several of the said colonies and plantations from this kingdom, it will be proper further to continue the said act for a short space, before any alterations and amendments shall take effect, in order that all persons concerned may have due and proper notice thereof; be it therefore enacted by the authority aforesaid, That the said act made in the sixth year of the reign of his late majesty King *George* the Second intituled, *An act for the better securing and encouraging the trade of his Majesty's sugar colonies in* America, shall be, and the same is hereby further continued, until the thirtieth day of *September,* one thousand seven hundred and sixty four.

V. And be it further enacted by the authority aforesaid, That from the twenty ninth day of *September,* one thousand seven hundred and sixty four, the said act, subject to such alterations and amendments as are herein after contained, shall be, and the same is hereby made perpetual.

VI. And be it further enacted by the authority aforesaid, That in lieu and instead of the rate and duty imposed by the said act upon melasses and syrups, there shall, from and after the said twenty ninth day of *September,* one thousand seven hundred and sixty four, be raised, levied, collected, and paid, unto his Majesty, his heirs and successors, for and upon every gallon of melasses or syrups, being the growth, product, or manufacture, of any colony or plantation in *America,* not under the dominion of his Majesty, his heirs or successors, which shall be imported or brought into any colony or plantation in *America,* which now is, or hereafter may be, under the dominion of his Majesty, his heirs or successors, the sum of three pence. . . .

XXVIII. And it is hereby further enacted by the authority aforesaid, That from and after the twenty ninth day of *September,* one thousand seven hundred and sixty four, no iron, nor any sort of wood, commonly called *Lumber,* as specified in an act passed in the eighth year of the reign of King *George* the First, intituled, *An act for giving further encouragement for the importation of naval stores, and for other purposes therein mentioned,* of the growth, production, or manufacture, of any *British* colony or plantation in *America,* shall be there loaden on board any ship or vessel to be carried from thence, until sufficient bond shall be given, with one surety besides the master of the vessel, to the collector or other principal officer of the customs at the loading port, in a penalty of double the value of the goods, with condition, that the said goods shall not be landed in any part of *Europe* except *Great Britain.* . . .

XLI. And it is hereby further enacted and declared, That from and after the twenty ninth day of *September,* one thousand seven hundred and sixty four, all sums of money granted and imposed by this act, and by an act made in the twenty fifth year of the reign of King *Charles* the Second, intituled, *An act for the encouragement of the* Greenland *and* Eastland *trades, and for the better securing the plantation trade,* as rates or duties; and also all sums of money imposed as penalties or forfeitures, by this or any other act of parliament relating to the customs, which shall be paid, incurred, or recovered, in any of the *British* colonies or plantations in *America;* shall be deemed, and are hereby declared to be sterling money of *Great Britain,* and shall be collected, recovered, and paid, to the amount of the value which such nominal sums bear in *Great Britain;* and that such monies shall and may be received and taken according to the proportion and value of five shillings and six pence the ounce in silver; and that all the forfeitures and penalties inflicted by this or any other act or acts of parliament relating to the trade and revenues of the said *British* colonies or plantations in *America,* which shall be incurred there, shall and may be prosecuted, sued for, and recovered in any court of record, or in any court of admiralty, in the said colonies or plantations where such offence shall be committed, or in any court of vice admiralty which may or shall be appointed over all *America* (which court of admiralty or vice admiralty are hereby respectively authorized and required to proceed, hear, and determine the same) at the election of the informer or prosecutor.

XLII. And it is hereby further enacted, That all penalties and forfeitures so recovered there, under this or any former act of parliament, shall be divided, paid, and applied, as follows; that is to say, after deducting the charges of prosecution from the gross produce thereof, one third part of the net produce shall be paid into the hands of the collector of his Majesty's customs at the port or place where such penalties or forfeitures shall be recovered, for the use of his Majesty, his heirs and successors; one third part to the governor or commander in chief of the said colony or plantation; and the other third part to the person who shall seize, inform, and sue for the same; excepting such seizures as shall be made at sea by the commanders or officers of his Majesty's ships or vessels of war duly authorized to make seizures; one moiety of which seizures, and of the penalties and forfeitures recovered thereon, first deducting the charges of prosecu-

tion from the gross produce thereof, shall be paid as aforesaid to the collector of his Majesty's customs, to and for the use of his Majesty, his heirs and successors, and the other moiety to him or them who shall seize, inform, and sue for the same; any law, custom, or usage, to the contrary notwithstanding; subject nevertheless to such distribution of the produce of the seizures so made at sea, as well with regard to the moiety herein before granted to his Majesty, his heirs and successors, as with regard to the other moiety given to the seizor or prosecutor, as his Majesty, his heirs and successors, shall think fit to order and direct by any order or orders of council, or by any proclamation or proclamations, to be made for that purpose.

XLIII. Provided always, and it is hereby further enacted by the authority aforesaid, That if the produce of any seizure made in *America,* shall not be sufficient to answer the expences of condemnation and sale; or if, upon the trial of any seizure of any ship or goods, a verdict or sentence shall be given for the claimant, in either of those cases, the charges attending the seizing and prosecuting such ship or goods shall and may, with the consent and approbation of any four of the commissioners of his Majesty's customs, be paid out of any branch of the revenue of customs arising in any of the *British* colonies or plantations in *America;* any thing in this or any other act of parliament to the contrary notwithstanding.

XLIV. And it is hereby further enacted by the authority aforesaid, That from and after the said twenty ninth day of *September,* one thousand seven hundred and sixty four, no person shall be admitted to enter a claim to any ship or goods seized in pursuance of this or any other act of parliament, and prosecuted in any of the *British* colonies or plantations in *America,* until sufficient security be first given, by persons of known ability, in the court where such seizure is prosecuted, in the penalty of sixty pounds, to answer the costs and charges of prosecution; and, in default of giving such security, such ship or goods shall be adjudged to be forfeited, and shall be condemned.

XLV. And it is hereby further enacted by the authority aforesaid, That from and after the twenty ninth day of *September,* one thousand seven hundred and sixty four, if any ship or goods shall be seized for any cause of forfeiture, and any dispute shall arise whether the customs and duties for such goods have been paid, or the same have been lawfully imported or exported, or concerning the growth, product, or manufacture, of such goods, or the place from whence such goods were brought, then, and in such cases, the proof thereof shall lie upon the owner or claimer of such ship or goods, and not upon the officer who shall seize or stop the same; any law, custom, or usage, to the contrary notwithstanding.

XLVI. And be it further enacted by the authority aforesaid, That from and after the twenty ninth day of *September,* one thousand seven hundred and sixty four, in case any information shall be commenced and brought to trial in *America,* on account of any seizure of any ship or goods as forfeited by this or any other act of parliament relating to his Majesty's customs, wherein a verdict or sentence shall be given for the claimer thereof; and

it shall appear to the judge or court before whom the same shall be tried, that there was a probable cause of seizure, the judge or court before whom the same shall be tried shall certify on the record or other proceedings, that there was a probable cause for the prosecutors seizing the said ship or goods; and, in such case, the defendant shall not be intitled to any costs of suit whatsoever; nor shall the persons who seized the said ship or goods, be liable to any action, or other suit or prosecution, on account of such seizure: and in case any action, or other suit or prosecution, shall be commenced and brought to trial against any person or persons whatsoever, on account of the seizing any such ship or goods, where no information shall be commenced or brought to trial to condemn the same, and a verdict or sentence shall be given upon such action or prosecution against the defendant or defendants, if the court or judge before whom such action or prosecution, shall certify in like manner as aforesaid that there was a probable cause for such seizure, then the plaintiff, besides his ship or goods so seized, or the value thereof, shall not be intitled to above two pence damages, nor to any costs of suit; nor shall the defendant in such prosecution be fined above one shilling.

2. The New York Petition to the House of Commons, October 18, 1764

[*Journal of the Votes and Proceedings of the General Assembly* (New York, 1766), II, 776-79.]

To the Honourable the Knights, Citizens and Burgesses, representing the Commons of Great-Britain, *in Parliament assembled.*

The Representation and Petition of the General-Assembly of the Colony of New-York.

Most humbly Shew,

That from the Year 1683, to this Day,

there have been three Legislative Branches in this Colony; consisting of the Governor and Council appointed by the Crown, and the Representatives chosen by the People, who, besides the Power of making Laws for the Colony, have enjoyed the Right of Taxing the Subject for the Support of the Government.

Under this Political Frame, the Colony

was settled by Protestant Emigrants from several Parts of *Europe,* and more especially from *Great-Britain* and *Ireland:* And as it was originally modelled with the Intervention of the Crown, and not excepted to by the Realm of *England* before, nor by *Great-Britain,* since the Union, the Planters and Settlers conceived the strongest Hopes, that the Colony had gained a civil Constitution, which, so far at least as the Rights and Privileges of the People were concerned, would remain permanent, and be transmitted to their latest Posterity.

It is therefore with equal Concern and Surprize, that they have received Intimations of certain Designs lately formed, if possible, to induce the Parliament of *Great-Britain,* to impose Taxes upon the Subjects *here,* by Laws to be passed *there;* and as we who have the Honour to represent them, conceive that this Innovation, will greatly affect the Interest of the Crown and the Nation, and reduce the Colony to absolute Ruin; it became our indispensible Duty, to trouble you with a seasonable Representation of the Claim of our Constituents, to an Exemption from the Burthen of all Taxes not granted by themselves, and their Foresight of the tragical Consequences of an Adoption of the contrary Principle, to the Crown, the Mother Country, themselves and their Posterity.

Had the Freedom from all Taxes not granted by ourselves been enjoyed as a *Privilege,* we are confident the Wisdom and Justice of the *British* Parliament, would rather establish than destroy it, unless by our abuse of it, the Forfeiture was justly incurred; but his Majesty's Colony of *New-York,* can not only defy the whole World to impeach their Fidelity, but appeal to all the Records of their past Transactions, as well for the fullest Proof of their steady Affection to the Mother Country, as for their strenuous Efforts to support the Government, and advance the general Interest of the whole *British* Empire.

It has been their particular Misfortune, to be always most exposed to the Incursions of the *Canadians,* and the more barbarous Irruptions of the Savages of the Desart, as may appear by all the Maps of this Country; and in many Wars we have suffered an immense Loss both of Blood and Treasure, to repel the Foe, and maintain a valuable Dependency upon the *British* Crown.

On no Occasion can we be justly reproached for with-holding a necessary Supply, our Taxes have been equal to our Abilities, and confessed to be so by the Crown; for Proof of which we refer to the Speeches of our Governors in all Times of War; and though we remember with great Gratitude, that in those grand and united Struggles, which were lately directed for the Conquest of *Canada,* Part of our Expences was reimbursed, yet we cannot suppress the Remark, that our Contribution surpassed our Strength, even in the Opinion of the Parliament, who under that Conviction, thought it but just to take off Part of the Burthen, to which we had loyally and voluntarily submitted; in a Word, if there is any Merit in facilitating on all Occasions, the publick Measures in the remote Extremes of the national Dominion, and in preserving untainted Loyalty and chearful Obedience, it is ours; and (with Submission) unabused, nay more, well improved Privileges cannot, ought not, to be taken away from any People.

But an Exemption from the Burthen of ungranted, involuntary Taxes, must be the grand Principle of every free State.— Without such a Right vested in themselves, exclusive of all others, there can be no Liberty, no Happiness, no Security; it is inseparable from the very Idea of Property, for who can call that his own, which may be taken away at the Pleasure of another? And so evidently does this appear to be the natural Right of Mankind, that even conquered tributary States, though subject to the Payment of a fixed periodical Tribute, never were reduced to so abject and forlorn a Condition, as to yield to all the Burthens which their Conquerors might at any future Time think fit to impose. The Tribute paid, the Debt was discharged; and the Remainder they could call their own.

And if conquered Vassals upon the Principle even of *natural Justice,* may claim a Freedom from Assessments unbounded and unassented to, without which they would sustain the Loss of every Thing, and Life itself become intolerable, with how much Propriety and Boldness may we proceed to inform the Commons of *Great-Britain,* who, to their distinguished Honour, have in all Ages asserted the Liberties of Mankind, that the People of this Colony, inspired by the Genius of their Mother Country, nobly disdain the thought of claiming that Exemption as *a Privilege.*— They found it on a Basis more honourable, solid and stable; they challenge it, and glory in it as their Right. That Right their Ancestors enjoyed in *Great-Britain* and *Ireland;* their Descendants returning to those Kingdoms, enjoy it again: And that it may be exercised by his Majesty's Subjects at Home, and justly denied to those who submitted to Poverty, Barbarian Wars, Loss of Blood, Loss of Money, personal Fatigues, and ten Thousand unutterable Hardships, to enlarge the Trade, Wealth, and Dominion of the Nation; or, to speak with the most unexceptionable Modesty, that when *as Subjects,* all have equal Merit; a Fatal, nay the most odious Discrimination should nevertheless be made between them, no Sophistry can recommend to the Sober, impartial Decision of common Sense.

Our Constituents exult in that glorious Model of Government, of which your Hon. House is so essential a Part; and earnestly pray the Almighty Governor of all, long to support the due Distribution of the Power of the Nation in the three great Legislative Branches. But the Advocates for divesting us of the Right to tax ourselves, would by the Success of their Machination, render the Devolution of all civil Power upon the *Crown alone,* a Government more favourable, and therefore more eligible to these *American* Dependences. The supreme Ruler in a Monarchy, even in a despotic Monarchy, will naturally consider his Relation to be, what it is, equal to all his good Subjects: And equal Dispensation of Favours will be the natural Consequence of those Views; and the Increase of mutual Affection must be productive of an Increase of the Felicity of *all.* But no History can furnish an Instance of a Constitution to permit one Part of a Dominion to be taxed by another, and that too in Effect, but by a Branch of that other Part; who in all Bills for public Aids, suffer not the least Alteration.— And if such an absurd and unequal Constitution should be adopted, who, that considers the natural Reluctance of Mankind to burthens, and their Inclination to cast them upon the Shoulders of others, cannot foresee, that while the People on one Side of the *Atlantic,* enjoy an Exemption from the Load, those on the other, must submit to the most unsupportable Oppression and Tyranny.

Against these Evils, the Indulgence of the present Parliament, of which we have had such large Experience, cannot provide, if the grand Right to tax ourselves is invaded. Depressed by the Prospect of an endless Train of the most distressing Mischiefs, naturally attendant upon such an Innovation, his Majesty's *American* Subjects, will think it no inconsiderable Augmentation of their Misery, that the Measure itself implies the most severe and unmerited Censure, and is urged, as far as they are acquainted, by no good Reasons of State.

They are unconscious of any Conduct, that brings the least Imputation upon their Love and Loyalty, and whoever has accused them, has abused both the Colonies and their Mother Country; more faithful Subjects his Majesty has not, in any Part of his Dominions, nor *Britain* more submissive and affectionate Sons.

And if our Contributions to the Support of the Government upon this Continent, or for the Maintenance of an Army, to awe and subdue the Savages should be thought necessary, why shall it be presumed, without a Trial, that we more than others, will refuse to hearken to a just Requisition from the Crown? To Requisitions for Aids salutary to our own Interests? Or why should a more incorrigible and unreasonable Spirit be imputed to us, than to the Parliament of *Ireland,* or any other of his Majesty's Subjects?

Left to the Enjoyment of our antient Rights, the Government will be truly informed when a Tax is necessary, and of the Abilities of the People; and there will be an equitable Partition of the Burthen. And as the publick Charges will necessarily increase with the Increase of the Country, and the Augmentation or Reduction of the Force kept up, be regulated by the Power and Temper of our barbarian Enemy, the Necessity for continuing the present Model must appear to be most strongly inforced.— At the remote Distance of the *British* Commons from the sequestered Shades of the interior Parts of this Desert, false Intelligence of the State of the *Indians* may be given; whereas the Vicinity of the Colonies will enable them, not only, to detect all false Alarms, and check all fraudulent Accounts, but urge them by the never failing Motive of Self-Preservation, to oppose any hostile Attempts upon their Borders.

Nor will the Candour of the Commons of *Great-Britain,* construe our Earnestness to maintain this Plea, to arise from a Desire of Independency upon the supreme Power of the Parliament. Of so extravagant a Disregard to our own Interests we cannot be guilty.— From what other Quarter can we hope for Protection? We reject the Thought with the utmost Abhorrence; and a perfect Knowledge of this Country will afford the fullest Proof, that nothing in our Temper can give the least Ground for such a Jealousy.

The peaceable and invariable Submission of the Colonies, for a Century past, forbids the Imputation, or proves it a Calumny.— What can be more apparent, than that the State which exercises a Sovereignty in Commerce, can draw all the Wealth of its Colonies into its own Stock? And has not the whole Trade of *North-America,* that growing Magazine of Wealth, been, from the Beginning, directed, restrained, and prohibited at the sole Pleasure of the Parliament? And whatever some may pretend, his Majesty's American Subjects are far from a Desire to invade the just Rights of *Great-Britain,* in all commercial Regulations. They humbly conceive, that a very manifest Distinction presents itself, which, while it leaves to the Mother Country an incontestible Power, to give Laws for the Advancement of her own Commerce, will, at the same Time, do no Violence to the Rights of the Plantations.

The Authority of the Parliament of *Great-Britain,* to model the Trade of the whole Empire, so as to subserve the Interest of her own, we are ready to recognize in the most extensive and positive Terms. Such a Preference is naturally founded upon her Superiority, and indissolubly connected with the Principle of Self-Preservation.— And therefore, to assign one Instance, instead of many, the Colonies cannot, would not ask for a Licence to import woolen Manufactures from *France;* or to go into the most lucrative Branches of Commerce, in the least Degree incompatible with the Trade and Interest of *Great-Britain.*

But a Freedom to drive all Kinds of Traffick in a Subordination to, and not inconsistent with, the *British* Trade; and an Exemption from all Duties in such a Course of Commerce, is humbly claimed by the Colonies, as the most essential of all the Rights to which they are intitled, as Colonists from, and connected, in the common Bond of Liberty, with the un-inslaved Sons of *Great-Britain*.

For, with Submission, since all Impositions, whether they be internal Taxes, or Duties paid, for what we consume, equally diminish the Estates upon which they are charged; what avails it to any People, by which of them they are impoverished? Every Thing will be given up to preserve Life; and though there is a Diversity in the Means, yet, the whole Wealth of a Country may be as effectually drawn off, by the Exaction of Duties, as by any other Tax upon their Estates.

And therefore, the General Assembly of *New-York,* in Fidelity to their Constituents, cannot but express the most earnest Supplication, that the Parliament will charge our Commerce with no other Duties, than a necessary Regard to the particular Trade of *Great-Britain,* evidently demands; but leave it to the legislative Power of the Colony, to impose all other Burthens upon it's own People, which the publick Exigences may require.

Latterly, the Laws of Trade seem to have been framed without an Attention to this fundamental Claim.

Permit us, also, in Defence of our Attachment to the Mother Country, to add, what your Merchants (to whom we boldly make the Appeal) know to be an undoubted Truth; that this Continent contains some of the *most useful* of her Subjects.— Such is the Nature of our Produce, that all we acquire is less than sufficient to purchase what we want of your Manufactures; and, be the Policy of your Commerce what it will, all our Riches must flow into *Great-Britain.*— Immense have been our Contributions to the National Stock.— Our Staple, Industry, Trade and Wealth, all conduce to the particular Advantage of our fellow Subjects there.— The natural State of this Country, necessarily forms the Ballance of Trade in her Favour.— Her growing Opulence must elevate her above all Fear and Jealousy of these Dependences. How much stronger then the

Reasons for leaving us free from ungranted Impositions? Whoever will give full Scope to his Meditations on this Topic, will see it the Interest of *Great-Britain,* to adopt the Maxim, that her own Happiness is most intimately connected with the Freedom, Ease and Prosperity of her Colonies: The more extensive our Traffick, the Greater her Gains; we carry all to her Hive, and consume the Returns; and we are content with any constitutional Regulation that inriches her, though it impoverishes ourselves. But a fuller Display of these Principles, being prepared by our Merchants, to be laid before the honourable House, at the last Sitting, we shall only beg Leave to add, that any Information, repugnant to this Account of the low State of our Traffick, must proceed from partial, or incompetent Witnesses; who may have formed their Estimate of the Wealth of the Colony, during the late War, when the *French* and *Spanish West-Indies,* were laid open to our Trade, and those immense Profits acquired there, for the Manufactures of *Great-Britain* and *Ireland,* flowed into the Colonies, and Luxury advanced upon us slower than our Gains.— But Trade being now confined to it's old Channels, and indeed still more restricted, and the late acquired Cash, remitted home for necessary Cloathing, other very indifferent Appearances begin to take place, and the *British* Merchants are, or will soon be convinced to their Sorrow, that our Splendor was not supported by solid Riches.

The honourable House will permit us to observe next, that the Act of the last Session of Parliament, inhibiting all Intercourse between the Continent and the foreign Sugar Colonies, will prove equally detrimental to us and *Great-Britain.*— *That* Trade, gave a value to a vast, but now alas unsaleable Staple, which being there converted into Cash and Merchandize, made necessary Remittances for the *British* Manufactures we consumed:— The same Law contains a Clause unfriendly to the Linen Manufactory in *Ireland,* for the Restraint upon the Exportation of Lumber to that Kingdom, prevents even our dunnaging the Flax-Seed Casks sent there with Staves.— And when we consider the Wisdom of our Ancestors in contriving Trials by Juries, we cannot stifle our Regret, that the Laws of Trade in general, change the Current of Justice from the common Law, and subject Controversies of the utmost Importance to the Decisions of the Vice-Admiralty Courts, who proceed not according the old wholesom Laws of the Land, nor are always filled with Judges of approved Knowledge and Integrity.— To this Objection, the aforementioned Statute will at first View appear to be so evidently open, that we shall content ourselves with barely suggesting, that the amazing Confidence it reposes in the Judges, gives great Grief to his Majesty's *American* Subjects; and pass on to a few Remarks on that other Law of the same Session, which renders our Paper Money no legal Tender.

The Use of this Sort of Currency in procuring a speedy Supply on Emergences, all the Colonies have often experienced.— We have had Recourse to this Expedient in every War, since the Reign of King *William* the Third; and without it we could not have co-operated so vigorously in the Reduction of *Canada,* that grand stroke which secured to *Great-Britain,* the immense Dominion of the Continent of *North-America.* We had no other Alternative but *that,* or the taking up Money upon Loan, Lenders could not have been easily found, and if they were, the Interest upon all the Sums raised in that Way, would have exceeded our Ability now to discharge. Happy for us, therefore, that we fell upon the Project of giving a Credit to Paper, which was always supported by seasonable Taxes on our Estates; the Currency of the Bills being prolonged only till we were able to burn up the Quantity from Time to Time emitted.— Our Laws, or the Copies transmitted to the Plantation Office, will evince that of the numerous Emissions we have made since the first, which was on the 8th of *June,* 1709, all were for the urgent Service of the Crown.— One Instance is so recent, and shews the Necessity of the Continuation of such a Power in the Colonies, in so striking a Point of Light, that it deserves more particular Notice. The Operations of the Year 1759, were nearly at a Stand for want of Money. The military Chest being exhausted, the General was alarmed, and seeing no other Method to ward of the impending Disaster, was obliged to ask the Colony for a Loan of *One Hundred and Fifty Thousand Pounds:* We immediately gratified his Request. —Such was our Concern for the publick Weal! We wish his Majesty's Service may suffer no Impediment, by this new Restraint in an Article which has been of so much Utility.— The Traffick of the Colony certainly will, for want of a competent Medium; and on that Account, and in behalf of those miserable Debtors, whose Estates, through the Scarcity of legal Cash, must be extended by Executions, and hastily sold beneath their true Value, to the Ruin of many Families, permit us to implore your tender Commiseration.

The General Assembly of this Colony have no desire to derogate from the Power of the Parliament of *Great-Britain;* but they cannot avoid deprecating the Loss of such Rights as they have hitherto enjoyed, Rights established in the first Dawn of our Constitution, founded upon the most substantial Reasons, confirmed by invariable Usage, conducive to the best Ends; never abused to bad Purposes, and with the Loss of which Liberty, Property, and all the Benefits of Life, tumble into Insecurity and Ruin: Rights, the Deprivation of which, will dispirit the People, abate their Industry, discourage Trade, introduce Discord, Poverty and Slavery; or, by depopulating the Colonies, turn a vast, fertile, prosperous Region, into a dreary Wilderness; impoverish *Great-*

Britain, and shake the Power and Independancy of the most opulent and flourishing Empire in the World.

All which your Petitioners (who repose the highest Confidence in your Wisdom and Justice) humbly pray, may be now taken into your seasonable Consideration, and such Measures pursued, as the

Event may prove to have been concerted for the Common-Weal, of all the Subjects of *Great-Britain,* both at home and abroad.

By Order of the General Assembly,
Wm. Nicoll, *Speaker.*

Assembly-Chamber,
City of New-York,
Oct. 18, 1764.

3. The Virginia Petitions to the King and Parliament, December 18, 1764

A. THE PETITION TO THE KING

[J. P. Kennedy, ed., *Journals of the House of Burgesses of Virginia, 1761-1765* (Richmond, 1907), 302.]

To the King's Most Excellent Majesty. Most gracious Sovereign,

We your Majesty's dutiful and loyal Subjects, the Council and Burgesses of your ancient Colony and Dominion of *Virginia,* now met in General Assembly, beg Leave to assure your Majesty of our firm and inviolable Attachment to your sacred Person and Government; and as your faithful Subjects here have at all Times been zealous to demonstrate this Truth, by a ready Compliance with the Royal Requisitions during the late War, by which a heavy and oppressive Debt of near Half a Million hath been incurred, so at this Time they implore Permission to approach the Throne with humble Confidence, and to intreat that your Majesty will be graciously pleased to protect your People of this Colony in the Enjoyment of their ancient and inestimable Right of being governed by such Laws respecting their internal Polity and Taxation as are

derived from their own Consent, with the Approbation of their Sovereign or his Substitute: A Right which as Men, and Descendents of *Britons,* they have ever quietly possessed since first by Royal Permission and Encouragement they left the Mother Kingdom to extend its Commerce and Dominion.

Your Majesty's dutiful Subjects of *Virginia* most humbly and unanimously hope that this invaluable Birthright, descended to them from their Ancestors, and in which they have been protected by your Royal Predecessors, will not be suffered to receive an Injury under the Reign of your Sacred Majesty, already so illustriously distinguished by your gracious Attention to the Liberties of the People.

That your Majesty may long live to make Nations happy is the ardent Prayer of your faithful Subjects, the Council and Burgesses of *Virginia.*

B. THE MEMORIAL TO THE HOUSE OF LORDS

[Kennedy, ed., *Journals of the House of Burgesses of Virginia, 1761-1765,* 302.]

To the Right Honourable the Lords Spiritual and Temporal in Parliament assembled: The Memorial of the Council and Burgesses of *Virginia,* now met in General Assembly,

Humbly represents,

That your Memorialists hope on Application to your Lordships, the fixed and hereditary Guardians of *British* Liberty, will not be thought improper at this Time, when Measures are proposed subversive, as they conceive, of that Freedom which all Men, especially those who derive their Constitution from *Britain,* have a Right to enjoy; and they flatter themselves that your Lordships will not look upon them as Objects so unworthy your Attention as to regard any Impropriety in the Form or Manner of their Application, for your Lordships Protection of their just and undoubted Rights as *Britons.*

It cannot be Presumption in your Memorialists to call themselves by this distinguished Name, since they are descended from *Britons* who left their native Country to extend its Territory and Dominion, and who happily for *Britain,* and as your Memorialists once thought for themselves too, effected this Purpose. As our Ancestors brought with them every Right and Privilege they could with Justice claim in their Mother Kingdom, their Descendants may conclude they cannot be deprived of those Rights without Injustice.

Your Memorialists conceive it to be a fundamental Principle of the *British* Constitution, without which Freedom can no Where exist, that the People are not subject to any Taxes but such as are laid on them by their own Consent, or by those who are legally appointed to represent them: Property must become too precarious for the Genius of a free People which can be taken from them at the Will of others, who cannot know what Taxes such People can bear, or the easiest Mode of raising them; and who are not under that Restraint, which is the greatest Security against a burthensome Taxation, when the Representatives themselves must be affected by every Tax imposed on the People.

Your Memorialists are therefore led into an humble Confidence that your Lordships will not think any Reason sufficient to support such a Power in the *British* Parliament, where the Colonies cannot be represented; a Power never before constitutionally assumed, and which if they

have a Right to exercise on any Occasion must necessarily establish this melancholy Truth, that the Inhabitants of the Colonies are the Slaves of *Britons,* from whom they are descended, and from whom they might expect every Indulgence that the Obligations of Interest and Affection can entitle them to.

Your Memorialists have been invested with the Right of taxing their own People from the first Establishment of a regular Government in the Colony, and Requisitions have been constantly made to them by their Sovereigns on all Occasions when the Assistance of the Colony was thought necessary to preserve the *British* Interest in America; from whence they must conclude they cannot now be deprived of a Right they have so long enjoyed, and which they have never forfeited.

The Expenses incurred during the last War, in Compliance with the Demands on this Colony by our late and present most gracious Sovereigns, have involved us in a Debt of near Half a Million; a Debt not likely to decrease under the continued Expense we are at in providing for the Security of the People against the Incursions of our savage Neighbours, at a Time when the low state of our Staple Commodity, the total Want of Specie, and the late Restrictions upon the Trade of the Colonies, render the Circumstances of the People extremely distressful, and which, if Taxes are accumulated upon them by the *British* Parliament, will make them truly deplorable.

Your Memorialists cannot suggest to themselves any Reason why they should not still be trusted with the Property of their People, with whose Abilities, and the least burthensome Mode of taxing (with great Deference to the superior Wisdom of Parliament) they must be best acquainted.

Your Memorialist hope they shall not be suspected of being actuated on this Occasion by any Principles but those of the purest Loyalty and Affection as they always endeavoured by their Conduct to demonstrate that they consider their Connexions with *Great Britain,* the Seat of Liberty, as their greatest Happiness.

The Duty they owe to themselves and their Posterity lays your Memorialists under the Necessity of endeavouring to establish their Constitution upon its proper Foundation; and they do most humbly pray your Lordships to take this Subject into your Consideration with the Attention that is due to the Well being of the Colonies, on which the Prosperity of *Great Britain* does in a great Measure depend.

C. THE REMONSTRANCE TO THE HOUSE OF COMMONS

[Kennedy, ed., *Journals of the House of Burgesses of Virginia, 1761-1765,* 303-4.]

To the Honourable the Knights, Citizens, and Burgesses of *Great Britain,* in Parliament assembled:

The Remonstrance of the Council and Burgesses of *Virginia.*

It appearing by the printed Votes of the House of Commons of *Great Britain* in Parliament assembled that in a Committee of the whole House, the 17th Day of *March* last, it was resolved that towards defending, protecting, and securing the *British* Colonies and Plantations in *America,* it may be proper to charge certain Stamp Duties in the said Colonies and Plantations; and it being apprehended that the same Subject, which was then declined, may be resumed and further pursued in a succeeding Session, the Council and Burgesses of *Virginia,* met in General Assembly, judge it their indispensable Duty, in a respectful Manner, but with decent Firmness, to remonstrate against such a Measure, that at least a cession of those Rights, which in their Opinion must be infringed by that Procedure, may not be inferred from their Silence, at so important a Crisis.

They conceive it is essential to *British* Liberty that Laws imposing Taxes on the People ought not to be made without the Consent of Representatives chosen by themselves; who, at the same Time that they are acquainted with the Circumstances of their Constituents, sustain a Proportion of the Burthen laid on them. This Privilege, inherent in the Persons who discovered and settled these Regions, could not be renounced or forfeited by their Removal hither, not as Vagabonds or Fugitives, but licensed and encouraged by their Prince and animated with a laudable Desire of enlarging the *British* Dominion, and extending its Commerce: On the contrary, it was secured to them and their Descendants, with all other Rights and Immunities of *British* Subjects, by a Royal Charter, which hath been invariably recognised and confirmed by his Majesty and his Predecessors in their Commissions to the several Governours, granting a Power, and prescribing a Form of Legislation; according to which, Laws for the Administration of Justice, and for the Welfare and good Government of the Colony, have been hitherto enacted by the Governour, Council, and General Assembly, and to them Requisitions and Applications for Supplies have been directed by the Crown. As an Instance of the Opinion which former Sovereigns entertained of these Rights and Privileges, we beg Leave to refer to three Acts of the General Assembly passed in the 32d Year of the Reign of King Charles II (one of which is entitled *An Act for raising a Publick Revenue for the better Support of the Government of his Majesty's Colony of* Virginia, imposing several Duties for that Purpose) which they thought absolutely necessary, were prepared in *England,* and sent over by their then Governour, the Lord *Culpeper,* to be passed by the General Assembly, with a full Power to give the Royal Assent thereto; and which were accordingly passed, after several

Amendments were made to them here: Thus tender was his Majesty of the Rights of his *American* Subjects; and the Remonstrants do not discern by what Distinction they can be deprived of that sacred Birthright and most valuable Inheritance by their Fellow Subjects, nor with what Propriety they can be taxed or affected in their Estates by the Parliament, wherein they are not, and indeed cannot, constitutionally be represented.

And if it were proper for the Parliament to impose Taxes on the Colonies at all, which the Remonstrants take Leave to think would be inconsistent with the fundamental Principles of the Constitution, the Exercise of that Power at this Time would be ruinous to *Virginia,* who exerted herself in the late War it is feared beyond her Strength, insomuch that to redeem the Money granted for that Exigence her People are taxed for several Years to come: This, with the large Expenses incurred for defending the Frontiers against the restless *Indians,* who have infested her as much since the Peace as before, is so grievous that an Increase of the Burthen will be intolerable; especially as the People are very greatly distressed already from the Scarcity of circulating Cash amongst them, and from the little Value of their Staple at the *British* Markets.

And it is presumed that adding to that Load which the Colony now labours under will not be more oppressive to her People than destructive of the Interests of *Great Britain:* For the Plantation Trade, confined as it is to the Mother Country, hath been a principal Means of multiplying and enriching her Inhabitants; and, if not too much discouraged, may prove an inexhaustible Source of Treasure to the Nation. For Satisfaction in this Point, let the present State of the *British* Fleets and Trade be compared with what they were before the Settlement of the Colonies; and let it be considered that whilst Property in Land may be acquired on very easy Terms, in the vast uncultivated Territory of *North America,* the Colonists will be mostly, if not wholly, employed in Agriculture; whereby the Exportation of their Commodities of *Great Britain,* and the Consumption of their Manufactures supplied from thence, will be daily increasing. But this most desirable Connexion between *Great Britain* and her Colonies, supported by such a happy Intercourse of reciprocal Benefits as is continually advancing the Prosperity of both, must be interrupted, if the People of the latter, reduced to extreme Poverty, should be compelled to manufacture those Articles they have been hitherto furnished with from the former.

From these Considerations, it is hoped that the Honourable House of Commons will not prosecute a Measure which those who may suffer under it cannot but look upon as fitter for Exiles driven from their native Country after ignominiously forfeiting her Favours and Protection, than for the Prosperity of *Britons* who have at all Times been forward to demonstrate all due Reverence to the Mother Kingdom, and are so instrumental in promoting her Glory and Felicity; and that *British* Patriots will never consent to the Exercise of anticonstitutional Power, which even in this remote Corner may be dangerous in its Example to the interiour Parts of the *British* Empire, and will certainly be detrimental to its Commerce.

4. The English Defense

[Thomas Whately, *The Regulations lately Made concerning the Colonies and the Taxes Imposed upon Them, Considered* (London, 1765), 100-14.]

As to the Revenue which the new Impositions will produce, I suppose it is very difficult, if not impossible to form any Calculation of its Amount: I will not even hazard a Conjecture upon it, as I can not presume that I should be right;

and I should be sorry to be wrong. Thus far however may be safely affirmed, that Duties so low, and now first laid, will not at present contribute largely to the Exigencies of the Public; for inconsiderable as they are, the Payment of them will be often avoided by Frauds and Subtilties, which no Penetration can foresee, and Experience only can discover and prevent. On the other hand, they will be an improving Revenue; because they are laid upon numerous Articles of general Consumption among an encreasing People; and if not productive of a great Fund immediately, will be at least a wide Foundation for a considerable future Revenue; but upon no Calculation can it be supposed to be equal to the Demand that must be made upon the Colonies; and therefore a further Tax has been proposed; it has been even resolved by a Vote of the House of Commons, that *it may be proper to charge certain Stamp Duties in the Plantations;* and here the Legislature stoped last Sessions out of Tenderness to the Colonies. A Stamp Duty, tho' often used in the Plantations for the Purposes of their own Government, has never been imposed there by Authority of Parliament, and time has been therefore very properly allowed, to enquire whether it will be attended with any Inconveniences, and to provide Expedients of Prevention or Remedy; but I believe the more it is examined, so much the more clearly will it appear, that this Mode of Taxation is the easiest, the most equal and the most certain that can be chosen; The Duty falls chiefly upon Property; but it is spread lightly over a great Variety of Subjects, and lies heavy upon none: The Act executes itself by annulling the Instruments that have not paid the small Sums they are charged with; and the Tax thus supported and secured, is collected by few Officers, without Expence to the Crown, or Oppression on the People.

The Revenue that may be raised by the Duties which have been already, or by these if they should be hereafter imposed, are all equally applied by Parliament, *towards defraying the necessary Expences of defending, protecting, and securing, the British Colonies and Plantations in America:* Not that on the one hand an *American* Revenue might not have been applied to different Purposes; or on the other, that *Great Britain* is to contribute nothing to these: The very Words of the Act of Parliament and of the Resolution of the House of Commons imply, that the whole of the Expence is not to be charged upon the Colonies: They are under no Obligation to provide for this or any other particular national Expence; neither can they claim any Exemption from general Burthens; but being a part of the *British* Dominions, are to share all necessary Services with the rest. This in *America* does indeed first claim their Attention: They are immediately, they are principally concerned in it; and the Inhabitants of their Mother-Country would justly and loudly complain, if after all their Efforts for the Benefit of the Colonies, when every Point is gained, and every wish accomplished, they, and they alone should be called upon still to answer every additional Demand, that the Preservation of these Advantages, and the Protection of the Colonies from future Dangers, may occasion: *Great Britain* has a Right at all Times, she is under a Necessity, upon this Occasion, to demand their Assistance; but still she requires it in the Manner most suitable to their Circumstances; for by appropriating this Revenue towards the Defence and Security of the Provinces where it is raised, the Produce of it is kept in the Country, the People are not deprived of the Circulation of what Cash they have amongst themselves, and thereby the severest Oppression of an *American* Tax, that of draining the Plantations of Money which they can so ill spare, is avoided. What Part they ought to bear of the national Expence, that is necessary for their Protection, must depend upon their Ability, which is not yet sufficiently known: to the whole they are certainly unequal, that would include all the military and all the naval Establishment, all Fortifications which it may be thought proper to erect, the Ordnance and Stores that must be furnished, and the Provisions which it is necessary to supply; but surely a Part of this great Disbursement, a large Proportion at least of some particular Branches of it, cannot be an intolerable Burthen upon such a Number of Subjects, upon a Territory so extensive, and upon the Wealth which they collectively possess. As to the Quota which each Individual must pay, it will be difficult to persuade the Inhabitants of this Country, where the neediest Cottager pays out of his Pittance, however scanty, and how hardly soever earned, our high Duties of Customs and Excise in the Price of all his Consumption; it will be difficult I say, to persuade those who see, who suffer, or who relieve such Oppression; that the *West Indian* out of his Opulence, and the *North American* out of his Competency, can contribute no more than it is now pretended they can afford towards the Expence of Services, the Benefit of which, as a Part of this Nation they share, and as Colonists they peculiarly enjoy. They have indeed their own civil Governments besides to support; but *Great Britain* has her civil Government too; she has also a large Peace Establishment to maintain; and the national Debt, tho' so great a Part, and that the heaviest Part of it has been incurred by a War undertaken for the Protection of the Colonies, lies solely still upon her.

The Reasonableness, and even the Necessity of requiring an *American* Revenue being admitted, the Right of the Mother Country to impose such a Duty upon her Colonies, if duly considered, cannot be questioned: they claim it is true the Privilege, which is common to all *British* Subjects, of being taxed only with their own Consent, given by their Repre-

sentatives; and may they ever enjoy the Privilege in all its Extent: May this sacred Pledge of Liberty be preserved inviolate, to the utmost Verge of our Dominions, and to the latest Page of our History! but let us not limit the legislative Rights of the *British* People to Subjects of Taxation only: No new Law whatever can bind us that is made without the Concurrence of our Representatives. The Acts of Trade and Navigation, and all other Acts that relate either to ourselves or to the Colonies, are founded upon no other Authority; they are not obligatory if a Stamp Act is not, and every Argument in support of an Exemption from the Superintendance of the *British* Parliament in the one Case, is equally applicable to the others. The Constitution knows no Distinction; the Colonies have never attempted to make one; but have acquiesced under several parliamentary Taxes. The 6 *Geo.* II. c. 13. which has been already refered to, lays heavy Duties on all foreign Rum, Sugar, and Melasses, imported into the *British* Plantations: the Amount of the Impositions has been complained of; the Policy of the Laws has been objected to; but the Right of making such a Law, has never been questioned. These however, it may be said, are Duties upon Imports only, and there some imaginary Line has been supposed to be drawn; but had it ever existed, it was passed long before, for by 25 *Charles* II. c. 7. enforced by 7 and 8 *Wil.* and *Mary,* c. 22. and by 1 *Geo.* I. c. 12. the Exports of the *West Indian* Islands, not the Merchandize purchased by the Inhabitants, nor the Profits they might make by their Trade, but the Property they had at the Time, the Produce of their Lands, was taxed, by the Duties then imposed upon Sugar, Tobacco, Cotton, Indigo, Ginger, Logwood, Fustick, and Cocoa, exported from one *British* Plantation to another.

It is in vain to call these only Regulations of Trade; the Trade of British Subjects may not be regulated by such Means, without the Concurrence of their Representatives. Duties laid for these Purposes, as well as for the Purposes of Revenue, are still Levies of Money upon the People. The Constitution again knows no Distinction between Impost Duties and internal Taxation; and if some speculative Difference should be attempted to be made, it certainly is contradicted by Fact; for an internal Tax also was laid on the Colonies by the Establishment of a Post Office there; which, however it may be represented, will, upon a Perusal of 9 *Anne* c. 10. appear to be essentially a Tax, and that of the most authoritative Kind; for it is enforced by Provisions, more peculiarly prohibitory and compulsive, than others are usually attended with: The Conveyance of Letters thro' any other Channel is forbidden, by which Restrictions, the Advantage which might be made by public Carriers and others of this Branch of their Business is taken away; and the Passage of Ferries is declared to be free for the Post, the Ferrymen being compellable immediately on Demand to give their Labour without pay, and the Proprietors being obliged to furnish the Means of Passage to the Post without Recompence. These Provisions are indeed very proper, and even necessary; but certainly Money levied by such Methods, the Effect of which is intended to be a Monopoly of the Carriage of Letters to the Officers of this Revenue, and by Means of which the People are forced to pay the Rates imposed upon all their Correspondence, is a public Tax to which they must submit, and not meerly *a* Price required of them for a private Accommodation. The Act treats this and the British Postage upon exactly the same Footing, and expressly calls them both a *Revenue.* The Preamble of it declares, that the new Rates are fixed in the Manner therein specified with a View *to enable her Majesty in some Measure to carry on and finish the War.* The Sum of 700 *1. per* Week out of all *the Duties arising from*

time to time by virtue of this Act is appropriated for that Purpose, and for other necessary Occasions; the Surplus after other Deductions, was made part of the civil List Revenues; it continued to be thus applied during the Reigns of *George* I. and *George* II. and on his present Majesty's Accession to the Throne, when the Civil List was put upon a different Establishment, the Post Office Revenues were carried with the others *to the aggregate Fund, to be applied to the Uses, to which the said Fund is or shall be applicable.* If all these Circumstances do not constitute a Tax, I do not know what do: the Stamp Duties are not marked with stronger Characters, to entitle them to that Denomination; and with respect to the Application of the Revenue, the Power of the Parliament of *Great Britain* over the Colonies was then held up much higher than it has been upon the present Occasion. The Revenue arising from the Postage in *America* is blended with that of *England,* is applied in Part to the carrying on of a continental War, and other public Purposes; the Remainder of it to the Support of the Civil List; and now the whole of it to the Discharge of the National Debt by Means of the aggregate Fund; all these are Services that are either national or particular to *Great Britain;* but the Stamp Duties and the others that were laid last Year, are appropriated to such Services only as more particularly relate to the Colonies; and surely if the Right of the *British* Parliament to impose the one be acknowledged; that of laying on the other cannot be disputed. The Post-Office has indeed been called a meer Convenience; which therefore the People always chearfully pay for. After what has been said, this Observation requires very little Notice; I will not call the Protection and Security of the Colonies, to which the Duties in question are applied, by so low a Name as a Convenience.

The Instances that have been mentioned prove, that the Right of the Parliament of *Great Britain* to impose Taxes of every Kind on the Colonies, has been always admitted; but were there no Precedents to support the Claim, it would still be incontestable, being founded on the Principles of our Constitution; for the Fact is, that the Inhabitants of the Colonies are represented in Parliament: they do not indeed chuse the Members of that Assembly; neither are Nine Tenths of the People of *Britain* Electors; for the Right of Election is annexed to certain Species of Property, to peculiar Franchises, and to Inhabitancy in some particular Places; but these Descriptions comprehend only a very small Part of the Land, the Property, and the People of this Island: all Copyhold, all Leasehold Estates, under the Crown, under the Church, or under private Persons, tho' for Terms ever so long; all landed Property in short, that is not Freehold, and all monied Property whatsoever are excluded: the Possessors of these have no Votes in the Election of Members of Parliament; Women and Persons under Age be their Property ever so large, and all of it Freehold, have none. The Merchants of *London,* a numerous and respectable Body of Men, whose Opulence exceeds all that *America* could collect; the Proprietors of that vast Accumulation of Wealth, the public Funds; the Inhabitants of *Leeds,* of *Halifax,* of *Birmingham,* and of *Manchester,* Towns that are each of them larger than the Largest in the Plantations; many of less Note that are yet incorporated; and that great Corporation the *East India* Company, whose Rights over the Countries they possess, fall little short of Sovereignty, and whose Trade and whose Fleets are sufficient to constitute them a maritime Power, are all in the same Circumstances; none of them chuse their Representatives; and yet are they not represented in Parliament? Is their vast Property subject to Taxes without their Consent? Are they all arbitrarily bound by Laws to which they have not agreed? The Colonies are in exactly the same Situation: All *British* Subjects are really in the same; none are actually, all are virtually represented in Parliament; for every Member of Parliament sits in the House, not as Representative of his own Constituents, but as one of that august Assembly by which all the Commons of *Great Britain* are represented. Their Rights and their Interests, however his own Borough may be affected by general Dispositions, ought to be the great Objects of his Attention, and the only Rules for his Conduct; and to sacrifice these to a partial Advantage in favour of the Place where he was chosen, would be a Departure from his Duty; if it were otherwise, *Old Sarum* would enjoy Privileges essential to Liberty, which are denied to *Birmingham* and to *Manchester;* but as it is, they and the Colonies and all *British* Subjects whatever, have an equal Share in the general Representation of the Commons of *Great Britain,* and are bound by the Consent of the Majority of that House, whether their own particular Representatives consented to or opposed the Measures there taken, or whether they had or had not particular Representatives there.

The Inhabitants of the Colonies however have by some been supposed to be excepted, because they are represented in their respective Assemblies. So are the Citizens of *London* in their Common Council; and yet so far from excluding them from the national Representation, it does not impeach their Right to chuse Members of Parliament: it is true, that the Powers vested in the Common Council of *London,* are not equal to those which the Assemblies in the Plantations enjoy; but still they are legislative Powers, to be exercised within their District, and over their Citizens; yet not exclusively of the general Superintendance of the great Council of the Nation: The Subjects of a By-law and of an Act of Parliament may possibly be the same; yet it never was imagined that the Privileges of *London* were incompatible with the Authority of

Parliament; and indeed what Contradiction, what Absurdity, does a double Representation imply? What difficulty is there in allowing both, tho' both should even be vested with equal legislative Powers, if the one is to be exercised for local, and the other for general Purposes? and where is the Necessity that the Subordinate Power must derogate from the superior Authority? It would be a singular Objection to a Man's Vote for a Member of Parliament, that being represented in a provincial, he cannot be represented in a national Assembly; and if this is not sufficient Ground for an Objection, neither is it for an Exemption, or for any Pretence of an Exclusion.

The Charter and the proprietary Governments in *America,* are in this Respect, on the same Footing with the Rest. The comprehending them also, both in a provincial and national Representation, is not necessarily attended with any Inconsistency, and nothing contained in their Grants can establish one; for all who took those Grants were *British* Subjects, inhabiting *British* Dominions, and who at the Time of taking, were indisputably under the Authority of Parliament; no other Power can abridge that Authority, or dispense with the Obedience that is due to it: those therefore, to whom the Charters were originally given, could have no Exemption granted to them: and what the Fathers never received, the Children cannot claim as an Inheritance; nor was it ever in Idea that they should; even the Charters themselves, so far from allowing guard against the Supposition.

And after all, does any Friend to the Colonies desire the Exemption? he cannot, if he will reflect but a Moment on the Consequences. We value the Right of being represented in the national Legislature as the dearest Privilege we enjoy; how justly would the Colonies complain, if they alone were deprived of it? They acknowledge Dependance upon their Mother Country; but that Dependance would be Slavery not Connection, if they bore no Part in the Government of the whole: they would then indeed be in a worse Situation than the Inhabitants of *Britain,* for these are all of them virtually, tho' few of them are actually represented in the *House of Commons;* if the Colonies were not, they could not expect that their Interests and their Privileges would be any otherwise considered there, than as subservient to those of *Great Britain;* for to deny the Authority of a Legislature, is to surrender all Claims to a Share in its Councils; and if this were the Tenor of their Charters, a Grant more insidious and more replete with Mischief, could not have been invented: a permanent Title to a Share in national Councils, would be exchanged for a precarious Representation in a provincial Assembly; and a Forfeiture of their Rights would be couched under the Appearance of Privileges; they would be reduced from Equality to Subordination, and be at the same Time deprived of the Benefits, and liable to the Inconveniences, both of Independency and of Connection. Happily for them, this is not their Condition. They are on the contrary a Part, and an important Part of the Commons of *Great Britain:* they are represented in Parliament, in the same Manner as those Inhabitants of *Britain* are, who have not Voices in Elections; and they enjoy, with the Rest of their Fellow-subjects, the inestimable Privilege of not being bound by any Laws, or subject to any Taxes, to which the Majority of the Representatives of the Commons have not consented.

If there really were any Inconsistency between a national and a provincial Legislature, the Consequence would be the Abolition of the latter; for the Advantages that attend it are purely local: the District it is confined to might be governed without it, by means of the national Representatives; and it is unequal to great general Operations; whereas the other is absolutely necessary for the Benefit and Preservation of the whole: But so far are they from being incompatible, that they will be seldom found to interfere with one another: The Parliament will not often have occasion to exercise its Power over the Colonies, except for those Purposes, which the Assemblies cannot provide for. A general Tax is of this Kind; the Necessity for it, the Extent, the Application of it, are Matters which Councils limited in their Views and in their Operations cannot properly judge of; and when therefore the national Council determine these Particulars, it does not encroach on the other, it only exercises a Power which that other does not pretend to, never claimed, or wished, nor can ever be vested with: The latter remains in exactly the same State as it was before, providing for the same Services, by the same Means, and on the same Subjects; but conscious of its own Inability to answer greater Purposes than those for which it was instituted, it leaves the care of more general Concerns to that higher Legislature, in whose Province alone the Direction of them always was, is, and will be. The Exertion of that Authority which belongs to its universal Superintendance, neither lowers the Dignity, nor depreciates the Usefulness of more limited Powers: They retain all that they ever had, and are really incapable of more.

The Concurrence therefore of the provincial Representatives cannot be necessary in great public Measures to which none but the national Representatives are equal: The Parliament of *Great Britain* not only may but must tax the Colonies, when the public Occasions require a Revenue there: The present Circumstances of the Nation require one now; and a Stamp Act, of which we have had so long an Experience in this, and which is not unknown in that Country, seems an eligible Mode of Taxation. From all these Considerations, and from many others which will occur upon Reflexion and need not be suggested, it must appear *proper to charge certain Stamp Duties in the Plantations to be applied towards defraying the necessary Expences of defending, protecting, and securing the British Colonies and Plantations in America.* This Vote of the House of Commons closed the Measures taken last Year on the Subject of the Colonies: They appear to have been founded upon true Principles of Policy, of Commerce, and of Finance; to be wise with respect to the Mother-Country; just and even beneficial to the Plantations; and therefore it may reasonably be expected that either in their immediate Operations, or in their distant Effects, they will improve the Advantages we possess, confirm the Blessings we enjoy, and promote the public Welfare.

CHAPTER II

THE GENESIS OF THE STAMP ACT

ON MARCH 9, 1764, when Grenville introduced in Parliament the resolutions which formed the substance of the Sugar Act, he included one stating that it might be proper to lay a stamp tax in the colonies. He explained at the time that he did not wish immediate passage of such a tax. Instead he wished to give the colonies time to take some sort of action that might make the tax unnecessary or undesirable. Exactly what he proposed that the colonies do is difficult to determine, because no one recorded his exact words. All we have is a number of unofficial accounts in letters, including some from the agents employed by the different colonies to look after their interests in London.

On March 10, the day after the speech, Cecilius Calvert, writing to Governor Horatio Sharpe of Maryland, described the speech and stated that no immediate action was to be taken on the stamp tax, in order "to apprise the Colonies if any they have they [may] make objection, only given I am told pro forma tantum, before it is fix next year, which the Agents are to expect unless very good reasons are produced to the House per Contra."[1] Eliphalet Dyer of Connecticut, in a letter written from London sometime in March, 1764, said, "The further Consideration of the proposed Stamp Act is referred over to the next sessions of Parliament, that the Colonies may be notified to make their Objections. . . ."[2] Charles Garth, agent for South Carolina, in a letter dated June 5, 1764, stated that Grenville had postponed action on the stamp tax "upon the principle of giving the Colonies the oppertunity of knowing the intention of Government that they might be able to remit their several objections for the consideration of Parliament."[3] When the Stamp Act was under debate a year later, in 1765, General Henry Seymour Conway, speaking against it, recalled that, at the time when the tax was first proposed,

1. *Archives of Maryland*, 14 (1895), 144.
2. *Connecticut Courant*, Sept. 16, 1765.
3. *English Historical Review*, 54 (1939), 646.

the ministry had stated its intention "to give to the Americans Time to represent their Inability, or to suggest the Propriety of a less burthensome Tax than the Stamp Duty" (No. 7B).

Conway, it will be noted, adds a second reason why the act was postponed: to give the Americans time to suggest another and less burdensome type of tax, some tax other than a stamp tax, but a tax to be levied, presumably, by Parliament. This point is also mentioned in a letter from Thomas Whately to Jared Ingersoll, a Connecticut lawyer. Whately's letter is not dated but seems to have been written in the spring of 1764. It states that the Stamp Act was not carried into execution "to give them [the colonies] time to furnish the necessary Information for this, or to suggest any better Mode of Taxation."[4]

Whately may have been speaking from private information (he had been given the task of drafting the Stamp Act) and may not have been referring to anything that Grenville said in the House of Commons on March 9. The next source of information, Jasper Mauduit, was probably not present when the speech was delivered, but his brother, Israel Mauduit, listened to it for him. Jasper was the agent for the colony of Massachusetts. On the basis of Israel's report he wrote to the Massachusetts House of Representatives on March 13, four days after the speech, enclosing a copy of the resolutions and commenting: "The Stamp duty you will see, is deferr'd till next Year. I mean the actual laying it: Mr. Grenville being willing to give to the Provinces their option to raise that or some equivalent tax, Desirous as he express'd himself to consult the Ease, the Quiet, and the Good will of the Colonies."[5]

Mauduit's account agrees substantially with that of Edward Montague, agent of Virginia, who heard the speech and wrote an account of it to the Virginia House of Burgesses on April 11, 1764. The part of the letter which deals with Grenville's proposal is as follows: "Mr. G—— then suggested that this [his?] great object, being the relief of this kingdom from the burthen which in justice America should bear, it would be as satisfactory to him if the several provinces would among themselves, and in modes best suited to their circumstances, raise a sum adequate to the expense of their defence."[6]

The colonial agents were apparently uncertain about what Grenville was proposing and met with him on May 17, 1764, in order to find out. There are three surviving eyewitness accounts of this meeting: a letter from Jasper Mauduit to the Massachusetts Assembly (No. 5A), one from Charles Garth to the South Carolina Assembly (No. 5B), and a printed version in a pamphlet by William Knox, agent of Georgia (No. 32). The British government

4. New Haven Colony Historical Society, *Papers*, 9 (1918), 294.
5. Massachusetts Archives, XXII, 359.
6. *Virginia Gazette* (Purdie and Dixon), Oct. 3, 1766.

sent no official communication to the colonial assemblies or to the colonial governors inviting objections or alternative proposals.

As a result of Mauduit's report that Grenville wished the colonies to tax themselves, popular leaders in Massachusetts proposed to take action. Governor Bernard described their efforts in a letter (No. 6) to Richard Jackson, one of Grenville's secretaries, who was interested in the colonies and had served as agent for Pennsylvania and for Connecticut.

Perhaps for the reasons indicated in Bernard's letter, perhaps because of the absence of any official communication from England, none of the colonies had done anything about taxing themselves before Grenville was ready to introduce the Stamp Act in Parliament. In a last-minute effort to prevent it, four of the agents held another conference with him on February 2, 1765. The most complete account of the meeting is in a letter from Jared Ingersoll to Governor Fitch of Connecticut, on February 11 (No. 7A). Ingersoll had gone to London on business in 1764 and had been specially commissioned by his colony to work against the proposed act.

Ingersoll's letter also described the various arguments offered for and against the bill in Parliament (Parliament kept no official record of debates) including the speech in behalf of the Americans by Colonel Isaac Barré. Barré's speech, widely publicized in America, was made in the first debate on the bill (February 6). General Conway spoke against it (No. 7B) on the second reading (February 15). At this time the agents presented colonial petitions against the bill, but these were not given a hearing on the ground that it had traditionally been the practice of the House of Commons to refuse petitions on money bills. Barré and Conway, because of their speeches, became instantly famous in America, where several towns were named or renamed after them. They were both adherents of the elder William Pitt, who was ill and unable to attend Parliament.

In spite of their arguments and those advanced by the colonists in pamphlets and petitions (see Chapter I), the act passed by a large majority (No. 8). The selections given from it include all the clauses specifying the amount of the tax on different items. The parts omitted consist mainly of interpretations and penalties for violations.

QUESTIONS

1. Did Grenville give the colonists an opportunity to avert the Stamp Act?

2. On what grounds was the act opposed in Parliament?

3. Were these different from the grounds on which the colonists opposed it?

4. What colonial activities would have been affected by the duties prescribed in the act?

5. What court or courts had authority to enforce collection of the duties prescribed by the act?

5. The Colonial Agents Confer with Grenville, May 17, 1764

A. Jasper Mauduit to the Massachusetts Assembly, May 26, 1764

[Massachusetts Archives, XXII, 375.]

A few days ago several of the Agents waited upon Mr. Grenville to know his intention upon that subject [stamp duties]. When he told us, that he was still of the same mind. That of the several Inland duties that of the stamps was the most equal, required the fewest officers, and was attended with the least Expence in the Collecting of it. That therefore, tho he doubted not but that the Colonies would wish rather to have no tax at all; yet as the necessities of Government rendered it an indispensable duty, he should certainly bring in such a Bill. and in the meantime he should leave it to each province to signify their Assent to such a Bill in General; or their requests about any particular modifications of it as they should think fit. My Brother [Israel Mauduit] took the Liberty of desiring to have the particular heads of the Bill; without which he said it would be asking the province to Assent to they did not know what. But was answered, that that was not necessary. That everyone knew the stamp laws here; and that this Bill is intended to be formd upon the same plan.

B. Charles Garth to the Committee of Correspondence of the South Carolina Assembly, June 5, 1764

[English Historical Review, 54 (1939), 646-48.]

Since I wrote last, the several Agents for the Colonies in America have had a meeting to consider of the steps proper on their part to be taken, in consequence of the Stamp Bill being postpon'd to the next Sessions of Parliament: in duty to our constituents to procure the best intelligence possible and as a mark of respect for the candour shown in not hurrying a measure so interesting to the subject in America, we came to a resolution of waiting upon Mr. Grenville.

On the 17th of May we attended him, and after expressing our thanks for waving the intended bill in the last session, upon the principle of giving the Colonies the oppertunity of knowing the intention of Government that they might be able to remit their several objections for the consideration of Parliament, we acquainted him with our wishes that he should be pleased to let us have copies of the Bill to transmit to America, in order that our respective constituents might have the whole, both substance and form under their deliberation, when they would be far better able to determine whether or how far, to approve or disapprove.—Mr. Grenville told us it was impossible for him to comply with our request, as the Bill was not yet thoroughly digested, and assured us that his motive for deferring it sprang from a desire of shewing his regard to the subjects in America, by previously consulting them on a measure, that if the principle upon which it was grounded should appear fair and just in itself, he believed could have the fewest objections of any that could be proposed:—the expence of maintaining, protecting and defending America, it was but natural for America to bear at a time when the revenue of the Mother Country stands in need of every relief and assistance to be had, in order to lessen and diminish as much as possible the immense load of debt upon the nation, that it may be able to exert itself upon every necessary occasion with that vigour, which the Colonies have happily experienced, and will at all times find essential to their immediate interest and wellfare. The method of raising this relief from America had employ'd much of his attention, from a desire of doing it by means the most easy and least exceptionable to the Colonies; the raising it within themselves and appropriating it would have been attended with very many difficulties even if it could be suppos'd that 26 colonies (including the Continent and West India Islands) would all have adopted such a recommendation, and which in case of refusal to enforce the power of Parliament must have been had recourse to, whereas his intention by this delay was to have the sense of the Colonies themselves upon the matter, and if they could point out any system or plan as effectual and more easy to them, he was open to every proposition to be made from the Colonies, but when the subject had been fully considered by them upon its proper grounds and principles, and no other method should upon the whole be suggested so proper for America in general, it would be a satisfaction to him to carry it into the House with their concurrence and approbation. Objections of inability might possibly come from some Colonies, but, he believed, would have very little weight with Parliament; and with regard to the power of Parliament, the sense of the House of Commons had been sufficiently declaratory thereof, even if there had been no precedent of a revenue from America granted to the Crown by Act of Parliament, meaning the Act establishing a Post Office at New York.—We then took the liberty of asking him (upon supposition of concurrence in the Colonies to the mode) if he had either determined in his mind what things he should make subject to this Stamp Duty, and whether the stamps, to be directed, were to be as high as are by law imposed in Great Britain, or what proportion they would bear, as it seemed to us to be unreasonable that if stamps were to be as great as in England, they should be so high, the object of Government being nothing more than as it were a reimbursement for the expence annually incurred on account of the American Dominions, which £400,000 would amply satisfy, and towards raising the same the Duty Bill last Sessions must not be forgot, the Legislature having so appropriated the income that redounds to the revenue from the duties therein impos'd: Mr. Grenville believed upon the plan thought of the objects for the Stamp Duty would be as extensive, but what the rate of the stamps might be, was not determin'd, and added he should be very ready to consult with us before the meeting of Parliament thereon to receive any propositions we might in the mean time be instructed upon by our respective constituents with regard to these points, if our Assemblies should, as he could not doubt, upon a due consideration they would, transmit us instructions with their assent to the plan for levying this money in the American Dominions.

6. Massachusetts Attempts to Forestall the Stamp Act

[Francis Bernard to Richard Jackson, Aug. 18, 1764, Bernard Papers, III, 248-49, Harvard College Library.]

Dear Sir

Yesterday the members for Boston came to me to signify that it was the desire of many Members of the House that the Assembly might meet as soon as possible, that proper measures might be taken to prevent an inland parliamentary Taxation. That their Agent had wrote word that Mr. Greenville had told him that such a taxation might be prevented, if they would tax themselves to the same purposes as were intended by the former. That they were desirous of immediately setting about such taxation themselves or at least of doing something to prevent a parliamentary tax.

I told them that in the present state of things I did not see that they could do anything more than they might have done last session: that is to signify their desire that they might be allowed to tax themselves and not be taxed by the parliament. That it was impossible at present to proceed to an actual taxation, untill the demands of the ministry should be further explained. That if every province was to be left to raise the Money in what manner they pleased, the particular sum expected from each province as their proportion must be first ascertained. That if a stamp Duty was to be imposed by provincial Acts as forming of itself a proportion of charge, The Duties themselves must be first settled, as they ought to be the same in every province; otherwise they will not be a proportional charge. That neither of these things can be done by the provinces themselves, they must be settled by some authority that can mediate between the Provinces and moderate their partialities for themselves. That in regard to the Provinces preferring to tax themselves rather than to be taxed by parliament,

there can be no doubt of that being the desire of the Ministry. The Friends of the Provinces had been long aware of that preferrence; you had particularly urged it: and I had wrote upon the same subject. In short it could never be doubted but that if the parliament should require certain sums of the provinces, It is of no little Consequence to them that such sums should be raised by provincial Acts. For thereby the forms of their priviledges (which are no little part of them) are kept up, tho' the Substance is impeached, as it frequently must be in Subordinate Governments, whose relation to the Sovereign power has never been formally settled nor is generally understood.

But I promised them that I would Call the Assembly together about the middle of october, when there would be time enough to send instructions to the agent before this business could be brought on in parliament. However, if the Ministry should be settling their plan before hand, I wish you would interpose on the behalf of the province that they may at least have the liberty of enacting internal taxations themselves: which I have no doubt, but that they will readily do, when it shall be positively required of them. I am Sir

your Most faithfull and obedient servant.

7. The Debate in Parliament

A. JARED INGERSOLL TO THOMAS FITCH, FEBRUARY 11, 1765

[New Haven Colony Historical Society, *Papers*, 9 (1918), 306-15.]

The principal Attention has been to the Stamp bill that has been preparing to Lay before Parliament for taxing America. The Point of the Authority of Parliament to impose such Tax I found on my Arrival here was so fully and Universally yielded, that there was not the least hopes of making any impressions that way. Indeed it has appeared since that the House would not suffer to be brought in, nor would any one Member Undertake to Offer to the House, any Petition from the Colonies that held forth the Contrary of that Doctrine. I own I advised the Agents if possible to get that point Canvassed that so the Americans might at least have the

Satisfaction of having the point Decided upon a full Debate, but I found it could not be done, and here before I proceed to acquaint you with the Steps that have been taken, in this Matter, I beg leave to give you a Summary of the Arguments which are made Use of in favour of such Authority.

The House of Commons, say they, is a branch of the supreme legislature of the Nation, & which in its Nature is supposed to represent, or rather to stand in the place of, the Commons, that is, of the great body of the people, who are below the dignity of peers; that this house of Commons Consists of a certain number of Men Chosen by certain people of certain places, which Electors, by the Way, they Insist, are not a tenth part of the people, and that the Laws, rules and Methods by which their number is ascertained have arose by degrees & from various Causes & Occasions, and that this house of Commons, therfore, is now fixt and ascertained & is a part of the Supreme unlimited power of the Nation, as in every State there must be some unlimited Power and Authority; and that when it is said they represent the Commons of England, it cannot mean that they do so because those Commons choose them, for in fact by far the greater part do not, but because by their Constitution they must themselves be Commoners, and not Peers, and so the Equals, or of the same Class of Subjects, with the Commons of the Kingdom. They further urge, that the only reason why America has not been heretofore taxed in the fullest Manner, has been merely on Account of their Infancy and Inability; that there have been, however, not wanting Instances of the Exercise of this Power, in the various regulations of the American trade, the Establishment of the post Office &c, and they deny any Distinction between what is called an internal & external Tax as to the point of the Authority imposing such taxes. And as to the Charters in the few provinces where there are any, they say, in the first place, the King cannot grant any that shall exempt them from the Authority of one of the branches of the great body of Legislation, and in the second place say the King has not done, or attempted to do it. In that of Pensilvania the Authority of Parliament to impose taxes is expressly mentioned & reserved; in ours tis said, our powers are generally such as are *According to the Course of other Corporations in England* (both which Instances by way of Sample were mentioned & referred to by Mr. Grenville in the House); in short they say a Power to tax is a necessary part of every Supreme Legislative Authority, and that if they have not that Power over America, they have none, & then America is at once a Kingdom of itself.

On the other hand those who oppose the bill say, it is true the Parliament have a supreme unlimited Authority over every Part & Branch of the Kings dominions and as well over Ireland as any other place, yet we believe a British parliament will never think it prudent to tax Ireland. Tis true they say, that the Commons of England & of the british Empire are all represented in and by the house of Commons, but this representation is confessedly on all hands by Construction & Virtually only as to those who have no hand in choosing the representatives, and that the Effects of this implied Representation here & in America must be infinitely different in the Article of Taxation. Here in England the Member of Parliament is equally known to the Neighbour who elects & to him who does not; the Friendships, the Connections, the Influences are spread through the whole. If by any Mistake an Act of Parliament is made that prove injurious and hard the Member of Parliament here sees with his own Eyes and is moreover very accessible to the people, not only so, but the taxes are laid equally by one Rule and fall as well on the Member himself as on the people. But as to America, from the great distance in point of Situation, from the almost total unacquaintedness, Especially in the more northern Colonies, with the Members of Parliament, and they with them, or with the particular Ability & Circumstances of one another, from the Nature of this very tax laid upon others not Equally & in Common with ourselves, but with express purpose to Ease ourselves, we think, say they, that it will be only to lay a foundation of great Jealousy and Continual Uneasiness, and that to no purpose, as we already by the Regulations upon their trade draw from the Americans all that they can spare, at least they say this Step should not take place untill or unless the Americans are allowed to send Members to Parliament; for *who of you,* said Coll Barre Nobly in his Speech in the house upon this Occasion, *who of you reasoning upon this Subject feels warmly from the Heart* (putting his hand to his own breast) *for the Americans as they would for themselves or as you would for the people of your own native Country?* and to this point Mr. Jackson produced Copies of two Acts of Parliament granting the priviledge of having Members to the County Palitine of Chester & the Bishoprick of Durham upon Petitions preferred for that purpose in the Reign of King Henry the Eighth and Charles the first, the preamble of which Statutes counts upon the Petitions from those places as setting forth that being in their general Civil Jurisdiction Exempted from the Common Law Courts &c, yet being Subject to the general Authority of Parliament, were taxed in Common with the rest of the Kingdom, which taxes by reason of their having no Members in Parliament to represent their Affairs, often proved hard and injurious &c and upon that ground they had the priviledge of sending Members granted them—& if this, say they, could be a reason in the case of Chester and Durham, how much more so in the case of America.

Thus I have given you, I think, the Substance of the Arguments on both sides of that great and important Question of the right & also of the Expediency of taxing America by Authority of Parliament. I cannot, however, Content myself without giving you a Sketch of what the aforementioned Mr. Barre said in Answer to some remarks made by Mr. Ch. Townsend in a Speech of his upon this Subject. I ought here to tell you that the Debate upon the American Stamp bill came on before the house for the first time last Wednesday, when the same was open'd by Mr. Grenville the Chanceller of the Exchequer, in a pretty lengthy Speech, & in a very able and I think in a very candid manner he opened the Nature of the Tax, Urged the Necessity of it, Endeavoured to obviate all Objections to it—and took Occasion to desire the house to give the bill a most Serious and Cool Consideration & not suffer themselves to be influenced by any resentments which might have been kindled from any thing they might have heard out of doors—alluding I suppose to the N. York and Boston Assemblys' Speeches & Votes—that this was a matter of revenue which was of all things the most interesting to the Subject &c. The Argument was taken up by several who opposed the bill (viz) by Alderman Beckford, who, and who only, seemed to deny the Authority of Parliament, by Col. Barre, Mr. Jackson, Sir William Meredith and some others. Mr. Barre, who by the way I think, & I find I am not alone in my Opinion, is one of the finest Speakers that the House can boast of, having been some time in America as an Officer in the Army, & having while there, as I had known before, contracted many Friendships with American Gentlemen, & I believe Entertained much more favourable Opinions of them than some of his profession have done, Delivered a very handsome and moving Speech upon the bill & against the same, Concluding by saying that he was very sure that Most who Should hold up their hands to the Bill must be under a Necessity of acting very much in the dark, but added, perhaps as well in the Dark as any way.

After him Mr. Charles Townsend spoke in favour of the Bill—took Notice of several things Mr. Barre had said, and concluded with the following or like Words:— And now will these Americans, Children planted by our Care, nourished up by our Indulgence untill they are grown to a Degree of Strength & Opulence, and protected by our Arms, will they grudge to contribute their mite to releive us from the heavy weight of that burden which we lie under? When he had done, Mr. Barre rose and having explained something which he had before said & which Mr. Townsend had been remarking upon, he then took up the beforementioned Concluding words of Mr. Townsend, and in a most spirited & I thought an almost inimitable manner, said—

"They planted by your Care? No! your Oppressions planted em in America. They fled from your Tyranny to a then uncultivated and unhospitable Country— where they exposed themselves to almost all the hardships to which human Nature is liable, and among others to the Cruelties of a Savage foe, the most subtle and I take upon me to say the most formidable of any People upon the face of Gods Earth. And yet, actuated by Principles of true english Lyberty, they met all these hardships with pleasure, compared with those they suffered in their own Country, from the hands of those who should have been their Friends.

"They nourished up by your indulgence? they grew by your neglect of Em: —as soon as you began to care about Em, that Care was Excercised in sending persons to rule over Em, in one Department and another, who were perhaps the Deputies of Deputies to some Member of this house—sent to Spy out their Lyberty, to misrepresent their Actions & to prey upon Em; men whose behaviour on many Occasions has caused the Blood of those Sons of Liberty to recoil within them; men pro-

moted to the highest Seats of Justice, some, who to my knowledge were glad by going to a foreign Country to Escape being brought to the Bar of a Court of Justice in their own.

"They protected by your Arms? they have nobly taken up Arms in your defence, have Exerted a Valour amidst their constant & Laborious industry for the defence of a Country, whose frontier, while drench'd in blood, its interior Parts have yielded all its little Savings to your Emolument. And believe me, remember I this Day told you so, that same Spirit of freedom which actuated that people at first, will accompany them still.—But prudence forbids me to explain myself further. God knows I do not at this Time speak from motives of party Heat, what I deliver are the genuine Sentiments of my heart; however superiour to me in general knowledge and Experience the reputable body of this house may be, yet I claim to know more of America than most of you, having seen and been conversant in that Country. The People I believe are as truly Loyal as any Subjects the King has, but a people Jealous of their Lyberties and who will vindicate them, if ever they should be violated—but the Subject is too delicate & I will say no more."

These Sentiments were thrown out so intirely without premeditation, so forceably and so firmly, and the breaking off so beautifully abrupt, that the whole house sat awhile as Amazed, intently Looking and without answering a Word.

I own I felt Emotions that I never felt before & went the next Morning & thank'd Coll Barre in behalf of my Country for his noble and spirited Speech.

However, Sir after all that was said, upon a Division of the house upon the Question, there was about 250 to about 50 in favour of the Bill.

The truth is I believe some who inclined rather against the Bill voted for it, partly because they are loth to break the Measures of the Ministry, and partly because they dont undertake to inform themselves in the fullest manner upon the Subject. The Bill comes on to a second Reading to-morrow, when ours and the Massachusetts Petitions will be presented & perhaps they may be some further Debate upon the Subject, but to no purpose I am very sure, as to the Stopping or preventing the Act taking Place.

The Agents of the Colonies have had several Meetings, at one of which they were pleased to desire Mr. Franklin & myself as having lately Come from America & knowing more Intimately the Sentiments of the people, to wait on Mr. Grenville, together with Mr. Jackson & Mr. Garth who being Agents are also Members of Parliament, to remonstrate against the Stamp Bill, & to propose in Case any Tax must be laid upon America, that the several Colonies might be permitted to lay the Tax themselves. This we did Saturday before last. Mr. Grenville gave us a full hearing—told us he took no pleasure in giving the Americans so much uneasiness as he found he did—that it was the Duty of his Office to manage the revenue—that he really was made to believe that considering the whole of the Circumstances of the Mother Country & the Colonies, the later could and ought to pay something, and that he knew of no better way than that now pursuing to lay such Tax, but that if we could tell of a better he would adopt it. We then urged the Method first mentioned as being a Method the people had been used to—that it would at least seem to be their own Act & prevent that uneasiness & Jealousy which otherwise we found would take place—that they could raise the Money best by their own Officers &c &c

Mr. Jackson told him plainly that he foresaw [by] the Measure now pursuing, by enabling the Crown to keep up an armed Force of its own in America & to pay the Governours in the Kings Goverments & all with the Americans own Money, the Assembles *in* the Colonys would be sub-

verted—that the Governors would have no Occasion, as for any Ends of their own or of the Crown, to call 'Em & that they never would be called to gether in the Kings Goverments. Mr. Grenville warmly rejected the thought, said no such thing was intended nor would he beleived take place. Indeed I understand since, there is a Clause added to the Bill Applying the monies that shall be raised to the protecting & Defending America *only*. Mr. Grenville asked us if we could agree upon the several proportions Each Colony should raise. We told him no. He said he did not think any body here was furnished with Materials for that purpose; not only so but there would be no Certainty that every Colony would raise the Sum enjoined & to be obliged to be at the Expence of making Stamps, to compel some one or two provinces to do their Duty & that perhaps for one year only, would be very inconvenient; not only so, but the Colonies by their constant increase will be Constantly varying in their proportions of Numbers & ability & which a Stamp bill will always keep pace with &c &c.

Upon the whole he said he had pledged his Word for Offering the Stamp Bill to the house, that the house would hear all our Objections & would do as they thought best; he said, he wished we would preserve a Coolness and Moderation in America; that he had no need to tell us, that resentments indecently & unbecomingly Express'd on one Side the Water would naturally produce resentments on tother Side, & that we could not hope to get any good by a Controversy with the Mother Country; that their Ears will always be open to any remonstrances from the Americans with respect to this bill both before it takes Effect & after, if it shall take Effect, which shall be exprest in a becoming manner, that is, as becomes Subjects of the same common Prince.

I acquainted you in my last that Mr. Whately, one of the Secretaries of the

Treasury, and who had under his Care and Direction the business of preparing the Stamp Bill, had often conferred with me on the Subject. He wanted, I know, information of the several methods of transfer, Law process &c made Use of in the Colony, & I believe has been also very willing to hear all Objections that could be made to the Bill or any part of it. This task I was glad to undertake, as I very well knew the information I must give would operate strongly in our favour, as the number of our Law Suits, Deeds, Tavern Licences & in short almost all the Objects of the intended taxation & Dutys are so very numerous in the Colony that the knowledge of them would tend to the imposing a Duty so much the Lower as the Objects were more in Number. This Effect I flatter myself it has had in some measure. Mr. Whately to be sure tells me I may fairly claim the Honour of having occasioned the Duty's being much lower than was intended, & three particular things that were intended to be taxed, I gave him no peace till he dropt; these were Licences for marriadge—a Duty that would be odious in a new Country where every Encouragement ought to be given to Matrimony & where there was little portion; Commissions of the Justices of peace, which Office was generally speaking not profitable & yet necessary for the good Order and Goverment of the people; and Notes of hand which with us were given & taken so very often for very small Sums.

After all I believe the people in America will think the Sums that will be raised will be quite Enough, & I wish they may'nt find it more Distressing than the people in power here are aware of.

The Merchants in London are alarmed at these things; they have had a meeting with the Agents and are about to petition Parliament upon the Acts that respect the trade of North America.

What the Event of these things will be I dont know, but am pretty certain that wisdom will be proper and even very necessary, as well as prudence and good Discretion to direct the Councils of America. . . .

I shall hope to see you the beginning of Summer at farthest.

Your Most Obedient Humble Servant.
J: Ingersoll.

B. General Conway's Speech, February 15, 1765

[Extract of a letter from London, dated Feb. 16, 1765, reprinted in the *Maryland Gazette*, June 13, 1765.]

General C —— y said in the House, "The last Session of Parliament we came to a Resolution, that it might be proper to Tax the Americans; at that Time it was thrown out.—I am sure I understood it so, that the Intention of this Resolution was, to give to the Americans Time to represent their Inability, or to suggest the Propriety of a less burthensome Tax than the Stamp Duty: This Time has been given; the Representations are come from the Colonies; and shall we shut our Ears against that Information, which, with an Affectation of Candour, we allotted sufficient Time to reach us? For my own part, I must declare myself just as much in the dark as I was the last Year; my way of Life does not engage me in Intercourse with commercial Gentlemen, or those who have any Knowledge of the Colonies. I declare upon my Honour, I expected, as a Member sitting in this House, to receive such Information, as in Consequence of the Notice given, might be transmitted by the Colonies, by which my Judgment might be directed, my Conduct regulated. In a Question so important, which regards Two Millions of unrepresented People, I lay aside every Consideration of Party, and shall therefore make no Scruple to declare my Opinion, that the *Jamaica* Petition is not admissible, because it does not come from the Colony, and of Course cannot contain those Lights, which I am sure, I am desirous of receiving, and which the Colonists themselves can only give. But there are, I am informed, other Petitions of the Nature which I describe, that I am for receiving. A great deal has been said of the standing and established Rule of this House, that no Petitions can be received against Money Bills. What is this Rule? I recollect no Order, no Resolution occurs to me; and it appears undeniable, from what has been advanced on both Sides, that the Practice is by no Means invariable; at best, it is but a Practice of Convenience; a Practice which in this Instance, if in no other, we ought to vary from: For from whom, unless from themselves, are we to learn the Circumstances of the Colonies, and the fatal Consequences that may attend the imposing of this Tax; I speak this with great Deference to the Abilities of the very few Agents who sit in Parliament; some of the Colonies have not this Advantage, and none of them, let Gentlemen say what they please, are Represented in Parliament. They can't be serious, when they insist even on their being virtually Represented: Will any Man in this House get up and say, he is one of the Representatives of the Colonies, when, so far from being an Object of their Choice, the most sensible Man in the Colonies scarce knows such a Gentleman exists. One Gentleman, in the Course of this Debate (G. *Elliott*) has observed, *That the Commons have maintained and asserted their Right against the Crown, and against the Lords, of solely voting Money without the Controul of either, any otherwise than by a Negative: And will you suffer your Colonies to impeach, to attack these Rights, to impede the Exercise of them, untouch'd, as they now are, by the other Branches of the Legislature.* This, I confess, appears to me the strangest Argument I ever heard: Can there be a more absolute Acknowledgment of your Right, a more declared Avowal of your Power, than a Petition, humbly submitting their Cause to your Wisdom and Justice, and praying to be heard before your Tribunal, against a Tax that will affect them in their tenderest Parts, in their Privileges, that at least you have suffered, and in their Property, acquired by your Protection. I am therefore, from a Principle of Lenity, Policy, and Justice, for receiving the Petitions of a numerous, useful, opulent People, from whom this Country derives its greatest Commerce, Strength, and Consideration."

8. The Stamp Act, March 22, 1765

[Pickering, ed., *The Statutes at Large*, XXVI, 179-87, 201-4. The act is designated as 5 George III, c. 12.]

An act for granting and applying certain stamp duties, and other duties, in the British *colonies and plantations in* America, *towards further defraying the expences of defending, protecting, and securing the same; and for amending such parts of the several acts of parliament relating to the trade and revenues of the said colonies and plantations, as direct the manner of determining and recovering the penalties and forfeitures therein mentioned.*

WHEREAS *by an act made in the last session of parliament, several duties were granted, continued, and appropriated, towards defraying the expences of defending, protecting, and securing, the* British *colonies and plantations in* America: *and whereas it is just and necessary, that provision be made for raising a further revenue within your Majesty's dominions in* America, *towards defraying the said expences:* we, your Majesty's most dutiful and loyal subjects, the commons of *Great Britain* in parliament assembled, have therefore resolved to give and grant unto your Majesty the several rates and duties herein after mentioned; and do most humbly beseech your Majesty that it may be enacted, and be it enacted by the King's most excellent majesty, by and with the advice and consent of the lords spiritual and temporal, and commons, in this present parliament assembled, and by the authority of the same, That from and after the first day of *November,* one thousand seven hundred and sixty five, there shall be raised, levied, collected, and paid unto his Majesty, his heirs, and successors, throughout the colonies and plantations in *America* which now are, or hereafter may be, under the dominion of his Majesty, his heirs and successors,

For every skin or piece of vellum or parchment, or sheet or piece of paper, on which shall be ingrossed, written or printed, any declaration, plea, replication, rejoinder, demurrer, or other pleading, or any copy thereof, in any court of law within the *British* colonies and plantations in *America,* a stamp duty of three pence.

For every skin or piece of vellum or parchment, or sheet or piece of paper, on which shall be ingrossed, written or printed, any special bail and appearance upon such bail in any such court, a stamp duty of two shillings.

For every skin or piece of vellum or parchment, or sheet or piece of paper, on which shall be ingrossed, written, or printed, any petition, bill, answer, claim, plea, replication, rejoinder, demurrer, or other pleading in any court of chancery or equity within the said colonies and plantations, a stamp duty of one shilling and six pence.

For every skin or piece of vellum or parchment, or sheet or piece of paper, on which shall be ingrossed, written, or printed, any copy of any petition, bill, answer, claim, plea, replication, rejoinder,

demurrer, or other pleading in any such court, a stamp duty of three pence.

For every skin or piece of vellum or parchment, or sheet or piece of paper, on which shall be ingrossed, written, or printed, any monition, libel, answer, allegation, inventory, or renunciation in ecclesiastical matters in any court of probate, court of the ordinary, or other court exercising ecclesiastical jurisdiction within the said colonies and plantations, a stamp duty of one shilling.

For every skin or piece of vellum or parchment, or sheet or piece of paper, on which shall be ingrossed, written, or printed, any copy of any will (other than the probate thereof) monition, libel, answer, allegation, inventory, or renunciation in ecclesiastical matters in any such court, a stamp duty of six pence.

For every skin or piece of vellum or parchment, or sheet or piece of paper, on which shall be ingrossed, written, or printed, any donation, presentation, collation, or institution of or to any benefice, or any writ or instrument for the like purpose, or any register, entry, testimonial, or certificate of any degree taken in any university, academy, college, or seminary of learning, within the said colonies and plantations, a stamp duty of two pounds.

For every skin or piece of vellum or parchment, or sheet or piece of paper, on which shall be ingrossed, written, or printed, any monition, libel, claim, answer, allegation, information, letter of request, execution, renunciation, inventory, or other pleading, in any admiralty court within the said colonies and plantations, a stamp duty of one shilling.

For every skin or piece of vellum or parchment, or sheet or piece of paper, on which any copy of any such monition, libel, claim, answer, allegation, information, letter of request, execution, renunciation, inventory, or other pleading shall be ingrossed, written, or printed, a stamp duty of six pence.

For every skin or piece of vellum or

parchment, or sheet or piece of paper, on which shall be ingrossed, written, or printed, any appeal, writ of error, writ of dower, *Ad quod damnum,* certiorari, statute merchant, statute staple, attestation, or certificate, by any officer, or exemplification of any record or proceeding in any court whatsoever within the said colonies and plantations (except appeals, writs of error, certiorari, attestations, certificates, and exemplifications, for or relating to the removal of any proceedings from before a single justice of the peace) a stamp duty of ten shillings.

For every skin or piece of vellum or parchment, or sheet or piece of paper, on which shall be ingrossed, written, or printed, any writ of covenant for levying of fines, writ of entry for suffering a common recovery, or attachment issuing out of, or returnable into, any court within the said colonies and plantations, a stamp duty of five shillings.

For every skin or piece of vellum or parchment, or sheet or piece of paper, on which shall be ingrossed, written, or printed, any judgment, decree, sentence, or dismission, or any record of *Nisi Prius* or *Postea,* in any court within the said colonies and plantations, a stamp duty of four shillings.

For every skin or piece of vellum or parchment, or sheet or piece of paper, on which shall ingrossed, written, or printed, any affidavit, common bail or appearance, interrogatory deposition, rule, order, or warrant of any court, or any *Dedimus Potestatem, Capias, Subpoena,* summons, compulsory citation, commission, recognizance, or any other writ, process, or mandate, issuing out of, or returnable into, any court, or any office belonging thereto, or any other proceeding therein whatsoever, or any copy thereof, or of any record not herein before charged, within the said colonies and plantations (except warrants relating to criminal matters, and proceeding thereon or relating thereto) a stamp duty of one shilling.

For every skin or piece of vellum or parchment, or sheet or piece of paper, on which shall be ingrossed, written, or printed, any licence, appointment, or admission of any counsellor, solicitor, attorney, advocate, or proctor, to practise in any court, or of any notary within the said colonies and plantations, a stamp duty of ten pounds.

For every skin or piece of vellum or parchment, or sheet or piece of paper, on which shall be ingrossed, written, or printed, any note or bill of lading, which shall be signed for any kind of goods, wares, or merchandize, to be exported from, or any cocket or clearance granted within the said colonies and plantations, a stamp duty of four pence.

For every skin or piece of vellum or parchment, or sheet or piece of paper, on which shall be ingrossed, written, or printed, letters of mart, or commission for private ships of war, within the said colonies and plantations, a stamp duty of twenty shillings.

For every skin or piece of vellum or parchment, or sheet or piece of paper, on which shall be ingrossed, written or printed, any grant, appointment, or admission of or to any publick beneficial, office or employment, for the space of one year, or any lesser time, of or above the value of twenty pounds *per annum* sterling money, in salary, fees, and perquisites, within the said colonies and plantations, (except commissions and appointments of officers of the army, navy, ordnance, or militia, of judges, and of justices of the peace) a stamp duty of ten shillings.

For every skin or piece of vellum or parchment, or sheet or piece of paper, on which any grant of any liberty, privilege, or franchise, under the seal of any of the said colonies or plantations, or under the seal or sign manual of any governor, proprietor, or publick officer alone, or in conjunction with any other person or persons, or with any council, or any council and assembly, or any exemplification of the same, shall be ingrossed, written, or printed, within the said colonies and plantations, a stamp duty of six pounds.

For every skin or piece of vellum or parchment, or sheet or piece of paper, on which shall be ingrossed, written, or printed, any licence for retailing of spirituous liquors, to be granted to any person who shall take out the same, within the said colonies and plantations, a stamp duty of twenty shillings.

For every skin or piece of vellum or parchment, or sheet or piece of paper, on which shall be ingrossed, written, or printed, any licence for retailing of wine, to be granted to any person who shall not take out a licence for retailing of spirituous liquors, within the said colonies and plantations, a stamp duty of four pounds.

For every skin or piece of vellum or parchment, or sheet or piece of paper, on which shall be ingrossed, written, or printed, any licence for retailing of wine, to be granted to any person who shall take out a licence for retailing of spirituous liquors, within the said colonies and plantations, a stamp duty of three pounds.

For every skin or piece of vellum or parchment, or sheet or piece of paper, on which shall be ingrossed, written, or printed, any probate of a will, letters of administration, or of guardianship for any estate above the value of twenty pounds sterling money; within the *British* colonies and plantations upon the continent of *America,* the islands belonging thereto, and the *Bermuda* and *Bahama* islands, a stamp duty of five shillings.

For every skin or piece of vellum or parchment, or sheet or piece of paper, on which shall be ingrossed, written or printed, any such probate, letters of administration or of guardianship, within all other parts of the *British* dominions in *America,* a stamp duty of ten shillings.

For every skin or piece of vellum or parchment, or sheet or piece of paper,

on which shall be ingrossed, written, or printed, any bond for securing the payment of any sum of money, not exceeding the sum of ten pounds sterling money, within the *British* colonies and plantations upon the continent of *America,* the islands belonging thereto, and the *Bermuda* and *Bahama* islands, a stamp duty of six pence.

For every skin or piece of vellum or parchment, or sheet or piece of paper, on which shall be ingrossed, written, or printed, any bond for securing the payment of any sum of money above ten pounds, and not exceeding the sum of twenty pounds sterling money, within such colonies, plantations, and islands, a stamp duty of one shilling.

For every skin or piece of vellum or parchment, or sheet or piece of paper, on which shall be ingrossed, written, or printed, any bond for securing the payment of any sum of money above twenty pounds, and not exceeding forty pounds sterling money, within such colonies, plantations, and islands, a stamp duty of one shilling and six pence.

For every skin or piece of vellum or parchment, or sheet or piece of paper, on which shall be ingrossed, written, or printed, any order or warrant for surveying or setting out any quantity of land, not exceeding one hundred acres, issued by any governor, proprietor, or any publick officer alone, or in conjunction with any other person or persons, or with any council, or any council and assembly, within the *British* colonies and plantations in *America,* a stamp duty of six pence.

For every skin or piece of vellum or parchment, or sheet or piece of paper, on which shall be ingrossed, written, or printed, any such order or warrant for surveying or setting out any quantity of land above one hundred, and not exceeding two hundred acres, within the said colonies and plantations, a stamp duty of one shilling.

For every skin or piece of vellum or parchment, or sheet or piece of paper, on which shall be ingrossed, written, or printed, any such order or warrant for surveying or setting out any quantity of land above two hundred, and not exceeding three hundred and twenty acres, and in proportion for every such order or warrant for surveying or setting out every other three hundred and twenty acres, within the said colonies and plantations, a stamp duty of one shilling and six pence.

For every skin or piece of vellum or parchment, or sheet or piece or paper, on which shall be ingrossed, written, or printed, any original grant, or any deed, mesne conveyance, or other instrument whatsoever, by which any quantity of land not exceeding one hundred acres shall be granted, conveyed, or assigned, within the *British* colonies and plantations upon the continent of *America,* the islands belonging thereto, and the *Bermuda* and *Bahama* islands (except leases for any term not exceeding the term of twenty one years) a stamp duty of one shilling and six pence.

For every skin or piece of vellum or parchment, or sheet or piece of paper, on which shall be ingrossed, written, or printed, any such original grant, or any such deed, mesne conveyance or other instrument whatsoever by which any quantity of land above one hundred, and not exceeding two hundred acres, shall be granted, conveyed, or assigned, within such colonies, plantations, and islands, a stamp duty of two shillings.

For every skin or piece of vellum or parchment, or sheet or piece of paper, on which shall be ingrossed, written, or printed, any such original grant, or any such deed, mesne conveyance, or other instrument whatsoever, by which any quantity of land above two hundred, and not exceeding three hundred and twenty acres, shall be granted, conveyed, or assigned, and in proportion for every such grant, deed, mesne conveyance, or other instrument, granting, conveying, or assigning, every other three hundred and twenty acres, within such colonies, planta-

tions, and islands, a stamp duty of two shillings and six pence.

For every skin or piece of vellum or parchment, or sheet or piece of paper, on which shall be ingrossed, written, or printed, any such original grant, or any such deed, mesne conveyance, or other instrument whatsoever, by which any quantity of land not exceeding one hundred acres shall be granted, conveyed, or assigned, within all other parts of the *British* dominions in *America,* a stamp duty of three shillings.

For every skin or piece of vellum or parchment, or sheet or piece of paper, on which shall be ingrossed, written, or printed, any such original grant, or any such deed, mesne conveyance, or other instrument whatsoever, by which any quantity of land above one hundred, and not exceeding two hundred acres, shall be granted, conveyed, or assigned, within the same parts of the said dominions, a stamp duty of four shillings.

For every skin or piece of vellum or parchment, or sheet or piece of paper, on which shall be ingrossed, written, or printed, any such original grant, or any such deed, mesne conveyance, or other instrument whatsoever, whereby any quantity of land above two hundred, and not exceeding three hundred and twenty acres, shall be granted, conveyed, or assigned, and in porportion for every such grant, deed, mesne conveyance, or other instrument, granting, conveying, or assigning, every other three hundred and twenty acres, within the same parts of the said dominions, a stamp duty of five shillings.

For every skin or piece of vellum or parchment, or sheet or piece of paper, on which shall be ingrossed, written, or printed, any grant, appointment, or admission, of or to any publick beneficial office or employment, not herein before charged, above the value of twenty pounds *per annum* sterling money in salary, fees, and perquisites, or any exemplification of the same, within the *British* colonies and plantations upon the continent of *America,* the islands belonging thereto, and the *Bermuda* and *Bahama* islands (except commissions of officers of the army, navy, ordnance, or militia, and of justices of the peace) a stamp duty of four pounds.

For every skin or piece of vellum or parchment, or sheet or piece of paper, on which shall be ingrossed, written, or printed, any such grant, appointment, or admission, of or to any such publick beneficial office or employment, or any exemplification of the same, within all other parts of the *British* dominions in *America,* a stamp duty of six pounds.

For every skin or piece of vellum or parchment, or sheet or piece of paper, on which shall be ingrossed, written, or printed, any indenture, lease, conveyance, contract, stipulation, bill of sale, charter party, protest, articles of apprenticeship, or covenant (except for the hire of servants not apprentices, and also except such other matters as are herein before charged) within the *British* colonies and plantations in *America,* a stamp duty of two shillings and six pence.

For every skin or piece of vellum or parchment, or sheet or piece of paper, on which any warrant or order for auditing any publick accounts, beneficial warrant, order, grant, or certificate, under any publick seal, or under the seal or sign manual of any governor, proprietor, or publick officer alone, or in conjunction with any other person or persons, or with any council, or any council and assembly, not herein before charged, or any passport or let-pass, surrender of office, or policy of assurance, shall be ingrossed, written, or printed, within the said colonies and plantations (except warrants or orders for the service of the navy, army, ordnance, or militia, and grants of offices under twenty pounds *per annum* in salary, fees, and perquisites) a stamp duty of five shillings.

For every skin or piece of vellum or parchment, or sheet or piece of paper, on which shall be ingrossed, written, or

printed, any notarial act, bond, deed, letter of attorney, procuration, mortgage, release, or other obligatory instrument, not herein before charged, within the said colonies and plantations, a stamp duty of two shillings and three pence.

For every skin or piece of vellum or parchment, or sheet or piece of paper, on which shall be ingrossed, written or printed, any register, entry, or inrollment of any grant, deed, or other instrument whatsoever herein before charged, within the said colonies and plantations, a stamp duty of three pence.

For every skin or piece of vellum or parchment, or sheet or piece of paper, on which shall be ingrossed, written, or printed, any register, entry, or inrollment of any grant, deed, or other instrument whatsoever not herein before charged, within the said colonies and plantations, a stamp duty of two shillings.

And for and upon every pack of playing cards, and all dice, which shall be sold or used within the said colonies and plantations, the several stamp duties following (that is to say)

For every pack of such cards, the sum of one shilling.

And for every pair of such dice, the sum of ten shillings.

And for and upon every paper, commonly called a *pamphlet,* and upon every news paper, containing publick news, intelligence, or occurrences, which shall be printed, dispersed, and made publick, within any of the said colonies and plantations, and for and upon such advertisements as are herein after mentioned, the respective duties following (that is to say)

For every such pamphlet and paper contained in half a sheet, or any lesser piece of paper, which shall be so printed, a stamp duty of one halfpenny, for every printed copy thereof.

For every such pamphlet and paper (being larger than half a sheet, and not exceeding one whole sheet) which shall be so printed, a stamp duty of one penny, for every printed copy thereof.

For every pamphlet and paper being larger than one whole sheet, and not exceeding six sheets in octavo, or in a lesser page, or not exceeding twelve sheets in quarto, or twenty sheets in folio, which shall be so printed, a duty after the rate of one shilling for every sheet of any kind of paper which shall be contained in one printed copy thereof.

For every advertisement to be contained in any gazette, news paper, or other paper, or any pamphlet which shall be so printed, a duty of two shillings.

For every almanack or calendar, for any one particular year, or for any time less than a year, which shall be written or printed on one side only of any one sheet, skin, or piece of paper parchment, or vellum, within the said colonies and plantations, a stamp duty of two pence.

For every other almanack or calendar for any one particular year, which shall be written or printed within the said colonies and plantations, a stamp duty of four pence.

And for every almanack or calendar written or printed within the said colonies and plantations, to serve for several years, duties to the same amount respectively shall be paid for every such year.

For every skin or piece of vellum or parchment, or sheet or piece of paper, on which any instrument, proceeding, or other matter or thing aforesaid, shall be ingrossed, written, or printed, within the said colonies and plantations, in any other than the *English* language, a stamp duty of double the amount of the respective duties before charged thereon.

And there shall be also paid in the said colonies and plantations, a duty of six pence for every twenty shillings, in any sum not exceeding fifty pounds sterling money, which shall be given, paid, contracted, or agreed for, with or in relation to any clerk or apprentice, which shall be put or placed to or with any master or mistress to learn any profession, trade, or employment.

* * * * *

LIV. And be it further enacted by the authority aforesaid, That all the monies which shall arise by the several rates and duties hereby granted (except the necessary charges of raising, collecting, recovering, answering, paying, and accounting for the same, and the necessary charges from time to time incurred in relation to this act, and the execution thereof) shall be paid into the receipt of his Majesty's exchequer, and shall be entered separate and apart from all other monies, and shall be there reserved to be from time to time disposed of by parliament, towards further defraying the necessary expences of defending, protecting, and securing, the said colonies and plantations.

* * * * *

LVIII. And it is hereby further enacted and declared by the authority aforesaid, That all sums of money granted and imposed by this act as rates or duties, and also all sums of money imposed as forfeitures or penalties, and all sums of money required to be paid, and all other monies herein mentioned, shall be deemed and taken to be sterling money of *Great Britain,* and shall be collected, recovered, and paid, to the amount of the value which such nominal sums bear in *Great Britain;* and that such monies shall and may be received and taken, according to the proportion and value of five shillings and six pence the ounce in silver; and that all the forfeitures and penalties hereby inflicted, and which shall be incurred, in the said colonies and plantations, shall and may be prosecuted, sued for, and recovered, in any court of record, or in any court of admiralty, in the respective colony or plantation where the offence shall be committed, or in any court of vice admiralty appointed or to be appointed, and which shall have jurisdiction within such colony, plantation, or place, (which courts of admiralty or vice admiralty are hereby respectively authorized and required to proceed, hear, and determine the same,) at the election of the informer or prosecutor; and that from and after the twenty ninth day of *September,* one thousand seven hundred and sixty five, in all cases, where any suit or prosecution shall be commenced and determined for any penalty or forfeiture inflicted by this act, or by the said act made in the fourth year of his present Majesty's reign, or by any other act of parliament relating to the trade or revenues of the said colonies or plantations, in any court of admiralty in the respective colony or plantation where the offence shall be committed, either party, who shall think himself aggrieved by such determination, may appeal from such determination to any court of vice admiralty appointed or to be appointed, and which shall have jurisdiction within such colony, plantation, or place, (which court of vice admiralty is hereby authorized and required to proceed, hear, and determine such appeal) any law, custom, or usage, to the contrary notwithstanding; and the forfeitures and penalties hereby inflicted, which shall be incurred in any other part of his Majesty's dominions, shall and may be prosecuted, sued for, and recovered, with full costs of suit, in any court of record within the kingdom, territory, or place, where the offence shall be committed, in such and the same manner as any debt or damage, to the amount of such forfeiture or penalty, can or may be sued for and recovered.

LIX. And it is hereby further enacted, That all the forfeitures and penalties hereby inflicted shall be divided, paid, and applied, as follows; (that is to say) one third part of all such forfeitures and penalties recovered in the said colonies and plantations, shall be paid into the hands of one of the chief distributors of stamped vellum, parchment, and paper, residing in the colony or plantation wherein the offender shall be convicted, for the use of his Majesty, his heirs, and successors; one third part of the penalties and forfeitures, so recovered, to the governor or commander in chief of such colony or plantation; and the other third part thereof, to the person who shall inform or sue for the same; and that one moiety of all such penalties and forfeitures recovered in any other part of his Majesty's dominions, shall be to the use of his Majesty, his heirs, and successors, and the other moiety thereof, to the person who shall inform or sue for the same.

LX. And be it further enacted by the authority aforesaid, That all the offences which are by this act made felony [counterfeiting or forging a stamped paper], and shall be committed within any part of his Majesty's dominions, shall and may be heard, tried, and determined, before any court of law within the respective kingdom, territory, colony, or plantation, where the offence shall be committed, in such and the same manner as all other felonies can or may be heard, tried, and determined, in such court.

LXI. And be it further enacted by the authority aforesaid, That all the present governors or commanders in chief of any *British* colony or plantation, shall, before the said first day of *November,* one thousand seven hundred and sixty five, and all who hereafter shall be made governors or commanders in chief of the said colonies or plantations, or any of them, before their entrance into their government, shall take a solemn oath to do their utmost, that all and every the clauses contained in this present act be punctually and *bona fide* observed, according to the true intent and meaning thereof, so far as appertains unto the said governors or commanders in chief respectively, under the like penalties, forfeitures, and disabilities, either for neglecting to take the said oath, or for wittingly neglecting to do their duty accordingly, as are mentioned and expressed in an act made in the seventh and eighth year of the reign of King *William* the Third, intituled, *An act for preventing frauds, and regulating abuses, in the plan-*

tation trade; and the said oath hereby required to be taken, shall be administered by such person or persons as hath or have been, or shall be, appointed to administer the oath required to be taken by the said act made in the seventh and eighth year of the reign of King *William* the Third.

LXII. And be it further enacted by the authority aforesaid, That all records, writs, pleadings, and other proceedings in all courts whatsoever, and all deeds, instruments, and writings whatsoever, hereby charged, shall be ingrossed and written in such manner as they have been usually accustomed to be ingrossed and written, or are now ingrossed and written within the said colonies and plantations.

LXIII. And it is hereby further enacted, That if any person or persons shall be sued or prosecuted, either in *Great Britain* or *America,* for any thing done in pursuance of this act, such person and persons shall and may plead the general issue, and give this act and the special matter in evidence; and if it shall appear so to have been done, the jury shall find for the defendant or defendants: and if the plaintiff or plaintiffs shall become non-suited, or discontinue his or their action after the defendant or defendants shall have appeared, or if judgement shall be given upon any verdict or demurrer against the plaintiff or plaintiffs, the defendant or defendants shall recover treble costs, and have the like remedy for the same, as defendants have in other cases by law.

CHAPTER III

THE ACTION OF THE COLONIAL ASSEMBLIES

NEWS OF THE Stamp Act reached America in April, 1765, but the colonial assemblies were not aroused to action until Patrick Henry introduced a number of resolutions in the Virginia House of Burgesses during the closing days of the May session. One of the most tantalizing problems of this period is the question of what exactly happened there. As Henry's biographer, William Wirt, told the story in 1817, Henry compared George III to Caesar and Charles I. When cries of treason interrupted him, he said that George III might profit by their example, and "if *this* be treason, make the most of it." Contemporary evidence, however, is not at all clear about what Henry said, what his resolutions said, or what the House of Burgesses did about them.

There are only three contemporary accounts of the episode. One is a single sentence in the *London Gazetteer* of August 13, 1765, from a letter written in Virginia on June 21, 1765. There is no indication whether the writer himself had been present. The sentence reads: "Mr —— has lately blazed out in the Assembly, where he compared —— to a Tarquin, a Caesar, a Charles the First, threatening him with a Brutus, or an Oliver Cromwell; yet Mr —— was not sent to the Tower: but having prevailed to get some ridiculous violent Resolves passed, rode off in Triumph."

The second account is from the journal of an anonymous French traveller (No. 9), who gives some hints about what resolves were debated by the House of Burgesses, but he does not say which ones were passed. Governor Fauquier, who was not present, informs us in the third account (No. 10) that five were passed, one of which was rescinded on May 31, and that Henry had two more in his pocket. Fauquier does not indicate the substance of the rescinded resolution, and the manuscript records of the Burgesses are not extant. The printed records say nothing of a rescinding but show only four resolutions (No. 11).

Henry himself left a copy of the resolves, five in number (No. 12), but it is impossible to tell whether he wrote it at the time of their passage or later (his endorsement on the reverse side was written after the Revolutionary War). When the resolves appeared in print for the first time in the *Newport Mercury,* June 24, 1765, there were six (No. 13). The *Mercury's* version was reprinted by most of the other colonial newspapers, but the *Maryland Gazette,* July 4, 1765, printed a different version with seven resolutions (No. 14).

Virginia's example was followed by most of the other colonies, each assembly composing its own resolutions (Nos. 15-22). Since the wording was arrived at after debate and discussion by representatives of the people, these resolutions are worthy of careful scrutiny. Together with the declarations and petitions of the Stamp Act Congress, they offer the most carefully formulated and most widely approved statements of the American position in 1765. All of them are included here, so that the reader may have before him the full materials for an authoritative understanding of that position.

All the declarations and petitions of the Stamp Act Congress (Nos. 23-26) are likewise included for the same reason. This congress, suggested to the other colonies by Massachusetts, assembled in New York on October 7, 1765. Virginia, North Carolina, and Georgia could not elect delegates, because their governors refused to convene the assemblies; and New Hampshire declined to attend. Twenty-seven delegates from the other nine colonies deliberated for twelve days before reaching agreement on the fourteen declarations of principle (No. 23); but with these settled the three petitions (Nos. 24-26) were drawn up and adopted in two days' time, and by October 24 the congress had adjourned. Very little is known about the debate which took place over the declarations; the petitions may be read as an aid in interpreting them.

The proceedings of the congress were officially approved by the assemblies of all the participating colonies and also by New Hampshire and Georgia.

QUESTIONS

1. What resolutions were passed by the Virginia House of Burgesses on May 30, 1765?

2. Which resolution was rescinded on May 31?

3. Was either of the last two resolutions as printed in the newspapers ever discussed in the House of Burgesses?

4. Do the resolutions differ in substance from the petitions sent to England the preceding year?

5. Why was there opposition to their passage?

6. Did the resolutions of any other colonial assembly or of the Stamp Act Congress advocate resistance to Parliament?

7. Did any of the colonial resolutions distinguish between internal and external taxation?

8. Did they object to duties levied for the regulation of trade?

9. Did they ask for representation in Parliament?

10. What authority did they allow Parliament in the colonies?

11. On what grounds did they claim an exemption from parliamentary taxation?

12. What did the Stamp Act Congress mean by the words "all Supplies to the Crown, being free gifts of the People" (resolution no. 6)?

13. Why did the Stamp Act Congress affirm "That the only Representatives of the People of these Colonies, are Persons chosen therein by themselves"?

The Virginia Resolves

9. The French Traveller's Account

[*American Historical Review*, 26 (1921), 745-46.]

May the 30th. Set out Early from halfway house in the Chair and broke fast at York, arived at williamsburg at 12, where I saw three Negroes hanging at the galous for haveing robed Mr. Waltho of 300 ps. I went imediately to the assembly which was seting, where I was entertained with very strong Debates Concerning Dutys that the parlement wants to lay on the american Colonys, which they Call or Stile stamp Dutys. Shortly after I Came in one of the members stood up and said he had read that in former times tarquin and Julus had their Brutus, Charles had his Cromwell, and he Did not Doubt but some good american would stand up, in favour of his Country, but (says he) in a more moderate manner, and was going to Continue, when the speaker of the house rose and Said, he, the last that stood up had spoke traison, and was sorey to see that not one of the members of the house was loyal Enough to stop him, before he had gone so far. upon which the Same member stood up again (his name is henery) and said that if he had afronted the speaker, or the house, he was ready to ask pardon, and he would shew his loyalty to his majesty King G. the third, at the Expence of the last Drop of his blood, but what he had said must be atributed to the Interest of his Countrys Dying liberty which he had at heart, and the heat of passion might have lead him to have said something more than he intended, but, again, if he said any thing wrong, he beged the speaker and the houses pardon. some other Members stood up and backed him, on which that afaire was droped.

May the 31th. I returned to the assembly today, and heard very hot Debates stil about the Stamp Dutys. the whole house was for Entering resolves on the records but they Differed much with regard the Contents or purport therof. some were for shewing their resentment to the highest. one of the resolves that these proposed, was that any person that would offer to sustain that the parlement of Engl'd had a right to impose or lay any tax or Dutys whats'r on the american Colonys, without the Consent of the inhabitants therof, Should be looked upon as a traitor, and Deemed an Enemy to his Country. there were some others to the same purpose, and the majority was for Entring these resolves, upon which the Governor Disolved the assembly, which hinderd their proceeding.

10. Governor Fauquier's Account

[Kennedy, ed., *Journals of the House of Burgesses of Virginia, 1761-1765*, lxvii.]

Williamsburg, June 5th, 1765

My Lords,

On *Saturday* the 1st instant I dissolved the Assembly after passing all the Bills, except one, which were ready for my assent. The four Resolutions which I have now the honor to inclose to your Lordships, will shew Your Lordships the reason of my conduct, and I hope justify it. I will relate the whole proceeding to your Lordships in as concise a manner as I am able.

On *Wednesday* the 29th of May, just at the end of the Session when most of the members had left the town, there being but 39 present out of 116 of which the House of Burgesses now consists, a motion was made to take into consideration the Stamp Act, a copy of which had crept into the House, and in a Committee of the whole House five resolutions were proposed and agreed to, all by very small majorities. On *Thursday* the 30th they were reported & agreed to by the House, the numbers being as before in the Committee; the greatest majority being 22 to 17; for the 5th Resolution, 20 to 19 only. On *Friday* the 31st there having happened a small alteration in the House there was an attempt to strike all the Resolutions off the Journals. The 5th which was thought the most offensive was accordingly struck off, but it did not succeed as to the other four. I am informed the gentlemen had two more resolutions in their pocket, but finding the difficulty they had in carrying the 5th which was by a single voice, and knowing them to be more virulent and inflammatory; they did not produce them. The most strenuous opposers of this rash heat were the late Speaker, the King's Attorney and Mr. *Wythe;* but they were overpowered by the young hot and giddy members. In the course of the debates I have heard that very indecent language was used by a Mr. *Henry* a young lawyer who had not been a month a Member of the House; who carried all the young Members with him; so that I hope I am authorised in saying there is cause at least to doubt whether this would have been the sense of the Colony if more of their Representatives had done their duty by attending to the end of the Session.

11. The Resolutions as Printed in *The Journal of the House of Burgesses*

[Kennedy, ed., *Journals of the House of Burgesses of Virginia, 1761-1765*, 360.]

Resolved, That the first Adventurers and Settlers of this his Majesty's Colony and Dominion of *Virginia* brought with them, and transmitted to their Posterity, and all other his Majesty's Subjects since inhabiting in this his Majesty's said Colony, all the Liberties, Privileges, Franchises, and Immunities, that have at any Time been held, enjoyed, and possessed, by the people of *Great Britain*.

Resolved, That by two royal Charters, granted by King *James* the First, the Colonists aforesaid are declared entitled to all Liberties, Privileges, and Immunities of Denizens and natural Subjects, to all Intents and Purposes, as if they had been abiding and born within the Realm of *England.*

Resolved, That the Taxation of the People by themselves, or by Persons chosen by themselves to represent them, who can only know what Taxes the People are able to bear, or the easiest Method of raising them, and must themselves be affected by every Tax laid on the People, is the only Security against a burthensome Taxation, and the distinguishing Characteristick of *British* Freedom, without which the ancient Constitution cannot exist.

Resolved, That his Majesty's liege People of this his most ancient and loyal Colony have without Interruption enjoyed the inestimable Right of being governed by such Laws, respecting their internal Polity and Taxation, as are derived from their own Consent, with the Approbation of their Sovereign, or his Substitute; and that the same hath never been forfeited or yielded up, but hath been constantly recognized by the Kings and People of *Great Britain.*

12. The Resolutions as Recalled by Patrick Henry

[From the original manuscript at Colonial Williamsburg.]

Resolved

That the first Adventurers and Settlers of this his Majesties Colony and Dominion brought with them and transmitted to their Posterity and all other his Majesties Subjects since inhabiting in this his Majestie's said Colony all the Priviledges, Franchises and Immunities that have at any Time been held, enjoyed, and possessed by the People of Great Britain.

Resolved

That by two royal Charters granted by King James the first the Colonists aforesaid are declared intituled to all the Priviledges, Liberties and Immunities of Denizens and natural born Subjects to all Intents and Purposes as if they had been abiding and born within the Realm of England.

Resolved

That the Taxation of the People by themselves or by Persons chosen by themselves to represent them who can only know what Taxes the People are able to bear and the easiest Mode of raising them and are equally affected by such Taxes Themselves is the distinguishing Characteristick of British Freedom and without which the ancient Constitution cannot subsist.

Resolved

That his Majestie's liege People of this most ancient Colony have uninterruptedly enjoyed the Right of being thus governed by their own assembly in the Article of their Taxes and internal Police and that the same hath never been forfeited or any other Way given up but hath been constantly recognized by the Kings and People of Great Britain.

Resolved

Therefore that the General Assembly of this Colony have the *only and sole exclusive* Right and Power to lay Taxes and Impositions upon the Inhabitants of this Colony and that every Attempt to vest such Power in any Person or Persons whatsoever other than the General Assembly aforesaid has a manifest Tendency to destroy British as well as American Freedom.

13. The Resolutions as Printed by the *Newport Mercury*, June 24, 1765

WHEREAS the Hon. House of Commons, in England, have of late drawn into Question, how far the General Assembly of this Colony hath Power to enact Laws for laying of Taxes and imposing Duties, payable by the People of this his Majesty's most antient Colony: For settling and ascertaining the same to all future Times, the House of Burgesses of this present General Assembly have come to the following Resolves:——

Resolved, That the first Adventurers, Settlers of this his Majesty's Colony and Dominion of Virginia, brought with them and transmitted to their Posterity, and all other his Majesty's Subjects since inhabiting in this his Majesty's Colony, all the Privileges and Immunities that have at any Time been held, enjoyed and possessed by the People of **Great-Britain.**

Resolved, That by two Royal Charters, granted by King *James* the First, the Colony aforesaid are declared and entitled to all Privileges and Immunities of natural born Subjects, to all Intents and Purposes, as if they had been abiding and born within the Realm of England.

Resolved, That his Majesty's liege People of this his antient Colony have enjoy'd the Right of being thus govern'd, by their own Assembly, in the Article of Taxes and internal Police; and that the same have never been forfeited, or any other Way yielded up, but have been constantly recogniz'd by the King and People of Britain.

Resolved, therefore, That the General Assembly of this Colony, together with his Majesty or his Substitutes, have, in their Representative Capacity, the only exclusive Right and Power to lay Taxes and Imposts upon the Inhabitants of this Colony: And that every Attempt to vest such Power in any other Person or Persons whatever, than the General Assembly afcresaid, is illegal, unconstitutional and unjust, and have a manifest Tendency to destroy British as well as American Liberty.

Resolved, That his Majesty's liege People, the Inhabitants of this Colony, are not bound to yield Obedience to any Law or Ordinance whatever, designed to impose any Taxation whatsoever upon them, other than the Laws or Ordinances of the General Assembly aforesaid.

Resolved, That any Person, who shall, by speaking or writing, assert or maintain, that any Person or Persons, other than the General Assembly of this Colony, have any Right or Power to impose or lay any Taxation on the People here, shall be deemed an Enemy to this his Majesty's. Colony.

14. The Resolutions as Printed by the *Maryland Gazette*, July 4, 1765

RESOLVES of the House of Burgesses in VIRGINIA, *June* 1765. That the first Adventurers and Settlers of this his Majesty's Colony and Dominion of *Virginia,* brought with them, and transmitted to their Posterity, and all other his Majesty's Subjects since inhabiting in this his Majesty's Colony, all the Liberties, Privileges, Franchises, and Immunities, that at any Time have been held, enjoyed, and possessed, by the People of *Great Britain.*

That by Two Royal Charters, granted by King *James* the First, the Colonies aforesaid are Declared Entitled, to all Liberties, Privileges and Immunities, of

Denizens and Natural Subjects (to all Intents and Purposes) as if they had been Abiding and Born within the Realm of *England*.

That the Taxation of the People by Themselves, or by Persons Chosen by Themselves to Represent them, who can only know what Taxes the People are able to bear, or the easiest Method of Raising them, and must themselves be affected by every Tax laid upon the People, is the only Security against a Burthensome Taxation; and the Distinguishing Characteristic of *British* FREEDOM; and, without which, the antient Constitution cannot exist.

That his Majesty's Liege People of this his most Ancient and Loyal Colony, have, without Interruption, the inestimable Right of being governed by such Laws, respecting their internal Polity and Taxation, as are derived from their own consent, with the Approbation of their Sovereign, or his Substitute; which Right hath never been Forfeited, or Yielded up; but hath been constantly recognized by the Kings and People of *Great Britain*.

Resolved therefore, That the General Assembly of this Colony, with the Consent of his Majesty, or his Substitute, HAVE the Sole Right and Authority to lay Taxes and Impositions upon It's Inhabitants: And, That every Attempt to vest such Authority in any other Person or Persons whatsoever, has a Manifest Tendency to Destroy AMERICAN FREEDOM.

That his Majesty's Liege People, Inhabitants of this Colony, are not bound to yield Obedience to any Law or Ordinance whatsoever, designed to impose any Taxation upon them, other than the Laws or Ordinances of the General Assembly as aforesaid.

That any Person who shall, by Speaking, or Writing, assert or maintain, That any Person or Persons, other than the General Assembly of this Colony, with such Consent as aforesaid, have any Right or Authority to lay or impose any Tax whatever on the Inhabitants thereof, shall be Deemed, AN ENEMY TO THIS HIS MAJESTY'S COLONY.

The Resolves of Other Colonies

15. The Rhode Island Resolves, September, 1765

[J. R. Bartlett, ed., *Records of the Colony of Rhode Island* (Providence, 1856-65), VI, 451-52, corrected from the original in the state archives.]

This Assembly taking into the most serious Consideration, an Act passed by the Parliament of Great Britain, at their last Session, for levying Stamp Duties, and other internal Duties, in North America, Do Resolve.

1. That the first Adventurers, Settlers of this His Majesty's Colony and Dominion of Rhode Island and Providence Plantations, brought with them and transmitted to their Posterity, and all other His Majesty's Subjects since inhabiting in this his Majesty's Colony, all the Privileges and Immunities that have at any Time been held, enjoyed and possessed by the People of Great Britain.

2. That by a Charter Granted by King Charles the Second, in the fifteenth Year of his Reign, the Colony aforesaid is declared and entituled to all the Privileges and Immunities of natural born Subjects, to all Intents and Purposes, as if they had been abiding and born within the Realm of England.

3. This His Majestys Liege People of this Colony have enjoyed the Right of being

governed by their own Assembly, in the Article of Taxes and internal Police; and that the same hath never been forfeited or any other Way yielded up, but hath been constantly recognized by the King and People of Britain.

4. That, therefore, the General Assembly, of this Colony, have, in their representative Capacity, the Only exclusive Right to lay Taxes and Imposts upon the Inhabitants of this Colony: And that every Attempt to vest such Power in any Person or Persons whatever, other than the General Assembly aforesaid, is unconstitutional, and hath a manifest Tendency to destroy the Liberties of the People of this Colony.

5. That his Majesty's liege People, the Inhabitants of this Colony, are not bound to yield Obedience to any Law or Ordinance, designed to impose any internal Taxation whatsoever upon them, other than the Laws or Ordinances of the General Assembly aforesaid.

6. That all the Officers in this Colony, appointed by the Authority thereof, be, and they are hereby directed, to proceed in the Execution of their respective Offices, in the same manner as usual: And that this Assembly will indemnify and save harmless all the said Officers, on Account of their Conduct, agreeable to this Resolution.

16. The Pennsylvania Resolves, September 21, 1765

[*Pennsylvania Archives*, 8th ser., 7 (1935), 5779-80.]

The House taking into Consideration, that an Act of Parliament has lately passed in *England*, for imposing certain Stamp Duties, and other Duties, on his Majesty's Subjects in *America*, whereby they conceive some of their most essential and valuable Rights, as *British* Subjects, to be deeply affected, think it a Duty they owe to themselves, and their Posterity, to come to the following Resolutions, *viz*.

Resolved, N. C. D. 1. That the Assemblies of this Province have, from Time to Time, whenever Requisitions have been made by his Majesty, for carrying on military Operations, for the Defence of *America*, most chearfully and liberally contributed their full Proportion of Men and Money for those Services.

Resolved, N. C. D. 2. That whenever his Majesty's Service shall, for the future, require the Aids of the Inhabitants of this Province, and they shall be called upon for that Purpose in a constitutional Way, it will be their indispensable Duty most chearfully and liberally to grant to his Majesty their Proportion of Men and Money for the Defence, Security, and other public Services of the *British American* Colonies.

Resolved, N. C. D. 3. That the inhabitants of this Province are entitled to all the Liberties, Rights and Privileges of his Majesty's Subjects in *Great-Britain*, or elsewhere, and that the Constitution of Government in this Province is founded on the natural Rights of Mankind, and the noble Principles of *English* Liberty, and therefore is, or ought to be, perfectly free.

Resolved, N. C. D. 4. That it is the inherent Birth-right, and indubitable Privilege, of every *British* Subject, to be taxed only by his own Consent, or that of his legal Representatives, in Conjunction with his Majesty, or his Substitutes.

Resolved, N. C. D. 5. That the only legal Representatives of the Inhabitants of this Province are the Persons they annually elect to serve as Members of Assembly.

Resolved, therefore, N. C. D. 6. That the Taxation of the People of this Province by any other Persons whatsoever than such their Representatives in Assembly, is unconstitutional, and subversive of their most valuable Rights.

Resolved, N. C. D. 7. That the laying Taxes upon the Inhabitants of this Province in any other Manner, being manifestly subversive of public Liberty, must, of necessary Consequence, be utterly destructive of public Happiness.

Resolved, N. C. D. 8. That the vesting and Authority in the Courts of Admiralty to decide in Suits relating to the Stamp Duty, and other Matters, foreign to their proper Jurisdiction, is highly dangerous to the Liberties of his Majesty's *American* Subjects, contrary to *Magna Charta,* the great Charter and Fountain of *English* Liberty, and destructive of one of their most darling and acknowledged Rights, that of Trials by Juries.

Resolved, N. C. D. 9. That it is the Opinion of this House, that the Restraints imposed by several late Acts of Parliament on the Trade of this Province, at a Time when the People labour under an enormous Load of Debt, must of Necessity be attended with the most fatal Consequences, not only to this Province, but to the Trade of our Mother Country.

Resolved, N. C. D. 10. That this House think it their Duty thus firmly to assert, with Modesty and Decency, their inherent Rights, that their Posterity may learn and know, that it was not with their Consent and Acquiescence, that any Taxes should be levied on them by any Persons but their own Representatives; and are desirous that these their Resolves should remain on their Minutes, as a Testimony of the Zeal and ardent Desire of the present House of Assembly to preserve their inestimable Rights, which, as *Englishmen,* they have possessed ever since this Province was settled, and to transmit them to their latest Posterity.

17. The Maryland Resolves, September 28, 1765

[Archives of Maryland, 59 (1942), 30-32.]

I:st Resolved Unanimously that the first Adventurers and Setlers of this Province of Maryland brought with them and transmitted to their Posterity and all other his Majestys Subjects since Inhabiting in this province all the Liberties privileges Franchises and Immunities that any time have been held enjoyed and possessed by the People of Great Britain

2.d Resolved Unanimously that it was Granted by Magna Charta and other the Good Laws and Statutes of England and Confirmed by the Petition and Bill of Rights that the Subject should not be Compelled to Contribute to any Tax Tallage Aid or other like Charge not set by common Consent of Parliament

3:d Resolved Unanimously that by a Royal Charter Granted by his Majesty King Charles the first in the eighth year of his Reign And in the Year of our Lord One thousand Six hundred and thirty two to Caecilius then Lord Baltimore it was for the Encouragement for People to Transport themselves and families in to this Province amongst other things Covenanted and Granted by his said Majesty for himself his heirs and Successors as followeth And we will also and for our more Special Grace for us our heirs and Successors we do strictly enjoin Constitute Ordain and Command that the said Province shall be of our Allegiance and that all and Singular the Subjects and liege People of us our heirs and Successors transported or to be Transported into the said Province and the Children of them and of such as shall descend from them there already born or hereafter to be born be and shall be Denizens and lieges of us our heirs and Successors of our Kingdoms of England and Ireland and be in all things held treated reputed and esteemed as the liege faithfull People of us our heirs and

Successors born within our Kingdom of England and likewise any Lands Tenements Revenues Services and other Hereditaments whatsoever within our Kingdom of England and other our Dominions may inherit or otherwise purchase receive take have hold buy and possess and them may Occupy and enjoy give Sell Alien and bequeath as likewise all Libertys Franchises and privileges of this our Kingdom of England freely quietly and peacably have and possess Occupy and enjoy as our liege people born or to be born within our said Kingdom of England without the Let Molestation Vexation trouble or Grievance of us our heirs and Successors Any Statute Act Ordinance or provision to the Contrary thereof Notwithstanding

And further our pleasure is and by these presents for us our heirs and Successors We do Covenant and Grant to and with the said now Lord Baltimore his heirs and Assigns that we our heirs and Successors shall at no time hereafter Set or make or cause to be Set any Imposition Custom or other Taxation Rate or Contribution whatsoever in or upon the Dwellers and Inhabitants of the aforesaid Province for their Lands Tenements Goods or Chattels within the said Province or in or upon any Goods or Merchandizes within the said Province to be laden or unladen within any the Ports or Harbours of the said Province And our Pleasure is and for us our heirs and Successors We Charge and Command that this our Declaration shall be hence forward from time to time received and allowed in all our Courts and before all the Judges of us our heirs and Successors for a Sufficient and lawfull Discharge Payment and Acquittance commanding all and Singular our Officers and Ministers of us our heirs and Successors and enjoyning them upon pain of our high Displeasure that they do not presume at any time to Attempt any thing to the Contrary of the Premisses or that they do in any Sort withstand the same but that they be at all times Aiding and Assisting as

is fitting unto the said now Lord Baltimore and his heirs and to the Inhabitants and Merchants of Maryland aforesaid their Servants Ministers factors and Assigns in the full use and Fruition of the Benefit of this our Charter

4:th Resolved that it is the Unanimous Opinion of this House that the said Charter is Declaratory of the Constitutional Rights and Privileges of the Freemen of this Province

5:th Resolved Unanimously That Tryals by Juries is the Grand Bulwark of Liberty the undoubted Birthright of every Englishman and Consequently of every British Subject in America and that the Erecting other Jurisdictions for the Tryal of Matters of fact is unconstitutional and renders the Subject insecure in his Liberty and Property

6:th Resolved That it is the Unanimous Opinion of this House that it cannot with any truth or Propriety be said that the Freemen of this Province of Maryland are Represented in the British Parliament

7:th Resolved Unanimously that his Majestys liege People of this Ancient Province have always enjoyed the Right of being Governed by Laws to which they themselves have consented in the Articles of Taxes and internal Polity and that the same hath never been forfeited or any other way Yielded up but hath been Constantly recognized by the King and People of Great Britain

8:th Resolved that it is the Unanimous Opinion of this House that the Representatives of the Freemen of this Province in their Legislative Capacity together with the other part of the Legislature have the Sole Right to lay Taxes and Impositions on the Inhabitants of this Province or their Property and effects And that the laying imposing levying or Collecting any Tax on or from the Inhabitants of Maryland under Colour of any other Authority is Unconstitutional and a Direct Violation of the Rights of the Freemen of this Province.

18. The Connecticut Resolves, October 25, 1765

[C. J. Hoadly, ed., *Public Records of the Colony of Connecticut* (Hartford, 1850-90), XII, 421-25, corrected from the original manuscript in the Connecticut State Library.]

The House of Representatives of his Majesty's Colony of Connecticut in New England, in general Court assembled,

Taking into their serious Consideration, that an Act of the Parliament of Great Britain has been lately past, for granting and applying certain stamp Duties etc. in the British Colonies and Plantations in America, find ourselves distressed with the most alarming Apprehensions, when wee observe, that grand Legislature to entertain Sentiments so different from Ours respecting what Wee ever, reconed among our most important, and essential Rights as, English-Men.—The Constitution of the British Government, Wee esteem the hapiest in the World, founded on Maxims of consummate Wisdom, and in the best Manner calculated to secure the Prerogatives of the Crown, while it maintains the just Rights and Liberties of the Subject. By Vertue of which Constitution, and the royal Grant and Charter of his Majesty King Charles the second, The Inhabitants of this Colony have enjoyed great and inestimable Liberties and Priviledges, of a civil and religious Nature for more than a Century past, And more especially under the auspicious Government of the illustrious House of Hanover. That royal House have ever held sacred and inviolable, those Rights and Priviledges of their loyal Subjects in this Colony, derived to them, as aforesaid. In Return for which, the Princes of that exalted Line, have ever had from this People, their ardent Desires of all Happiness to their Persons, and Glory to their Empire. Inspired with the warmest Sentiments of affectionate Loyalty and Duty, The Colonists have been ever ready to sacrifice their Lives and Fortunes, to the Service of their King and Country, And believing that his Majesty's Interest in this Colony cannot be more firmly established and perfectly secured, nor the Hapiness of the British Nation more effectually promoted by us, than in our full Possession and continued Enjoyment of the Rights and Priviledges of the British Constitution, which wee have not forfeited, but ought to hold as Englishmen, and which are if possible, rendered more sacred and indefeasible by the royal Grant and Charter aforesaid, which We conceive to stand upon the same Basis with the grand Charters and Fountains of English Liberty. —And as the aforesaid Act tends (as we conceive) to deprive us of the most interesting, important, and essential of those Rights, which we hold most dear, and cannot on any possible Considerations be induced willingly to part with, Wee are therefore filled with the most sensible Grief, and Concern, And think it a Duty, wee owe to his Majesty, to the Nation, to Ourselves and to Posterity to express and declare the Sense wee have respecting the Rights and Priviledges which wee may justly claim, and humbly hope to enjoy, under his Majestys gracious Protection and Government; And do therefore declare and make it known, in the following Declarations and Resolves.

1. In the first Place, Wee do most expresly declare, recognize and acknowledge His Majesty King George the third, to be lawful and rightful King of Great Britain, and all other the Dominions and Countries thereto belonging, And that it is the indispensible Duty of the People of this Colony, as being Part of his Majesty's Dominions, always to bear faithful and true Allegiance to his Majesty, and him to defend to the Utmost of their Power against all Attempts, against his Person, Crown and Dignity.

2. That, this Colony or the greatest

Part thereof, was purchased and obtained for great and valuable Considerations, and some other Part thereof gained by Conquest, with much Difficulty, and at the only Endeavours, expences and Charges, of our fore-Fathers, And that thereby considerable Addition was made to his Majesty's Dominions and Interest, And that in Consideration of such Purchase etc. as aforesaid His Majesty King Charles the 2d. in the fourteenth Year of his Reign, did for himself his Heirs and Successors, ordain declare and grant, unto the Governor and Company of this Colony, and their Successors, That all and every of the Subjects of Him, his Heirs and Successors, which should go to inhabit within the said Colony, and every of their Children, which should be born there, or on the Sea in going thither or returning from thence, should have, and enjoy, all Liberties, and Immunities of free and natural Subjects, within any of the Dominions of the said King, his Heirs or Successors, to all Intents Constructions and Purposes whatsoever, as if they and every of them, were born within the Realm of England.

3. That the free natural Subjects of Great Britain, born within the Realm of England have a Property in their own Estate, and are to be taxed only by their own Consent, given in Person or by their Representatives, And are not to be disseized of their Liberties or free Customes, sentenced or condemned but by lawful Judgment of their Peers, And that the said Rights and Immunities, were granted to, and conferred on the Inhabitants of this Colony, by the royal Grant and Charter aforesaid, And therefore are their Rights to all Intents, Constructions, and Purposes, whatsoever.

4. That the Consent of the Inhabitants of this Colony was not given to the said Act of Parliament personally or by Representation, actual or virtual, in any Sense or Degree, that at all comports, with the True intendment, Spirit, or equitable Construction of the British Constitution.

5. That, his Majestys's liege Subjects of this Colony have enjoyed the Right and Priviledge of being governed by their general Assembly, in the Article of taxing and internal Police, agreeable to the Powers and Priviledges granted and contained in the royal Charter aforesaid, for more than a Century past, And that the same have never been forfeited or any Way yielded up, but have been constantly recognized by the King and Parliament of Great Britain.

6. That in the Opinion of this House, An Act for raising Money by Duties or Taxes differs from other Acts of Legislation, in that it is always considered as a free Gift of the People made by their legal, and elected Representatives, And that we cannot conceive, that the People of great Britain, or their Representatives, have Right, to dispose of our Property.

7. That the only legal Representatives of the Inhabitants of this Colony are the Persons they elect to serve as Members of the General Assembly thereof.

8. That the vesting an Authority, in the Courts of Admiralty as in said Act is provided to judge and determine in Sutes relating to the Duties and Forfeitures contained in said Act and other Matters, foreign to their accustomed and established Jurisdiction, is in the Opinion of this House, highly dangerous to the Liberties of his Majesty's american Subjects, contrary to the great Charter of English Liberty, and destructive of one of their most darling Rights, that of Tryal by Juries, which is justly esteemed one chief Excellence of the British Constitution and principal Bulwark of English Liberty.

9. That it is the Opinion of this House, that the said Act for granting and applying certain Stamp Duties etc. as aforesaid, is unprecedented, and unconstitutional.

10. That, whenever his Majesty's Service shall require the Aid of the Inhabitants of this Colony, the same fixed Principles of Loyalty, as well as Self

Preservation, which have hitherto induced us fully to comply, with his Majesty's Requisitions, will, together with the deep Sense Wee have, of its being our indispensible Duty (in the Opinion of this House) ever hold us under the strongest Obligations which can be given or desired, most cheerfully to grant his Majesty from Time to Time, our further Proportion, of Men and Money for the Defence Security, and other Services of the British american Dominions.

11. That wee look upon the well being and greatest Security of this Colony to depend (under God) on our Connections with Great Britain, which wee ardently wish, may continue to the latest Posterity, And that it is the humble Opinion of this House That the Constitution of this Colony being understood and practised upon, as it has been ever since it existed, is the surest Band of Union, Confidence, and mutual Prosperity of our Mother-Country, and Us, and the best Foundation, on which to build the good of the whole, whether considered in a civil, military or mercantile Light, And of the Truth of this Opinion, Wee are the more confident as it is not founded on Speculation only, but has been verified in Fact, and by long Experience, found to produce, according to our Extent, and other Circumstances, as many loyal, virtuous, industrious, and well governed Subjects, as any Part of his Majesty's Dominions, And as truely zealous, and as warmly engaged to promote the best good, and real Glory of the grand whole, which constitutes the British Empire.

19. The Massachusetts Resolves, October 29, 1765

[*Journal of the Honourable House of Representatives . . . Begun and held at Boston, in the County of Suffolk, on Wednesday the Twenty-ninth Day of May, Annoque Domini, 1765* (Boston, 1765), 151-53.]

Whereas the just Rights of His Majesty's Subjects of this Province, derived to them from the *British Constitution,* as well as the *Royal Charter,* have been lately drawn into Question: In order to ascertain the same, this House do UNANIMOUSLY come into the following Resolves.

1. *Resolved,* That there are certain essential Rights of the *British* Constitution of Government, which are founded in the Law of God and Nature, and are the common Rights of Mankind—Therefore

2. *Resolved,* That the Inhabitants of this Province are *unalienably* entitled to those essential Rights in common with all Men: And that no Law of Society can consistent with the Law of God and Nature divest them of those Rights.

3. *Resolved,* That no Man can justly take the Property of another without his Consent: And that upon this *original* Principle the Right of Representation in the same Body, which exercises the Power of making Laws for levying Taxes, which is one of the main Pillars of the British Constitution, is evidently founded.

4. *Resolved,* That this *inherent* Right, together with all other, essential Rights, Liberties, Privileges and Immunities of the People of *Great Britain,* have been fully confirmed to them by *Magna Charta,* and by former and later Acts of Parliament.

5. *Resolved,* That His Majesty's subjects in *America,* are in Reason and common Sense, entitled to the same Extent of Liberty with His Majesty's Subjects in *Britain.*

6. *Resolved,* That by the Declaration of the Royal Charter of this Province the Inhabitants are entitled, to all the Rights, Liberties, and Immunities of free and

natural Subjects of *Great-Britain,* to all Intents, Purposes and Constructions whatever.

7. Resolved, That the Inhabitants of this Province appear to be entitled to all the Rights aforementioned, by an Act of Parliament, 13th of *Geo.* 2d.

8. Resolved, That those Rights do belong to the Inhabitants of this Province, upon Principles of *common Justice;* their Ancestors having settled this Country at their *sole Expence;* and *their* Posterity, having constantly approved themselves most loyal and faithful Subjects of *Great-Britain.*

9. Resolved, That every Individual in the Colonies is as advantageous to *Great-Britain,* as if he were in *Great-Britain,* and held to pay his full Proportion of Taxes there: And as the Inhabitants of this Province pay their full Proportion of Taxes, for the Support of his Majesty's Government *here,* it is unreasonable for them to be called upon, to pay any Part of the Charges of the Government *there.*

10. Resolved, That the Inhabitants of this Province are not, and never have been, represented in the Parliament of *Great-Britain;* And that such a Representation *there,* as the Subjects in *Britain* do actually and rightfully enjoy, is *impracticable* for the subjects *in America:*—And further, That in the Opinion of this House, the several subordinate Powers of Legislation in *America,* were constituted, upon the Apprehensions of this *Impracticability.*

11. Resolved, That the *only* Method, whereby the constitutional Rights of the Subjects of this Province can be secure, consistent with a Subordination to the supreme Power of *Great-Britain,* is by the continued Exercise of such Powers of Government as are granted in the Royal Charter, and a firm Adherence to the Privileges of the same.

12. Resolved, As a just Conclusion from some of the foregoing Resolves, That all Acts made, by any Power whatever, other than the General Assembly of this Province, imposing Taxes on the Inhabitants are Infringements of our *inherent* and *unalienable* Rights, as *Men* and *British Subjects:* and render void the most valuable Declarations of our *Charter.*

13. Resolved, That the Extension of the Powers of the Court of Admiralty within this Province, is a most violent Infraction of the Right of Trials by Juries.—A Right, which this House upon the Principles of their *British Ancestors,* hold most dear and sacred; it being the only Security of the Lives, Liberties and Properties of his Majesty's Subjects here.

14. Resolved, That this House owe the strictest Allegiance to his Most Sacred Majesty King GEORGE the Third: That they have the greatest Veneration for the Parliament: And that they will, after the Example of *all* their Predecessors, from the Settlement of this Country, exert themselves to their utmost, in supporting his Majesty's Authority in the Province,—in promoting the true Happiness of his Subjects: and in enlarging the Extent of his Dominion.

Ordered, That all the foregoing Resolves be kept in the Records of this House; that a just Sense of Liberty, and the firm Sentiments of Loyalty may be transmitted to Posterity.

20. The South Carolina Resolves, November 29, 1765

[Mss. Journal of the Commons House of Assembly, in the South Carolina Archives Department.]

THIS HOUSE, Sincerely devoted, with the warmest Sentiments of Affection and Duty to His Majesty's Person and Government, inviolably attached to the present happy Establishment of the Protestant Succession; and with minds deeply impressed by a sense of the present and impending Misfortunes of the People of this Province; esteem it their indispensable Duty to their Constituents, to themselves, and to Posterity, to come to the following RESOLUTIONS, respecting their most essential Rights and Liberties, and the Grievances under which they labour, by reason of several late Acts of Parliament.

1st. RESOLVED, That His Majesty's Subjects in this Province owe the same Allegiance to the Crown of Great Britain, that is due from His Subjects born there.

2d. THAT His Majesty's Liege Subjects in this Province, are intitled to all the inherent Rights and Liberties of His natural born Subjects within the Kingdom of Great Britain.

3d. THAT the Inhabitants of this Province appear also to be confirmed in all the Rights aforementioned, not only by their Charter, but by an Act of Parliament of the 13th George 2d.

4th. THAT it is inseperably essential to the Freedom of a People, and the undoubted Right of Englishmen, that no Taxes be imposed on them, but with their own Consent, given personally, or by their Representatives.

5th. THAT the People of this Province are not, and, from their local Circumstances, cannot be, represented in the House of Commons of Great Britain, And farther, That, in the Opinion of this House, the several Powers of Legislation in America were constituted, in some Measure, upon the Apprehention of this Impracticability.

6th. THAT the only Representatives of the People of this Province are Persons chosen therein by themselves; and that no Taxes ever have been, or can be, constitutionally imposed on them, but by the Legislature of this Province.

7th. THAT all Supplies to the Crown being free Gifts of the People, it is unreasonable and inconsistent with the Principles and Spirit of the British Constitution, for the People of Great Britain to grant to His Majesty the Property of the People of this Province.

8th. THAT Trial by Jury, is the inherent and invaluable Right of every British Subject in this Province.

9th. THAT the late Act of Parliament, intituled, "an Act for granting and applying certain Stamp Duties and other Duties on the British Colonies and Plantations in America," &c. by imposing Taxes on the Inhabitants of this Province; and the said Act and several other Acts, by extending the Jurisdiction of the Courts of Admiralty, beyond its ancient Limits, have a Manifest Tendency to subvert the Rights and Liberties of the People of this Province.

10th. THAT the Duties imposed, by several late Acts of Parliament, on the People of this Province, will be extreamly burthensome and grievous, and, from the Scarcity of Gold and Silver, the Payment of them absolutely impracticable.

11th. THAT, as the Profits of the Trade of the People of this Province ultimately center in Great Britain, to pay for the Manufactures which they are obliged to take from thence, they eventually contribute very largely to all the Supplies granted there to the Crown; And besides, as every Individual in this Province, is as advantageous at least to Great Britain, as if he were in Great Britain; and as they pay their full Proportion of Taxes for the Support of His Majesty's Government here (which Taxes are equal, or more, in Proportion to our Estates, than those paid by our Fellow Subjects in Great Britain upon theirs); it is unreasonable, for them to be called upon, to pay any farther part of the Charges of the Government there.

12th. THAT the Assemblies of this Province have, from Time to Time, whenever Requisitions have been made by His Majesty, for carrying on Military Operations, either for the Defence of themselves, or that of America in general, most chearfully and liberally contributed their full

Proportion, of Men and Money, for these Services.

13th. THAT, though the Representatives of the People of this Province had equal Assurances and reasons, with those of the other Provinces, to expect a proportional Reimbursement, of those immense Charges they had been at, for His Majesty's Service, in the late War, out of the several Parliamentary Grants for the use of America; yet, they have obtained only their Proportion of the first of those Grants; and the small Sum of Two Hundred and Eighty five Pounds Sterling received since.

14th. THAT notwithstanding, whenever His Majesty's Service shall, for the future, require the Aids of the Inhabitants of this Province, and they shall be called upon for that Purpose in a Constitutional Way, it shall be their indispensable Duty, most chearfully and liberally, to grant to His Majesty, their Proportion, according to their ability, of Men and Money, for the Defence, Security, and other public Services of the British American Colonies.

15th. THAT the Restrictions on the Trade of the People of this Province, together with the late Duties and Taxes, imposed on them by Acts of Parliament, must necessarily greatly lessen the Consumption of British Manufactures amongst them.

16th. THAT the Increase, Prosperity, and Happiness of the People of this Province, depend on the full and free Enjoyment of their Rights and Liberties, and an affectionate Intercourse with Great Britain.

17th. THAT the Readiness of the Colonies to comply with His Majestys Requisitions, as well as their Inability to bear any additional Taxes, beyond what is laid on them by their respective Legislatures, is apparent, from the several Grants of Parliament, to reimburse them Part of the heavy Expences they were at in the late War in America.

18th. THAT it is the Right of the British Subjects in this Province, to petition the King or either House of Parliament.

ORDERED that these VOTES AND RESOLUTIONS, be Signed by the Speaker, and be Printed, and made Public, that a just Sense of Liberty, and a firm Sentiments of the Loyalty, of the Representatives of the People of this Province, may be known to their Constituents, and transmitted to Posterity.

21. The New Jersey Resolves, November 30, 1765

[*Pennsylvania Gazette*, Dec. 5, 1765.]

Whereas the late Act of Parliament called the Stamp Act, is found to be utterly subversive of Privileges inherent in and originally secured by, Grants and Confirmations from the Crown of Great-Britain to the Settlers of this Colony: In Duty therefore to ourselves, our Constituents, and Posterity, this House think it absolutely necessary to leave the following Resolves on our Minutes.

1. Resolved, N. C. D. That his Majesty's Subjects Inhabiting this Province are, from the strongest Motives of Duty, Fidelity and Gratitude, inviolably attached to his Royal Person and Government, and have ever shewn, and we doubt not ever will, their utmost Readiness and Alacrity in, acceding to the constitutional Requisitions of the Crown, as they have been from time to time made to this colony.

2. Resolved, N. C. D. That his Majesty's liege Subjects in this Colony, are entitled to all the inherent Rights and Liberties of his natural born Subjects within the Kingdom of Great-Britain.

3. Resolved, N. C. D. That it is inseparably essential to the Freedom of a People, and the undoubted right of Eng-

lishmen, that no Taxes be imposed on them but with their own Consent, given personally, or by their Representatives.

4. Resolved, N. C. D. That the People of this Colony are not, and from their remote situations cannot be, represented in the Parliament of Great-Britain. And if the Principle of taxing the Colonies without their own Consent should be adopted, the People here would be subjected to the Taxation of two Legislatures, a grievance unprecedented, and not to be thought of without the greatest Anxiety.

5. Resolved, N. C. D. That the only Representatives of the People of this Colony are Persons chosen by themselves, and that no Taxes ever have been, or can be imposed on them, agreeable to the Constitution of this Province, granted and confirmed by his Majesty's most gracious Predecessors, but by their own Legislature.

6. Resolved, N. C. D. That all Supplies being free Gifts, for the People of Great-Britain to grant to his Majesty the Property of the People of this Colony, without their Consent, and being represented, would be unreasonable, and render useless Legislation in this Colony, in the most essential Point.

7. Resolved, N. C. D. That the Profits of Trade arising from this Colony, centering in Great Britain, eventually contribute to the supplies granted there to the Crown.

8. Resolved, N. C. D. That the giving unlimited Power to any Subject or Subjects, to impose what Taxes they please in the Colonies, under the Mode of regulating the Prices of stamped Vellum, Parchment and Paper, appears to us unconstitutional, contrary to the Rights of the Subject, and apparently dangerous in its Consequences.

9. Resolved, N. C. D. That any Incumbrances which, in Effect, restrains the Liberty of the Press in America, is an infringement upon the Subjects' Liberty.

10. Resolved, N. C. D. That the Extension of the Powers of the Court of Admiralty within this Province, beyond its antient Limits, is a violent Innovation of the Right of trials by jury, a Right which this House, upon the Principles of their British Ancestors, hold most dear and invaluable.

11. Resolved, N. C. D. That as the Tranquility of this Colony hath been interrupted, through Fear of the dreadful Consequences of the Stamp Act, that therefore the Officers of the Government, who go on in their Offices for the Good and Peace of the Province, in the accustomed Manner, while Things are in their present unsettled Situation, will, in the Opinion of this House, be intitled to the Countenance of the Legislature. And it is recommended to our Constituents, to use what Endeavours lie in their Power, to preserve the Peace, Quiet, Harmony, and good Order of the Government; that no Heats, Disorders or Animosities, may in the least obstruct the united Endeavours that are now strongly engaged, for the Repealing the Act above mentioned, and other Acts affecting the Trade of the Colonies.

22. The New York Resolves, December 18, 1765

[*Journal of the Votes and Proceedings of the General Assembly* (New York, 1766), II, 807-8.]

The General Assembly of the Colony of *New-York*, taking into their most serious Consideration, several Acts of Parliament lately passed, granting Stamp, and other Duties to his Majesty, and restricting the Trade of this Colony, apprehending an Abolition of that Constitution under which they have so long and happily enjoyed the Rights and Liberties of *Englishmen*, and being clearly of Opinion that it is the Interest of *Great-Britain*, a Dependence on which they esteem their Felicity, to confirm them in the Enjoyment of those Rights, think it their indispensible Duty to make a Declaration of their Faith and Allegiance to his Majesty King GEORGE the Third, of their Submission to the Supreme Legislative Power; and at the same Time to shew that the Rights claimed by them are in no Manner inconsistent with either: For which Purpose they are come to the following Resolutions, *that is to say:*

Resolved, Nemine Contradicente,

That the People of this Colony owe the same Faith and Allegiance to his Majesty King GEORGE the Third, that are due to him from his Subjects in *Great-Britain.*

Resolved, Nemine Contradicente,

That they owe Obedience to all Acts of Parliament not inconsistent with the essential Rights and Liberties of *Englishmen,* and are intitled to the same Rights and Liberties which his Majesty's *English* Subjects both within and without the Realm have ever enjoyed.

Resolved, Nemine Contradicente,

That his Majesty's Subjects in *England,* are secured in the superior Advantages they enjoy principally, by the Privilege of an Exemption from Taxes not of their own Grant, and their Right to Trials by their Peers.—The First secures the People collectively from unreasonable Impositions; and without the Second, Individuals are at the arbitrary Disposition of the executive Powers.

Resolved, Nemine Contradicente,

That the Colonists did not forfeit these essential Rights by their Emigration; because *this* was by the Permission and Encouragement of the Crown; and that they rather merit Favour, than a Deprivation of those Rights, by giving an almost boundless Extent to the *British* Empire, expanding its Trade, increasing its Wealth, and augmenting that Power which renders it so formidable to all *Europe.*

Resolved, Nemine Contradicente,

That the Acts of Trade giving a Right of Jurisdiction to the Admiralty Courts, in Prosecutions for Penalties and Forfeitures, manifestly infringes the Right of Trials by Jury; and that the late Act for granting *Stamp Duties,* not only exposes the *American* Subjects to an intolerable Inconvenience and Expence, by compelling them to a Defence at a great Distance from Home; but, by imposing a Tax, utterly deprives them of the essential Right of being the *sole* Disposers of their own Property.

Resolved, Nemine Contradicente,

That all Aids to the Crown, in *Great-Britain,* are Gifts of the People by their Representatives in Parliament, as appears from the Preamble of every Money Bill, in which the Commons are said to give and grant to his Majesty.

Resolved, Nemine Contradicente,

That it involves the greatest Inconsistency with the known Principles of the *English* Constitution, to suppose that the honourable House of Commons of *Great-Britain,* can without divesting the Inhabitants of this Colony of their most essential Rights, grant to the Crown their, or any Part of their Estates for any Purpose whatsoever.

Resolved, Nemine Contradicente,

That from the first Settlement of the Colonies, it has been the Sense of the Government at Home, that such Grants could not be constitutionally made; and therefore Applications for the Support of Government, and other publick Exigencies, have always been made to the Representatives of the People of this Colony; and frequently during the late War by immediate Orders from the Crown, upon which they exerted themselves with so much Liberality, that the Parliament thought proper to contribute to their Reimbursement.

Resolved, Nemine Contradicente,

That if the People of this Colony should be deprived of the *sole* Right of Taxing themselves, or presenting such Sums as the publick Exigencies require, they would be laid under the greatest Disadvantages, as the united Interest of the Electors, or Elected, which constitute the Security of his Majesty's Subjects in *Great-Britain,* will operate strongly against them.

Resolved, Nemine Contradicente,

That the Impracticability of inducing the Colonies to grant Aids in an equal Manner, proportioned to their several Abilities, does by no Means induce a Necessity of divesting the Colonies of their *essential Rights.*

Resolved, Nemine Contradicente,

That it is the Duty of every Friend to *Great-Britain,* and this Colony to cultivate a hearty Union between them.

Resolved, Nemine Contradicente,

That if the honourable House of Commons insist on their Power of Taxing this Colony, and by that Means deprive its Inhabitants of what they have always looked upon as an undoubted Right, though this Power should be exerted in the mildest Manner, it will teach them to consider the People of *Great-Britain,* as vested with absolute Power to dispose of all their Property, and tend to weaken that Affection for the Mother Country, which this Colony *ever had,* and is *extremely* desirous of retaining.

Resolved, Nemine Contradicente,

That in order to keep the Colonies in due Subjection to, and Dependence upon *Great-Britain,* it is not necessary to deprive them of the Right they have long enjoyed, of Taxing themselves; since the same Right has been enjoyed by the Clergy within the Realm, and by all the Subjects of *Great-Britain* without the Realm, until the late Innovation.

Resolved, Nemine Contradicente,

That the Duties lately imposed by Act of Parliament on the Trade of this Colony, are very grievous and burthensome; and in the Apprehension of this House, impossible to be paid: Have already greatly diminished the advantageous Traffic heretofore carried on with the foreign Islands in the *West-Indies;* and in consequence, must render us unable to purchase the Manufactures of *Great-Britain.*

The Stamp Act Congress, October 7-24, 1765

23. The Declarations of the Stamp Act Congress

[Proceedings of the Congress at New York (Annapolis, 1766), 15-16.]

The Members of this Congress, sincerely devoted, with the warmest Sentiments of Affection and Duty to his Majesty's Person and Government, inviolably attached to the present happy Establishment of the Protestant Succession, and with Minds deeply impressed by a Sense of the present and impending Misfortunes of the *British* Colonies on this Continent; having considered as maturely as Time will permit, the Circumstances of the said Colonies, esteem it our indispensable Duty, to make the following Declarations of our humble Opinion, respecting the most Essential Rights and Liberties of the Colonists, and of the Grievances under which they labour, by Reason of several late Acts of Parliament.

I. That his Majesty's Subjects in these Colonies, owe the same Allegiance to the Crown of *Great-Britain,* that is owing from his Subjects born within the Realm, and all due Subordination to that August Body the Parliament of *Great-Britain.*

II. That his Majesty's Liege Subjects in these Colonies, are entitled to all the inherent Rights and Liberties of his Natural born Subjects, within the Kingdom of *Great-Britain.*

III. That it is inseparably essential to

the Freedom of a People, and the undoubted Right of *Englishmen,* that no Taxes be imposed on them, but with their own Consent, given personally, or by their Representatives.

IV. That the People of these Colonies are not, and from their local Circumstances cannot be, Represented in the House of Commons in *Great-Britain.*

V. That the only Representatives of the People of these Colonies, are Persons chosen therein by themselves, and that no Taxes ever have been, or can be Constitutionally imposed on them, but by their respective Legislature.

VI. That all Supplies to the Crown, being free Gifts of the People, it is unreasonable and inconsistent with the Principles and Spirit of the *British* Constitution, for the People of *Great-Britain,* to grant to his Majesty the Property of the Colonists.

VII. That Trial by Jury, is the inherent and invaluable Right of every *British* Subject in these Colonies.

VIII. That the late Act of Parliament, entitled, *An Act for granting and applying certain Stamp Duties, and other Duties, in the* British *Colonies and Plantations in* America, *&c.* by imposing Taxes on the Inhabitants of these Colonies, and the said Act, and several other Acts, by extending the Jurisdiction of the Courts of Admiralty beyond its ancient Limits, have a manifest Tendency to subvert the Rights and Liberties of the Colonists.

IX. That the Duties imposed by several late Acts of Parliament, from the peculiar Circumstances of these Colonies, will be extremely Burthensome and Grievous; and from the scarcity of Specie, the Payment of them absolutely impracticable.

X. That as the Profits of the Trade of these Colonies ultimately center in *Great-Britain,* to pay for the Manufactures which they are obliged to take from thence, they eventually contribute very largely to all Supplies granted there to the Crown.

XI. That the Restrictions imposed by several late Acts of Parliament, on the Trade of these Colonies, will render them unable to purchase the Manufactures of *Great-Britain.*

XII. That the Increase, Prosperity, and Happiness of these Colonies, depend on the full and free Enjoyment of their Rights and Liberties, and an Intercourse with *Great-Britain* mutually Affectionate and Advantageous.

XIII. That it is the Right of the *British* Subjects in these Colonies, to Petition the King, or either House of Parliament.

Lastly, That it is the indispensable Duty of these Colonies, to the best of Sovereigns, to the Mother Country, and to themselves, to endeavour by a loyal and dutiful Address to his Majesty, and humble Applications to both Houses of Parliament, to procure the Repeal of the Act for granting and applying certain Stamp Duties, of all Clauses of any other Acts of Parliament, whereby the Jurisdiction of the Admiralty is extended as aforesaid, and of the other late Acts for the Restriction of *American* Commerce.

24. The Petition to the King

[*Proceedings of the Congress at New York* (Annapolis, 1766), 17-19.]

To the King's most Excellent Majesty.

The PETITION of the Freeholders and other Inhabitants of the *Massachu-* *setts-Bay, Rhode-Island,* and *Providence* Plantations,   ,[1]   , *New-Jersey, Pennsylvania,* the Government of

1. The blank spaces in this and in the other petitions are for the names of Connecticut, New York, and South Carolina, which did not empower their delegates to sign the documents and did not formally approve the proceedings until later.

the Counties of *New-Castle, Kent,* and *Sussex,* upon *Delaware,* Province of *Maryland,*

Most humbly Sheweth,

That the Inhabitants of these Colonies, Unanimously devoted with the warmest Sentiments of Duty and Affection to your Majesty's Sacred Person and Government, Inviolably attached to the present Happy Establishment of the Protestant Succession in your Illustrious House, and deeply sensible of your Royal Attention to their Prosperity and Happiness, humbly beg Leave to approach the Throne, by representing to your Majesty, That these Colonies were Originally Planted by Subjects of the *British* Crown, who, animated with the Spirit of Liberty, encouraged by your Majesty's Royal Predecessors, and confiding in the Public Faith for the Enjoyment of all the Rights and Liberties essential to Freedom, emigrated from their Native Country to this Continent, and by their successful Perseverance in the midst of innumerable Dangers and Difficulties, together with a Profusion of their Blood and Treasure, have happily added these vast and valuable Dominions to the Empire of *Great-Britain.* That for the Enjoyment of these Rights and Liberties, several Governments were early formed in the said Colonies, with full Power of Legislation, agreeable to the Principles of the *English Constitution.*

That under those Governments, these Liberties, thus vested in their Ancestors, and transmitted to their Posterity, have been exercised and enjoyed, and by the inestimable Blessings thereof (under the Favour of Almighty GOD), the inhospitable Desarts of *America* have been converted into Flourishing Countries; Science, Humanity, and the Knowledge of Divine Truths, diffused through Remote Regions of Ignorance, Infidelity, and Barbarism; the Number of *British* Subjects wonderfully Increased, and the Wealth and Power of *Great-Britain* proportionably Augmented.

That by Means of these Settlements, and the unparallelled Success of your Majesty's Arms, a Foundation is now laid for rendering the *British* Empire the most Extensive and Powerful of any Recorded in History. Our Connection with this Empire, we esteem our greatest Happiness and Security, and humbly conceive it may now be so established by your Royal Wisdom, as to endure to the latest Period of Time; This, with most humble Submission to your Majesty, we apprehend will be most effectually Accomplished, by fixing the Pillars thereof on Liberty and Justice, and securing the inherent Rights and Liberties of your Subjects here, upon the Principles of the *English* Constitution. To this Constitution these Two Principles are essential, the Right of your faithful Subjects, freely to grant to your Majesty, such Aids as are required for the Support of your Government over them, and other Public Exigencies, and Trials by their Peers: By the One they are secured from unreasonable Impositions; and by the Other from Arbitrary Decisions of the executive Power.

The Continuation of these Liberties to the Inhabitants of *America* we ardently Implore, as absolutely necessary to Unite the several Parts of your wide extended Dominions, in that Harmony so Essential to the Preservation and Happiness of the Whole. Protected in these Liberties, the Emoluments *Great-Britain* receives from us, however great at present, are inconsiderable, compared with those she has the fairest Prospect of acquiring. By this Protection she will for ever secure to herself the Advantage of conveying to all *Europe,* the Merchandizes which *America* furnishes, and of Supplying through the same Channel whatever is wanted from thence. Here opens a boundless Source of Wealth and Naval Strength; yet these immense Advantages, by the Abridgment of those invaluable Rights and Liberties, by which our Growth has been Nourished, are in Danger of being for ever Lost; and our subordinate Legislatures, in Effect, rendered useless, by the late Acts of Parliament imposing Duties and Taxes on these Colonies, and extending the Jurisdiction of the Courts of Admiralty here, beyond its antient Limits: Statutes by which your Majesty's Commons in *Britain* undertake, absolutely to dispose of the Property of their Fellow Subjects in *America*, without their Consent, and for the enforcing whereof, they are subjected to the Determination of a single Judge in a Court unrestrained by the wise Rules of the Common Law, the Birthright of *Englishmen*, and the Safeguard of their Persons and Properties.

The invaluable Rights of Taxing ourselves, and Trial by our Peers, of which we implore your Majesty's Protection, are not, we most humbly conceive Unconstitutional; but confirmed by the Great CHARTER of *English* Liberty. On the First of these Rights the Honourable the House of Commons Found their Practice of Originating Money Bills, a Right enjoyed by the Kingdom of *Ireland*, by the Clergy of *England*, until relinquished by themselves,

a Right, in fine, which all other your Majesty's *English* Subjects, both within, and without the Realm, have hitherto enjoyed.

With Hearts therefore impressed with the most indelible Characters of Gratitude to your Majesty, and to the Memory of the Kings of your Illustrious House, whose Reigns have been Signally distinguished by their Auspicious Influence on the Prosperity of the *British* Dominions, and convinced by the most affecting Proofs of your Majesty's Paternal Love to all your People, however distant, and your unceasing and benevolent Desires to promote their Happiness, We most humbly beseech your Majesty, that you will be graciously pleased to take into your Royal Consideration, the Distresses of your faithful Subjects on this Continent, and to lay the same before your Majesty's Parliament, and to afford them such Relief, as in your Royal Wisdom their unhappy Circumstances shall be judged to require.

And your Petitioners as in Duty bound will pray.

25. The Memorial to the House of Lords

[*Proceedings of the Congress at New York* (Annapolis, 1766), 19-21.]

To the Right Honourable the Lords Spiritual and Temporal of Great-Britain, *in Parliament assembled.*

The MEMORIAL of the Freeholders and other Inhabitants of the *Massachusetts-Bay, Rhode-Island,* and *Providence* Plantations,   , *New-Jersey, Pennsylvania,* the Government of the Counties of *New-Castle, Kent,* and *Sussex,* upon *Delaware,* Province of *Maryland,*

Most humbly Sheweth,

That his Majesty's Liege Subjects in his *American* Colonies, tho' they acknowledge a due Subordination to that August Body the *British* Parliament, are entitled,

in the Opinion of your Memorialists, to all the inherent Rights and Liberties of the Natives of *Great-Britain,* and have ever since the Settlement of the said Colonies, exercised those Rights and Liberties, as far as their local Circumstances would permit.

That your Memorialists humbly conceive one of the most essential Rights of these Colonies, which they have ever, till lately, uninterruptedly enjoyed, to be Trial by Jury.

That your Memorialists also humbly conceive another of these essential Rights to be the Exemption from all Taxes, but such as are imposed on the People by the several Legislatures in these Colonies, which Right also they have, till of late, freely enjoyed.

But your Memorialists humbly beg Leave to represent to your Lordships, That the Act for granting certain Stamp Duties in the *British* Colonies in *America, &c.* fills his Majesty's *American* Subjects with the deepest Concern, as it tends to deprive them of the Two fundamental and invaluable Rights and Liberties above mentioned, and that several other late Acts of Parliament, which extend the Jurisdiction and Powers of Courts of Admiralty in the Plantations, beyond their Limits in *Great-Britain,* thereby make an unnecessary and unhappy Distinction as to the Modes of Trial, between us and our Fellow Subjects there, by whom we never have been excelled in Duty and Loyalty to our Sovereign.

That from the natural Connection between *Great-Britain* and *America,* the perpetual Continuance of which your Memorialists most ardently desire, they conceive that nothing can Conduce more to the Interest of both, than the Colonists free Enjoyment of their Rights and Liberties, and an affectionate Intercourse between *Great-Britain* and them. But your Memorialists (not waving their Claim to these Rights, of which with the most becoming Veneration and Deference to the Wisdom and Justice of your Lordships, they apprehend they cannot Reasonably be deprived) humbly Represent, That from

the peculiar Circumstances of these Colonies, the Duties imposed by the aforesaid Act, and several other late Acts of Parliament, are extremely Grievous and Burthensome, and the Payment of the said Duties will very soon, for want of Specie, become absolutely impracticable; and that the Restrictions on Trade by the said Acts, will not only greatly distress the Colonies, but must be extremely detrimental to the Trade and true Interest of *Great-Britain.*

Your Memorialists therefore, impressed with a just Sense of the unfortunate Circumstances of the Colonies, and the impending destructive Consequences which must necessarily ensue from the Execution of those Acts, animated with the warmest Sentiments of filial Affection for their Mother Country, most earnestly and humbly entreat, That your Lordships will be pleased to Hear their Counsel in Support of this Memorial, and take the Premisses into your most serious Consideration, and that your Lordships will also be thereupon pleased to pursue such Measures for Restoring the just Rights and Liberties of the Colonies, and preserving them for ever inviolate, for redressing their present, and preventing future Grievances, thereby promoting the united Interest of *Great-Britain* and *America,* as to your Lordships in your great Wisdom shall seem most Conducive and Effectual to that important End.

And your Memorialists as in Duty bound will ever pray.

26. The Petition to the House of Commons

[*Proceedings of the Congress at New York* (Annapolis, 1766), 21-24.]

To the Honourable the Knights, Citizens, and Burgesses of Great-Britain, *in Parliament assembled.*

The PETITION of his Majesty's dutiful and loyal Subjects, the Freeholders and other Inhabitants of the Colonies of the *Massachusetts-Bay, Rhode-Island,* and *Providence* Plantations,

    , *New-Jersey, Pennsylvania,* the Government of the Counties of *New-Castle, Kent,* and *Sussex,* upon *Delaware, Maryland,*

    Most humbly Sheweth,

    That the several late Acts of Parliament imposing divers Duties and Taxes on the Colonies, and laying the Trade and Commerce thereof under very Burthensome Restrictions, but above all the Act for granting and applying certain Stamp Duties, &c. in *America,* have fill'd them with the deepest Concern and Surprize; and they humbly conceive the Execution of them will be attended with Consequences very Injurious to the Commercial Interest of *Great-Britain* and her Colonies, and must terminate in the eventual Ruin of the latter.

Your Petitioners therefore most ardently implore the Attention of the Honourable House, to the united and dutiful Representation of their Circumstances, and to their earnest Supplications for Relief, from those Regulations which have already involv'd this Continent in Anxiety, Confusion, and Distress.

We most sincerely recognize our Allegiance to the Crown, and acknowledge all due Subordination to the Parliament of *Great-Britain,* and shall always retain the most grateful Sense of their Assistance and Protection. It is from and under the *English* Constitution, we derive all our Civil and Religious Rights and Liberties: We Glory in being Subjects of the best of Kings, and having been Born under the most perfect Form of Government; but it is with most ineffable and humiliating Sorrow, that we find ourselves, of late, deprived of the Right of Granting our own Property for his Majesty's Service, to which our Lives and Fortunes are entirely devoted, and to which, on his Royal Requisitions, we have ever been ready to contribute to the utmost of our Abilities.

We have also the Misfortune to find, that all the Penalties and Forfeitures mentioned in the Stamp Act, and in divers late Acts of Trade extending to the Plantations, are, at the Election of the Informer, Recoverable in any Court of Admiralty in *America.* This, as the newly erected Court of Admiralty has a general Jurisdiction over all *British America,*

renders his Majesty's Subjects in these Colonies, liable to be carried, at an immense Expence, from one End of the Continent, to the other.

It gives us also great Pain, to see a manifest Distinction made therein, between the Subjects of our Mother Country, and those in the Colonies, in that the like Penalties and Forfeitures recoverable there only in his Majesty's Courts of Record, are made cognizable here by a Court of Admiralty: By these Means we seem to be, in Effect, unhappily deprived of Two Privileges essential to Freedom, and which all *Englishmen* have ever considered as their best Birthrights, that of being free from all Taxes but such as they have consented to in Person, or by their Representatives, and of Trial by their Peers.

Your Petitioners further shew, That the remote Situation, and other Circumstances of the Colonies, render it impracticable that they should be Represented, but in their respective subordinate Legislature; and they humbly conceive, that the Parliament, adhering strictly to the Principles of the Constitution, have never hitherto Tax'd any, but those who were actually therein Represented; for this Reason, we humbly apprehend, they never have Tax'd *Ireland,* or any other of the Subjects without the Realm.

But were it ever so clear, that the Colonies might in Law, be reasonably deem'd to be Represented in the Honourable House of Commons, yet we conceive, that very good Reasons, from Inconvenience, from the Principles of true Policy, and from the Spirit of the *British* Constitution, may be adduced to shew, that it would be for the real Interest of *Great-Britain,* as well as her Colonies, that the late Regulations should be rescinded, and the several Acts of Parliament imposing Duties and Taxes on the Colonies, and extending the Jurisdiction of the Courts of Admiralty here, beyond their ancient Limits, should be Repeal'd.

We shall not Attempt a minute Detail

of all the Reasons which the Wisdom of the Honourable House may suggest, on this Occasion, but would humbly submit the following Particulars to their Consideration.

That Money is already become very scarce in these Colonies, and is still decreasing by the necessary Exportation of Specie from the Continent, for the Discharge of our Debts to *British* Merchants.

That an immensly heavy Debt is yet due from the Colonies for *British* Manufactures, and that they are still heavily burthen'd with Taxes to discharge the Arrearages due for Aids granted by them in the late War.

That the Balance of Trade will ever be much against the Colonies, and in Favour of *Great-Britain,* whilst we consume her Manufactures, the Demand for which must ever Increase in Proportion to the Number of Inhabitants settled here, with the Means of Purchasing them. We therefore humbly conceive it to be the Interest of *Great-Britain,* to increase, rather than diminish, those Means, as the Profits of all the Trade of the Colonies ultimately center there to pay for her Manufactures, as we are not allowed to purchase elsewhere; and by the Consumption of which, at the advanced Prices the British Taxes oblige the Makers and Venders to set on them, we eventually contribute very largely to the Revenue of the Crown.

That from the Nature of *American* Business, the Multiplicity of Suits and Papers used in Matters of small Value, in a Country where Freeholds are so minutely divided, and Property so frequently transferr'd, a Stamp Duty must ever be very Burthensome and Unequal.

That it is extremely improbable that the Honourable House of Commons, shou'd at all Times, be thoroughly acquainted with our Condition, and all Facts requisite to a just and equal Taxation of the Colonies.

It is also humbly submitted, Whether there be not a material Distinction in Reason and sound Policy, at least, between the necessary Exercise of Parliamentary Jurisdiction in general Acts, for the Amendment of the Common Law, and the Regulation of Trade and Commerce through the whole Empire, and the Exercise of that Jurisdiction, by imposing Taxes on the Colonies.

That the several subordinate Provincial Legislatures have been moulded into Forms, as nearly resembling that of their Mother Country, as by his Majesty's Royal Predecessors was thought convenient; and their Legislatures seem to have been wisely and graciously established, that the Subjects in the Colonies might, under the due Administration thereof, enjoy the happy Fruits of the *British* Government, which in their present Circumstances, they cannot be so fully and clearly availed of, any other Way under these Forms of Government we and our Ancestors have been Born or Settled, and have had our Lives, Liberties, and Properties, protected. The People here, as every where else, retain a great Fondness for their old Customs and Usages, and we trust that his Majesty's Service, and the Interest of the Nation, so far from being obstructed, have been vastly promoted by the Provincial Legislatures.

That we esteem our Connections with, and Dependance on *Great-Britain,* as one of our greatest Blessings, and apprehend the latter will appear to be sufficiently secure, when it is considered, that the Inhabitants in the Colonies have the most unbounded Affection for his Majesty's Person, Family, and Government, as well as for the Mother Country, and that their Subordination to the Parliament, is universally acknowledged.

We therefore most humbly entreat, That the Honourable House would be pleased to hear our Counsel in Support of this Petition, and take our distressed and deplorable Case into their serious Consideration, and that the Acts and Clauses of Acts, so grievously restraining our Trade and Commerce, imposing Duties and Taxes on our Property, and extending the Jurisdiction of the Court of Admiralty beyond its ancient Limits, may be repeal'd; or that the Honourable House would other- wise relieve your Petitioners, as in your great Wisdom and Goodness shall seem meet.

And your Petitioners as in Duty bound shall ever pray.

CHAPTER IV

THE AMERICAN PRESS

WHILE COLONIAL assemblies were formulating resolutions and petitions, various individuals were arguing the colonial cause in pamphlets and in letters to the newspapers. Here we may find some of the reasoning that lay behind the official resolutions.

News that Parliament had refused to consider the colonial petitions and was preparing to pass the Stamp Act reached the colonies about the same time as the defense of parliamentary taxation contained in *The Regulations lately Made*. The colonial response was immediate and continuous. One of the earliest writers to argue the colonial position against the ministry appeared in the *Providence Gazette* on May 11, 1765, under the pseudonym of "A Plain Yeoman" (No. 27), and the piece was widely reprinted in other colonial newspapers. The author has not been identified, but the quotation from Dean Swift suggests that he may have been Stephen Hopkins, who quoted Swift in other essays.

The most popular exponent of the colonial objections to taxation was Daniel Dulany, a Maryland lawyer, whose *Considerations on the Propriety of Imposing Taxes in the British Colonies for the purpose of raising a Revenue by Act of Parliament* first appeared in October, 1765. Dulany, who had been educated at Eton, Cambridge, and the Middle Temple, may have conceded more than other Americans would have, in allowing that constituents could not instruct their representatives; but he followed other colonial spokesmen in giving his first attention to the doctrine of virtual representation. He perceived that the ministry had rested its case for taxing the Americans on the ground that they were represented in Parliament. By showing that they were not represented he could prove that Parliament, by the ministry's own admission, had no right to tax them. Having established this point, he devoted the rest of his pamphlet to other arguments, grounded on equity and expediency, and to stating what he thought the limits of Parliament's authority to be. The selections contain the argument against virtual representation and the principal attempt to define the limits of parliamentary authority (No. 28).

Although American writers vigorously attacked the doctrine of virtual representation, probably few would have found actual representation in Parliament attractive. James Otis proposed it in 1764, but the reasons why Americans might have rejected it if offered were well stated by an anonymous contributor to the *Pennsylvania Journal,* March 13, 1766 (No. 29).

The newspapers reacted to the Stamp Act, not only with sober disquisitions on colonial rights, but also with violent exhortation and invective against persons suspected of insufficient hostility to it. In some cases this type of writing helped to bring on rioting. In Connecticut, for example, the piece signed "Cato" (No. 30) was the prelude to an attack on Jared Ingersoll, who, after opposing passage of the Stamp Act, accepted a position as collector of the tax. Cato was Naphtali Daggett, Professor of Divinity at Yale. The author of the last selection is unknown (No. 31).

QUESTIONS

1. Do any of the writings in this section go beyond the position taken by the assemblies in setting limits to parliamentary authority?

2. What connection is allowed between mother country and colonies in selections 27 and 29?

3. Does Dulany concede Parliament any authority to tax for revenue?

4. Does he distinguish between internal and external taxation?

5. What authority does he admit Parliament to possess?

6. What does he mean by the statement: "I am upon a Question of Propriety, not of Power"?

27.   A Letter from a Plain Yeoman

[*Providence Gazette,* May 11, 1765.]

The following is said to be a copy of a letter, sent by a plain yeoman in New-England, *to a certain great personage in* Old-England.

My Lord,

At a time when the respective legislatures of *Great-Britain,* and of these his majesty's dominions in *America,* are as wide apart in sentiment of each one's extent of power in point of legislation, as they are east and west of each other in point of situation; more especially when we are not permitted to assert, or contend for, exclusive rights from those of our fellow-subjects on the other side of the Atlantic, an appeal to your lordship from a plain *American,* who never was among the great, in regard to parliamentary resolutions for taxing us, and otherwise abridging such privileges as we have long enjoyed, and humbly conceive have a right to, may be thought highly presumptuous. However, the character which your lordship bears, of a vindicator of all the just and established rights of the king's subjects, emboldens me to address you, in full reliance, that so far as the matters contained in the following address are founded on the known principles of the *British* government, and managed with decency, they will find with your lordship candor and countenance.

I am told from good authority, that the parliament would not permit any petitions to be heard from the colonies, claiming as a right an exemption from parliamentary taxation. It is very hard, my lord, that so large a portion of the king's subjects, as are contained in *North-America,* and who have ever been distinguished for their loyalty, cannot be heard on a subject, in which they are so deeply interested. Can it come within possibility, that all the individuals in the northern colonies should, without previous conference, minutely concur in sentiment, that the *British* parliament cannot, agreeable with the inherent privileges of the colonists, tax them without a representation on their part, unless there was some color for such exemption?—I have always been instructed, and perhaps truly, that to claim a right was as well the subjects privilege, as to remonstrate against any particular grievance: And suppose, my lord, that the parliament of *Great-Britain* should order a tax to be assessed and levied on the real and personal estate in *Ireland,* without any reference to the legislature of that kingdom, or representation of the people there, could it be thought presumption, or a project of *independance* in that people, *freely* to remonstrate against such unconstitutional measures? The northern colonies fall but little short in numbers with *Ireland;* and of what importance they are to the crown, your lordship is a fit judge. Why then is it deemed near or quite *criminal* even to expostulate, when they universally look on the late measures resolved on concerning them, as so many privations of their just rights as freemen? Our zeal for his majesty's person and government, and our loyalty, have been always testified, and of late especially, in a manner so much for the national advantage, and our own honour, that we verily thought that every right, which we had heretofore enjoyed, with the full concurrence of the *British*

government, would have been amply secured to us; not to mention the hopes we had conceived of such further privileges and immunities, as the tenderness of a maternal state should dictate, for the emolument of her dutiful children. But to our infinite regret and disappointment, we have not only been deprived in a great measure of some of our ancient and invaluable rights, but virtually forbid the liberty even of complaining!

The ministry have held forth, that a plea on the side of the colonies, expressive of their rights, and contesting the power of parliament to tax them without their own agreement, is not to be *endured,* and looks like *aiming at independance. Ministerial* threats too, if we are rightly informed, have been directed at us, to terrify us into a compliance with such new regulations, as must operate to our ruin. All the colonies on the continent, in their several petitions and remonstrances, dutifully, though firmly, assert their right of exclusion from parliamentary taxation, founded on the principles of the *British* government, and the terms of their colonization.—The parliament expresses indignation at such pretensions, and will not hear the colonies on that plea. If there be any color, my lord, for a claim of the exemption in question, the whole world will judge, that the parliament's refusal to hear the colonies on that point, must convince them what reception they are to expect any future applications for the preservation of their liberties will meet with. Would not any men, other than the constituent members of the commons house, pay so much deference to the opinions of above a *million* of loyal subjects of the crown, in a matter of right and privilege, as to think that at least there was color for their pretensions? The dignity of so many legislatives, composed of great and good men, one would think should have some attraction upon the virtue of the grand legislative of the nation, and operate in a manner at least to induce a hearing. However dignified men may be, they are not absolved from their obligations of doing right to the lowest subject, and consulting the security and protection of all his righteous claims. On the other hand, should those in rule and power roughly dismiss him, who would lay his grievances before them, and instead of alleviating his burdens, should increase them, *because he dared to expostulate,* all indifferent spectators of such an use of power would judge that it presaged no good to the governed. *Pharaoh, Caligula,* and but a few more, have been instances of such abusers of power, and thereby rendered themselves so detestable to mankind, that instead of imitation, rulers in general shudder at a bare recital of their horrid impieties. I do not mention those monsters with any design of making an odious parallel between them and any persons now in authority, but only to color high an ignominious condition of slavery, that so the state of free *Englishmen,* free *Britons,* may appear the more illustrious in contrast; and to shew that every little infraction of their famed privileges, whether casual or designed, tends consequentially to the introduction of tyranny. If our arguments are frivolous, it will be the easier to confute them; and most certainly among brother subjects a serious refutation ought to be tried before a contemptuous treatment, or a discharge of menaces.

But it is said that such doctrine as we have embraced is *dangerous,* and looks like *aiming at independance.* These are very general charges, and unless the terms be defined with some precision, we shall never know what defences to make against them. If by *dangerous* be intended that we challenge something contrary to the *fundamentals* of the *British* constitution, it will be begging the question: For we contend that unless our claim be admitted, we shall be deprived of that, which by the *fundamentals* of the *British* constitution we ought to enjoy. And what *danger,* my lord, can result from a discussion in parliament of the question? As to the words *dependance* and *independance,* I take it, that they are more used for their sound, than for any meaning which they can possibly bear, as applied to the colonies. I could wish that some *civilian* would settle how far the *people of America* are dependant on the *people of Britain:* I know of no *dependance* or relation, only that we are all the common subjects of the same king; and by any thing that hath been said in the present controversy, I cannot find that the inhabitants of the colonies are *dependant* on the *people* of *Britain,* or the *people* of *Britain* on them, any more than *Kent* is on *Sussex,* or *Sussex* on *Kent.*— If by *aiming at independance* be meant, that the colonies are about to shake off their allegiance to the crown, we utterly deny that such intentions ever entered into our breasts. Here I cannot pass by in silence the *jealous* and baseless supposition, formed on the other side of the water, that the colonies want only a favorable opportunity of setting up for themselves. This charge against us hath for many years been kept a going in *Britain,* with such diligence and management, that the minds of the people there are almost universally imbittered against us; and the prejudice, *to represent the colonies in fact,* hath taken it's seat in the grand legislative of the nation, to our infinite detriment; although nothing can be more fictitious than the suggestion. We are esteemed as rivals and enemies by a country, who ought and might put the surest confidence in us, and who have the greatest reason in the world to lend us their kind assistance, and upon the least application for the purpose to consider and redress our griefs. This jealousy towards us, although utterly groundless, accounts for the unfavorable light in which all our conduct and petitions are viewed, and so far hath a pernicious effect.

But if by *independance* be intended our maintenance of argument against the levying taxes upon us without our own consent, then it is so far true that we do *aim at independance.* Such *independance* is the main pillar of our happy frame of government, and hath ever been claimed and enjoyed, from the times of the *Saxons* down to this day, by our fellow-subjects in *Britain,* excepting when for short durations in tyrannous times it was interrupted; and how it hath come to pass that the colonists, as part of the king's natural subjects, have forfeited such ancient privileges, always heretofore acknowledged to be the *birth-right* of all the king's free subjects without distinction, hath not been yet told us. How then, my lord, can it be deemed as *aiming at independance,* in the worst sense of the words, *i.e.* an effort to cast off our allegiance, for the dominions in *America* to assert and claim that as a right, which all the rest of the king's subjects have ever claimed and enjoyed.

I must now beg your lordship's patience, whilst I consider a little two objections, which have been made against the matters of our remonstrances. One is *precedents,* and the other is a round assertion, that we are in *fact* represented in parliament.

As to the first, it is objected to us that the erecting a post-office in *America* is a tax upon the people, and that we made no such plea, as the present one, when the act of the 9th of *Anne* was made for the establishment of that office here. In answer to which let it be observed, that such an institution, if not made too expensive, is so manifestly for the convenience of a country, that it is not to be wondered at that the colonists put up with an undesigned bordering too close upon a meer right, which might arise from want of due attention to it, when instead of evil consequences, there sprung a general convenience. It is well known by all, who are but a little versed in history, by what silent and almost imperceptible degrees the liberties of subjects may be encroached upon, and how much they will endure before they will make any general complaint; and it is unfair to cite as a *precedent* our sub-

mission to an unconstitutional proceeding, although then unattended with any evil consequences. But it is now apparent that that measure, by only being brought into *example,* hath been of *dangerous* consequence; and very likely the colony of *South-Carolina,* who, I am told, would never permit the postmaster-general to exercise any authority there, foresaw the evil tendency of such a *precedent.* Mr. *Locke* supposes that absolute monarchy would be the best form of government, if the monarch was always a wise and good man; but yet I very much doubt if such doctrine, supposing it be true, could justify the legislative in a departure from the established principles of the constitution, even upon a supposition that such unconstitutional proceedings appeared salutary and good for the governed: For the very *example* would be a proof that the laws of the country were no security to the subject, and might be got over, when it should be thought convenient. But here with respect to the statute of the 9th of *Anne,* let it be considered that the colonies on the continent are so distinct from each other, and so different in their situation, interest and modes of government, that it would have been next to impossible for them to have ever established regular posts through their several extensive jurisdictions, for want of a concurrence of council; and therefore it became needful for that matter to be regulated by some power *superior to all the colonies;* but with submission to your lordship's better judgment, I think, from the nature of our territorial rights such a regulation might have come with much more propriety from the king, who is supreme lord of these dominions, than from the parliament, and then the concurrence of the colonies would have been of course given thereto.

But further I am in doubt if there be so much in the matter of *precedents* as some would have. I know that the *lawyers* have carried the authority of *precedents* so far, that if a point be to be gained, nothing is required or sought after but a *precedent,* and if that can be found among the various and contrary resolutions, they form a conclusion that the point is *clearly established;* whether the *precedent* be footed on justice and reason or on whim and arbitrariness. "It is a maxim among these men, that whatever has been done before, may legally be done again, and therefore they take special care to record all the decisions formerly made, even those, which have, through ignorance or corruption, contradicted the rules of common justice, and the general reason of mankind. These, under the name of *precedents,* they produce as authorities, and thereby endeavour to justify the most iniquitous opinions; and they are so lucky in this practice, that it rarely fails of decrees answerable to their intent and expectation." [Dean Swift] *Precedents* of infringing the liberties of the subject are to be met with plentifully in history; yet I humbly conceive that if any such could be found in the *British* annals, it would not be much to the credit of a *British writer against the liberties of America,* to cite them in vindication of a measure, which a whole continent of people thought to be an aggression of their plain and certain privileges.

The second objection made to our remonstrances is, that the inhabitants of the colonies are in *fact* represented in parliament. This proposition, one would think, would be sufficiently refuted by only saying, that not one *American* ever gave, or can give, his suffrage for the choice of any of these pretended representatives. It is very strange, my lord, and looks like being under the power of magic, that such a vast extent of an inhabited country as this, should be represented in parliament, and that yet the people here should never have found it out. How can a colony, shire, city or borough be represented, when not one individual inhabitant ever did the least thing towards procuring such representation? This position is the last shift, the dernier subterfuge, of such as would reconcile the proceedings of parliament, respecting laying taxes on us, with *British* liberties; but if it be preached forever, the utter falsity of it, (pardon a plain expression) is so notorious, that not one single *American* will ever believe it. The arguments in support of this *mushroom* proposition are so fallacious and weak, that they scarcely deserve a serious attention. It is urged that because a great number of the inhabitants of *Britain* are not electors there, and seeing that it is unquestionably true that the house of commons, notwithstanding, actually represent the whole people, that therefore they represent a vast dominion at three thousand miles distance, and who have not a single voice in their election, although multitudes in such distant country in point of estate would be well qualified to vote, were they with their estates in *Britain,* and actually do vote for persons to represent them in their own assemblies. If such argument be of any force, it will prove, that all the people in *Britain* might be as well represented by the members of any single borough town, as by the whole house of commons. How came it necessary at the union, to provide that *Scotland* should send members to parliament? Were they not according to the foregoing doctrine in *fact* represented by the *English* members? A right of election is annexed to a certain species of property, franchises, &c. and every man in *England,* who falls under these descriptions, hath a right to vote, either for knights, citizens, or burgesses; but can any man in the colonies be admitted to a voice, let him come under what description he will? Every person in *England* is not qualified to be an elector, yet the country is represented;—but doth it follow that the colonies too are therefore represented, who give not a single voice, although multitudes here have as much freehold estate as serves to qualify their fellow subjects in *England?* But it is said that persons under age, women and children are not electors, but yet are represented. I wonder these subtle politicians had not shewn, that ideots, madmen, and cattle were not electors, and from thence infer that we are represented. Women have not a share in government, but yet by their strict connexion with the other sex, all their liberties are as amply secured as those of the men, and it is impossible to represent the one sex, without the other. As to any inference which can be drawn against us, on the present point, from infants being represented notwithstanding their incapacity to elect, it seems to me that a writer must be put to a sorry shift indeed, to rest any part of his cause on so weak a foundation.

To infer, my lord, that the *British* members actually represent the colonies, who are not permitted to do the least act towards their appointment, because *Britain* is unequally represented, although every man in the kingdom, who hath certain legal qualifications can vote for some one to represent him, is such a piece of sophistry that I had half a mind to pass by the cobweb without blowing it to pieces. Is there no difference between a country's having a privilege to choose 558 members to represent them in parliament, though in unequal proportions to the several districts, which cannot be avoided, and not having liberty to choose any? To turn the tables, —if the *Americans* only had leave to send members to parliament, could such sophistry ever persuade the people of *Britain* that they were represented and had a share in the national councils? A right of election hath its origin from having property of freehold estate, and such only have a right to a share in government. Mens estates are represented, and such as have great and noble estates actually sit in parliament for their own estates. All who have freehold in *England* to a small value, share in the administration; but in *America,* where almost every head of a family and most other men have freehold, and very many are owners of great landed estates, they can have no share in government; and those estates are not represented, be-

cause the owners cannot elect. Suppose none of the 558 members were chosen by the people, but enjoyed the right of sitting in parliament by hereditary descent; could the common people be said to share in the national councils? How trifling then is the supposition, that we in *America* virtually have such share in the national councils, by those members whom we never chose? If we are not their constituents, they are not our representatives. But it is said that we are represented in the same manner as the non-electors are in *Britain*. This, may it please your lordship, is a strange paradox; for the very reason why the non-electors in *Britain* are such, is because they are not qualified in point of estate, which I hope will not be said of all the colonists; and it was observed before, that having property or freehold, necessarily inferred a right to be an elector, or which is all one, to have a share in government. Lastly it is really a piece of mockery to tell us that a country, detached from *Britain,* by an ocean of immense breadth, and which is so extensive and populous, should be represented by the *British* members, or that we can have any interest in the house of commons.

It therefore remains fully disproved, that the inhabitants of the colonies are in *fact* represented in parliament; and therefore our most darling privilege, namely an immunity from taxes without our own consent, hath been nullified by the late parliamentary resolutions.

It is beside my present purpose to examine how far other acts, *to wit,* such as regulate trade, &c. are obligatory upon us, or what sort of connections subsist between a parent state and distant colonies. These may be the subjects of some abler pen: But I would just observe, that the commons of *Great-Britain* have ever held the right of not being taxed without their own assent, the most sacred of all others.

It gives me pain, my lord, that so much untenderness, approaching near to wrath, on the part of the present administration is exercised towards us. We are not conscious of having done any thing to deserve it; and in our turn, having all the feelings of human nature, must be irritated at what we must think ill-treatment. Broad hints have been given that *standing forces* are to be sent amongst us, to humble us, and to enforce execution of such laws, as we must esteem grievances. Such is the delicacy of the *British* constitution, that it instantly dies under the hands of such *executive red-coats,* and every privilege wings it's flight. If such measures should be pursued, permit me, my lord, to think that the people of *Britain* may then begin to tremble for their own liberties. It amounts almost to demonstration, that when the whole *British* empire in *America* are dissatisfied, there must be some foundation for such dissatisfaction: And whether it would not be for the benefit of the whole nation in general, as well as just in itself, to hear our complaints, and to endeavour by a mild and gentle treatment to secure our love and *good-will,* instead of exciting our *ill-will,* I chearfully submit to the judgment of your lordship.

Thus I have with much freedom and plainness, which I doubt not your candor will excuse, gone through what I proposed to consider. I have only to add that I am in sure and certain hopes, that what I have written will meet with a better reception from your lordship, than the humble petitions of an innumerable multitude of people did lately from the parliament.

I am, my lord, your lordship's most obedient and most humble servant.

28. Daniel Dulany on the Authority of Parliament

[Dulany, *Considerations on the Propriety of Imposing Taxes in the British Colonies for the purpose of raising a Revenue by Act of Parliament* (2nd ed.; Annapolis, 1765), 3-11, 14-15, 28-35.]

PREFACE

It would, now, be an unfashionable Doctrine, whatever the ancient Opinion might be, to affirm that the Constituent can bind his Representative by Instructions; but, tho' the obligatory Force of these Instructions is not insisted upon, yet their persuasive Influence, in most Cases, may be: for a Representative, who should act against the explicit Recommendation of his Constituents, would most deservedly forfeit their Regard and all Pretension to their future Confidence.

When it is under Deliberation, whether a new Law shall be Enacted, in which the Electors of England *are interested,* THEY *have Notice of it, and an Opportunity of declaring their Sense—*THEY *may point out every dangerous Tendency, and are not restrain'd in their Representations, from shewing, in the plainest Language, the Injustice or Oppression of it.*

When a Law, in it's Execution, is found to be repugnant to the Genius of Liberty, or productive of Hardships or Inconvenience, THEY *may also instruct their Deputies to exert themselves in procuring a Repeal of it, and in the Exercise of this Right are not constrain'd to whine in the Style of humble Petitioners.—*THEY *are expos'd to no Danger in explaining their Reasons—*THEIR *Situation does not become so delicate as to make it prudent, to weaken, by not urging them, with their full Force, and to their utmost Extent. But who are the Representatives of the Colonies? To whom shall* THEY *send their Instructions, when desirous to obtain the Repeal of a Law striking at the Root and Foundation of every Civil Right, should such an one take Place? Instructions to all the Members who compose the House of Commons would not be proper. To them the Application must be by Petition, in* *which an unreserved Style would, probably, be deemed Indecency, and strong Expressions Insolence, in which a Claim of Rights may not, perhaps, be explained, or even insinuated, if to impugn, or glance at their Authority whose Relief is supplicated. To soften and deprecate must be the Hope and Endeavour, tho' a guiltless Freeman would, probably, be aukward in ringing all the Changes of* Parce, Precor, [*O spare, I beseech you.*]

Under these Circumstances, the Liberty of the Press is of the most momentous Consequence, for if Truth is not allowed to speak thence in it's genuine Language of Plainness and Simplicity, nor Freedom to vindicate it's Privileges with decent Firmness, we shall have too much Reason to acknowledge his Foresight who predicted, that, "the Constitution of the British *Government was too excellent to be permanent." The Train for the Accomplishment of that Prophecy hath not yet catched in* America, *nor, I trust, been laid.*

That there have been Laws extremely unjust and oppressive, the Declarations of subsequent Parliaments, fixing this Stigma upon them, evince; but whilst the Power which introduced them prevailed, it was not prudent to give them their deserved Characters. The Parliament of Henry III, *or that of* Henry VI, *need not be cited; there are many other Instances, tho' not branded with Epithets so remarkably opprobrious.*

In the Opinion of a great Lawyer, an Act of Parliament may be void, and of a great Divine, "all Men have natural, and Freemen legal Rights, which they may justly maintain, and no legislative Authority can deprive them of."

Cases may be imagined in which the Truth of these Positions might, in Theory, be admitted; but in Practice, unless there should be very peculiar Circumstances, such as can't be supposed to exist during the Prevalence of the Power that introduced it, who would rely upon the Authority of Opinions, or the Principles of them,

for his Protection against the Penalties of any positive Law?

When the Judges were ask'd by Henry VIII, *Whether a Man might be attainted of High Treason by Parliament, tho' not called to answer, they declared that it was a dangerous Question, and gave the evasive Answer that, "the High Court of Parliament ought to give Examples of Justice to the inferior Courts, none of which could do the like." But tho' it might be dangerous to declare against the Authority of Parliament, we are not bound to acknowledge it's Inerrability, nor precluded from examining the Principles and Consequences of Laws, or from pointing out their Improprieties, and Defects. Upon this Ground I have proceeded in the following* Considerations, *and shall not be disappointed if they should appear to be too free, or too reserved, to Readers of different Complexions.*

CONSIDERATIONS, &c.

In the Constitution of *England*, the Three principal Forms of Government, Monarchy, Aristocracy, and Democracy, are blended together in certain Proportions; but each of these Orders, in the Exercise of the legislative Authority, hath its peculiar Department, from which the other are excluded. In this Division, the *Granting of Supplies,* or *Laying Taxes,* is deemed to be the Province of the House of Commons, as the Representative of the People.—All Supplies are supposed to flow from their Gift; and the other Orders are permitted only to Assent, or Reject generally, not to propose any Modification, Amendment, or partial Alteration of it.

This Observation being considered, it will undeniably appear, that, in framing the late *Stamp Act,* the Commons acted in the Character of Representative of the Colonies. They assumed it as the Principle of that Measure, and the *Propriety* of it must therefore stand, or fall, as the Principle is true, or false: For the Preamble sets forth, That the Commons of

Great-Britain had resolved to *Give and Grant* the several Rates and Duties imposed by the Act; but what Right had the Commons of *Great-Britain* to be thus Munificent at the Expence of the Commons of *America?*—To give Property, not belonging to the Giver, and without the Consent of the Owner, is such evident and flagrant Injustice, in *ordinary Cases*, that few are hardy enough to avow it; and therefore, when it really happens, the Fact is disguised and varnished over by the most plausible Pretences the Ingenuity of the Giver can suggest.—But it is alledged that there is a *Virtual,* or *implied Representation* of the Colonies springing out of the Constitution of the *British* Government: And, it must be confessed on all Hands, that, as the Representation is not actual, it is virtual, or it doth not exist at all; for no Third Kind of Representation can be imagined. The Colonies claim the Privilege, which is common to all *British Subjects,* of being Taxed *only* with their own Consent, given by their Representatives, and all the Advocates for the *Stamp-Act* admit this Claim. Whether, therefore, upon the whole Matter, the Imposition of the *Stamp Duties* is a *proper* Exercise of Constitutional Authority, or not, depends upon the single Question, Whether the Commons of *Great-Britain* are *virtually* the Representatives of the Commons of *America,* or not.

The Advocates for the Stamp-Act admit, in express Terms, that "the Colonies do not chuse Members of Parliament," but they assert that "the Colonies are *virtually* represented, in the same Manner with the Non-Electors resident in *Great-Britain.*"

How have they proved this Position? Where have they defined, or precisely explained what they mean by the Expression, *Virtual Representation?* As it is the very Hinge upon which the Rectitude of the Taxation turns, something more satisfactory than mere Assertion, more solid than a Form of Expression, is necessary; for, how can it be seriously expected, that

Men, who think themselves injuriously affected in their Properties and Privileges, will be convinced and reconciled by a fanciful Phrase, the Meaning of which can't be precisely ascertained by those who use it, or properly applied to the Purpose for which it hath been advanced.

They argue, that "the Right of Election being annexed to certain Species of Property, to Franchises, and Inhabitancy in some particular Places, a very small Part of the Land, the Property, and the People of *England,* is comprehended in those Descriptions. All Landed Property, not Freehold, and all Monied Property, are *excluded.* The Merchants of *London,* the Proprietors of the Public Funds, the Inhabitants of *Leeds, Halifax, Birmingham,* and *Manchester,* and that great Corporation of the *East-India* Company, *None of Them* chuse their Representatives, and yet are they all represented in Parliament, and the Colonies being *exactly* in *their* Situation, are represented in the *same* Manner."

Now, this Argument, which is all that their Invention hath been able to supply, is totally defective; for, it consists of Facts not true, and of Conclusions inadmissible.

It is so far from being true, that all the Persons enumerated under the Character of *Non-Electors,* are in that Predicament, that it is indubitably certain there is *no* Species of Property, Landed, or Monied, which is not possessed by *very many* of the *British Electors.*

I shall undertake to disprove the supposed Similarity of Situation, whence the same Kind of Representation is deduced of the Inhabitants of the Colonies, and of the *British* Non-Electors; and, if I succeed, the Notion of a *virtual Representation* of the Colonies must fail, which, in Truth, is a mere Cob-web, spread to catch the unwary, and intangle the weak. I would be understood. I am upon a Question of *Propriety,* not of Power; and, though some may be inclined to think it is to little Purpose to discuss the one, when the other is irresistible, yet are they different Considerations; and, at the same Time that I invalidate the Claim upon which it is founded, I may very consistently recommend a Submission to the Law, whilst it endures. I shall say Nothing of the Use I intend by the Discussion; for, if it should not be perceived by the Sequel, there is no Use in it, and, if it should appear then, it need not be premised.

Lessees for Years, Copyholders, Proprietors of the Public Funds, Inhabitants of *Birmingham, Leeds, Halifax,* and *Manchester,* Merchants of the City of *London,* or Members of the Corporation of the *East-India* Company, are, *as such,* under no personal Incapacity to be Electors; for they may acquire the Right of Election, and there are *actually* not only a considerable Number of Electors in each of the Classes of Lessees for Years, &c. but in many of them, if not all, even Members of Parliament. The Interests therefore of the Non-Electors, the Electors, and the Representatives, are individually the same; to say nothing of the Connection among Neighbours, Friends, and Relations. The Security of the Non-Electors against Oppression, is, that their Oppression will fall also upon the Electors and the Representatives. The one can't be injured, and the other indemnified.

Further, if the Non-Electors should not be taxed by the *British* Parliament, they would not be taxed *at all;* and it would be iniquitous, as well as a Solecism, in the political System, that they should partake of all the Benefits resulting from the Imposition, and Application of Taxes, and derive an Immunity from the Circumstance of not being qualified to vote. Under this Constitution then, a double or virtual Representation may be reasonably supposed.— The Electors, who are inseparably connected in their Interests with the Non-Electors, may be justly deemed to be the Representatives of the Non-Electors, at the same Time they exercise their personal Privilege in their Right of Election, and the Members chosen, therefore, the Repre-

sentatives of both. This is the only rational Explanation of the Expression, *virtual Representation.* None has been advanced by the Assertors of it, and their Meaning can only be inferred from the Instances, by which they endeavour to elucidate it, and no other Meaning can be stated, to which the Instances apply.

It is an essential Principle of the *English* Constitution, that the Subject shall not be Taxed without his Consent, which hath not been introduced by any particular Law, but necessarily results from the Nature of that mixed Government; for, without it, the Order of Democracy could not exist.

Parliaments were not formerly so Regular in Point of Form as they now are. Even the Number of Knights for each Shire were not ascertained. The first Writs now extant for their Choice, are 22d *Edward* I, by which, Two, as at this Day, were directed to be chosen for each County; but the King not being satisfied with that Number, other Writs were issued for chusing Two more. This discretionary Power being thought inconvenient, was afterwards restrained by the Statutes of *Richard* II, *Henry* IV, and subsequent Acts.

In earlier Times there was more Simplicity in the Rules of Government, and Men were more solicitous about the Essentials, than the Forms of it. When the Consent of those who were to perform, or pay any Thing extra-feudal, was fairly applied for and obtained, the Manner was little regarded; but, as the People had reason to be jealous of Designs to impose Contributions upon them without their Consent, it was thought expedient to have Formalities regulated, and fixed, to prevent this Injury to their Rights, not to destroy a Principle, without which, they could not be said to have any Rights at all.

Before the Introduction of those Formalities, which were framed with a View to restrain the Excursions of Power, and to secure the Privileges of the Subject, as the Mode of proceeding was more simple, so perhaps this Foundation of Consent was more visible than it is at present, wherefore it may be of Use to adduce some Instances, which directly point out this necessary and essential Principle of *British Liberty.*

The Lords and Commons have separately given Aids and Subsidies to the Crown. In 13th *Edward* III, the Lords granted the Tenth of all the Corn, *&c.* growing upon their Demesnes, the Commons then granting Nothing, nor concerning themselves with what the Lords thought fit to grant out of their own Estates.—At other Times, the Knights of Shires, separating from the rest of the Commons, and joining with the Lords, have granted a Subsidy, and the Representatives of Cities and Boroughs have likewise granted Subsidies to the Crown separately, as appears by a Writ in 24th *Edward* I, which runs in these Words: *Rex, &c.—Cum Comites, Barones, Milites Nobis, &c. fecerunt undecimam de omnibus Bonis suis mobilibus, et Cives et Burgenses, &c. septimam de omnibus Bonis suis mobilibus, &c. nobis curialiter concesserint, &c.—[The earls, barons, and knights, having given unto us in parliament, the eleventh part, and the citizens and burgesses the seventh part of their goods and chattels, &c.]* When an Affair happened, which affected only some Individuals, and called for an Aid to the Crown, it was common for those Individuals *alone* to be summoned; to which Purpose several Writs are extant. In 35th *Edward* III, there is a Writ (which *Dugdale* has printed in his Collection of Writs of Summons to Parliament) directed to the Earl of *Northampton,* which, after reciting the Confusion the Affairs of *Ireland* were in, and that he, and some other *English* Lords had Possessions in that Kingdom, and were therefore more particularly obliged to the Defence of it, follows in these Words: *Volumus Vobiscum, et cum aliis de eodem Regno (Angliae scilicet) Terras in dicta Terra habentibus Collo-*

quium habere, &c. [*We will confer with you, and others of the same kingdom, (viz. England) possessed of lands in the said country.*]

But, that the Reader may perceive how strictly the Principle of no Person's being Taxed without their Consent, hath been regarded, it is proper to take Notice, that, upon the same Occasion, Writs were likewise directed even to Women, who were Proprietors of Land in *Ireland,* to send their Deputies to consult, and consent to what should be judged necessary to be done on the Occasion; e.g. *Rex, &c.— Mariae, &c. Salutem, &c. Vobis, &c. Mandamus quod aliquem, vel aliquos de quibus confidatis apud Westmon. mittatis ad loquendum nobiscum super dictis Negotiis, et ad faciendum et consentiendum Nomine vestro, super hoc quod ibidem ordinari contigerit.* [*We command you to send to Westminster, some person or persons, whom you may confide in, to confer with us, on the above said affair, and to do and assent, in your name, to whatever shall be there decreed.*]

A reflection naturally arises from the Instances cited—When, on a particular Occasion, *some* Individuals *only* were to be taxed, and not the *whole* Community, *their* Consent *only* was called for, and in the last Instance it appears, that they, who upon an Occasion of a general Tax, would have been bound by the Consent of their *virtual Representatives* (for in that Case they would have had no *actual Representatives*) were in an Affair calling for a *particular* Aid from them, *separate* from the rest of the Community, required to send their *particular Deputies:* But how different would be the Principle of a Statute, imposing Duties without *their* Consent who are to pay them, upon the Authority of *their* Gift, who should undertake to give, what doth not belong to them.

That great King, *Edward* I, inserted in his Writs of Summons, as a first Principle of Law, that *quod omnes tangat ab omnibus approbetur,* [*what concerns all, must be approved by all,*] which by no Torture can be made to signify that their Approbation or Consent *only* is to be required in the Imposition of a Tax, who are to pay *no* Part of it.

The Situation of the Non-Electors in *England*—their Capacity to become Electors—their inseparable Connection with those who are Electors, and their Representatives—their Security against Oppression resulting from this Connection, and the Necessity of imagining a double or virtual Representation, to avoid Iniquity and Absurdity, have been explained—The Inhabitants of the Colonies are, *as such,* incapable of being Electors, the Privilege of Election being exerciseable only in Person, and therefore if *every* Inhabitant of *America* had the requisite Freehold, not *one* could vote, but upon the Supposition of his ceasing to be an Inhabitant of *America,* and becoming a Resident in *Great-Britain,* a Supposition which would be impertinent, because it shifts the Question—Should the Colonies not be Taxed by *Parliamentary Impositions,* their respective Legislatures have a regular, adequate, and constitutional Authority to Tax them, and therefore there would not necessarily be an iniquitous and absurd Exemption, from their not being represented by *the House of Commons.*

There is not that intimate and inseparable Relation between the *Electors of* Great-Britain and the *Inhabitants of the Colonies,* which must inevitably involve both in the same Taxation; on the contrary, not a single *actual* Elector in *England,* might be immediately affected by a Taxation in *America,* imposed by a Statute which would have a general Operation and Effect, upon the Properties of the Inhabitants of the Colonies. The latter might be oppressed in a Thousand Shapes, without any Sympathy, or exciting any Alarm in the former. Moreover, even Acts, oppressive and injurious to the Colonies in an extreme Degree, might become popular in *England,* from the Promise or Expectation, that the very Measures which depressed the Colonies, would give Ease to the Inhabitants of *Great-Britain.* It is indeed true, that the Interests of *England* and the Colonies are allied, and an Injury to the Colonies produced into all it's Consequences, will eventually affect the Mother-Country, yet these Consequences being generally remote, are not at once foreseen; they do not immediately alarm the Fears, and engage the Passions of the *English* Electors, the Connection between a Freeholder of *Great-Britain,* and a *British American* being deducible only through a Train of Reasoning, which few will take the Trouble, or can have an Opportunity, if they have Capacity, to investigate; wherefore the Relation between the *British-Americans,* and the *English Electors,* is a Knot too infirm to be relied on as a competent Security, especially against the Force of a present counter-acting, Expectation of Relief.

If it would have been a just Conclusion, that the *Colonies* being exactly in the *same* Situation with the *Non-Electors* of *England,* are *therefore* represented in the same Manner, it ought to be allowed, that the Reasoning is solid, which, after having evinced a total *Dissimilarity* of Situation, infers that their Representation is *different.*

If the Commons of *Great-Britain* have no Right by the Constitution, to GIVE AND GRANT Property *not* belonging to themselves, but to others, without their Consent actually or virtually given—If the Claim of the Colonies not to be Taxed *without their Consent,* signified by their Representatives, is well founded, if it appears that the Colonies are not actually represented by the Commons of *Great-Britain,* and that the Notion of a double or virtual Representation, doth not with any Propriety apply to the People of *America;* then the Principle of the *Stamp Act,* must be given up as indefensible on the Point of Representation, and the Validity of it rested upon the *Power* which they who framed it, have to carry it into Execution. . . .

But it has been alledged, that if the Right to *Give and Grant* the Property of the Colonies by an internal Taxation is denied to the House of Commons, the Subordination or Dependance of the Colonies, and the Superintendence of the *British* Parliament can't be consistently establish'd—That any supposed Line of Distinction between the Two Cases, is but "a whimsical Imagination, a chimerical Speculation against Fact and Experience." —Now, under Favour, I conceive there is more Confidence, than Solidity in this Assertion, and it may be satisfactorily and easily proved, that the Subordination and Dependance of the Colonies may be preserved, and the *supreme Authority* of the Mother-Country be firmly supported, and yet the Principle of Representation, and the Right of the *British* House of Commons flowing from *it*, to *Give and Grant* the Property of the Commons of *America*, be denied.

The Colonies are Dependent upon *Great-Britain*, and the supreme Authority vested in the King, Lords, and Commons, may justly be exercised to secure, or preserve their Dependence, whenever necessary for that Purpose. This Authority results from, and is implied in the Idea of the Relation subsisting between *England* and her Colonies; for, considering the Nature of human Affections, the Inferior is not to be trusted with providing Regulations to prevent his Rising to an Equality with his Superior. But, tho' the Right of the Superior to use the proper Means for preserving the Subordination of his Inferior is admitted, yet, it does not necessarily follow, that he has a Right to seize the Property of his Inferior when he pleases, or to command him in every Thing, since, in the Degrees of it, there may very well exist a *Dependence* and *Inferiority*, without absolute *Vassalage* and *Slavery*. In what the Superior may *rightfully* controul, or compel, and in what the Inferior ought to be at Liberty to act without Controul or Compulsion, depends upon the Nature of the Dependence, and the Degree of the Subordination; and, these being ascertained, the Measure of Obedience, and Submission, and the Extent of the Authority and Superintendence will be settled. When Powers, compatible with the Relation between the Superior and Inferior, have, by express Compact, been granted to, and accepted by the latter, and have been, after that Compact, repeatedly recognized by the former—When they may be exercised effectually upon every Occasion without any Injury to that Relation, the Authority of the Superior can't properly interpose; for, by the Powers vested in the Inferior, is the Superior limited.

By their Constitutions of Government, the Colonies are impowered to impose internal Taxes. This Power is compatible with their Dependence, and hath been expressly recognized by *British* Ministers and the *British* Parliament, upon many Occasions; and it may be exercised effectually without striking at, or impeaching, in any Respect, the Superintendence of the *British* Parliament. May not then the Line be distinctly and justly drawn between such Acts as are necessary, or proper, for preserving or securing the Dependence of the Colonies, and such as are not necessary or proper for that very important Purpose; and would moreover Destroy the fundamental and necessary Principle of Constitutional Liberty?

* * * * *

The Right of Exemption from all Taxes *without their Consent*, the Colonies claim as *British* Subjects. They derive this Right from the Common Law, which their Charters have declared and confirmed, and they conceive that when stripped of this Right, whether by Prerogative or by any other Power, they are at the same Time deprived of every Privilege distinguishing Free-Men from Slaves.

On the other Hand, they acknowledge themselves to be subordinate to the Mother-Country, and that the Authority vested in the supreme Council of the Nation, may be justly exercised to support and preserve that Subordination.

Great and just Encomiums have been bestow'd upon the Constitution of *England,* and their Representative is deservedly the Favourite of the Inhabitants in *Britain.* But it is not because the supreme Council is called *Parliament,* that they boast of their Constitution of Government; for there is no particular magical Influence from the Combination of the Letters which form the Word; it is because they have a Share in that Council, that they appoint the Members who constitute one Branch of it, whose Duty and Interest it is to consult their Benefit, and to assert their Rights, and who are vested with an Authority, to prevent any Measures taking Effect dangerous to their Liberties, or injurious to their Properties.

But the Inhabitants in the Colonies have no Share in this great Council. None of the Members of it are, or can be of their Appointment, or in any respect Dependent upon them. There is no immediate Connection, on the Contrary, there may be an Opposition of Interest; how puerile then is the Declamation, "what will become of the Colonies Birthright, and the glorious Securities which their Forefathers handed down to them, if the Authority of the *British* Parliament *to impose Taxes* upon them should be given up? To deny the Authority of the *British* Legislature, is to surrender all Claim to a Share in its Councils, and if this were the Tenor of their Charters, a Grant more insidious or replete with Mischief, could not be imagined, a Forfeiture of their Rights would be couched under the Appearance of Privilege, *&c.*"

We claim an Exemption from all *Parliamentary* Impositions, that we may enjoy those Securities of our Rights and Properties, which we are entitled to by the Constitution. For those Securities are derived to the Subject from the Principle *that he is not to be Taxed without his own Consent,* and an Inhabitant in *America* can give his Consent in no other Manner than in Assembly. It is in the Councils that exist there, and there *only,* that he hath a Share, and whilst he enjoys it, his Rights and Privileges are as well secured as any Elector's in *England,* who hath a Share in the National Councils there; for the Words *Parliament* and *Assembly* are, in this Respect, only different Terms to express the same Thing.

But it is argued, that "if the Common Law of *England* is to be brought, as justifying a Claim of Exemption in any Subject of *Great-Britain* from a Parliamentary Tax, it will plead against a Tax imposed by a Provincial Assembly; for, as all the Colony Assemblies, derive their Authority from the mere Grant of the Crown only, it might be urged that any Tax imposed by them, is imposed by Authority of the Prerogative of the Crown, and not by full Consent of Parliament. That if this Right in the Crown, is acknowledged to exempt the Subject from the Jurisdiction of Parliament in the Case of Taxation, its Power to dispense with Acts of Parliament, or to deprive the same Subject of the Benefit of the Common Law, can't be denied."

One would be inclined to suspect that it is supposed, something else than Reason, may, on this Occasion, conduce to Persuasion.

The *English* Subjects, who left their *native* Country to settle in the Wilderness of *America,* had the Privileges of *other Englishmen.* They knew their Value, and were desirous of having them perpetuated to their Posterity. They were aware that, as their Consent whilst they should reside in *America,* could neither be ask'd, nor regularly given, in the National Legislature, and that, if they were to be bound by Laws without Restriction affecting the Property they should earn by the utmost Hazard and Fatigue, they would lose every other Privilege which they had enjoyed in their native Country, and become mere Tenants at Will, dependent upon the Moderation of their Lords and Masters, without any other Security.—That, as their Settlement was to be made under the Protection of the *English* Government, they knew, that in Consequence of their Relation to the Mother-Country, they and their Posterity would be subordinate to the supreme National Council, and expected that Obedience and Protection would be considered as reciprocal Duties.

Considering themselves, and being considered in this Light, they entered into a Compact with the Crown, the Basis of which was, *That their Privileges as* English *Subjects, should be effectually secured to Themselves, and transmitted to their Posterity*. And as for this Purpose, precise Declarations and Provisions formed upon the Principles, and according to the Spirit of the *English Constitution* were necessary; CHARTERS were accordingly framed and conferred by the Crown, and accepted by the Settlers, by which all the Doubts and Inconveniencies which might have arisen from the Application of general Principles to a new Subject, were prevented.

By these Charters, founded upon the unalienable Rights of the Subject, and upon the most sacred Compact, the Colonies claim a Right of Exemption from Taxes *not imposed with their Consent.*— They claim it upon the Principles of the Constitution, as once *English,* and now *British* Subjects, upon Principles on which their Compact with the Crown was originally founded.

The Origin of other Governments is covered by the Veil of Antiquity, and is differently traced by the Fancies of different Men; but, of the Colonies, the Evidence of it is as clear and unequivocal as of any other Fact.

By these declaratory Charters the Inhabitants of the Colonies claim an Exemption from *all* Taxes not imposed by their own Consent, and to infer from their Objection to a Taxation, to which their Consent is not, nor can be given, *that They are setting up a Right in the Crown to dis-*

pense with Acts of Parliament, and to deprive the British *Subjects in* America *of the Benefits of the Common Law,* is so extremely absurd, that I should be at a Loss to account for the Appearance of so strange an Argument, were I not apprized of the unworthy Arts employed by the Enemies of the Colonies to excite strong Prejudices against them in the Minds of their Brethren at Home, and what gross Incongruities prejudiced Men are wont to adopt.

Tho' I am persuaded that this Reasoning hath already been sufficiently refuted, and that no sensible and dispassionate Man can perceive any Force in it, yet I can't help remarking, that it is grounded upon a Principle, which, if it were possible for the Examiner to establish it, would entitle him to the Applause of the Inhabitants in *Great-Britain,* as little as to the Thanks of the Colonies.

From what Source do the Peers of *England* derive their Dignity, and the Share they have in the *British Legislature?* Are there no Places in *England* that derive their Power of chusing Members of Parliament from Royal Charters? Will this Writer argue, that the Crown may, by Prerogative, Tax the Inhabitants of *Great-Britain,* because the Peers of *England,* and some Representatives of the People, exercise a legislative Authority under Royal Patents and Charters? It must be admitted, that all the Members of the House of Commons are freely chosen by the People, and are not afterwards subject to any Influence of the Crown or the Ministry: And are not the Members of the Lower House of Assembly as freely chosen also by the People; and, in Fact, as independent as the Members of the House of Commons? If the Truth were confessed, the Objection would not be, *that the Colonies are too dependent upon the Crown,* or that their Claim of Exemption from all Taxes, not imposed by their own Consent, *is founded upon a Principle leading to Slavery.* At one Time, the *North-*

Americans are called *Republicans;* at another, *the Assertors of Despotism.* What a strange Animal must a *North-American* appear to be from these Representations to the Generality of *English* Readers, who have never had an Opportunity to admire, that he may be neither black, nor tawny, may speak the *English* Language, and, in other Respects, seem, for all the World, like one of them!

"The Common Law, the Great Charter, the Bill of Rights," are so far from "declaring, with one Voice, that the Inhabitants of the Colonies shall be Taxed by no other Authority than that of the *British Parliament,*" that they prove the contrary; for the Principle of the Common Law is, *that no Part of their Property shall be drawn from* British *Subjects, without their Consent, given by those whom they depute to represent them;* and this Principle is enforced by the Declaration of the GREAT CHARTER, and *the Bill of Rights,* neither the one nor the other, introducing any *new* Privilege. In *Great-Britain,* the Consent of the People is given by the House of Commons; and, as Money had been levied there for the Use of the Crown, *by Pretence of Prerogative, without their Consent,* it was properly declared at the Revolution, in Support of the Constitution, and in Vindication of the People's Rights, that the levying of Money, by *Pretence of Prerogative,* without Grant of Parliament, *i.e.* without their Consent who are to Pay it, is illegal, which Declaration was most suitable to the Occasion, and effectually establishes the very Principle contended for by the Colonies.

The Word *Parliament,* having been made use of, the *Letter* of the Declaration is adheard to, and the Consequence drawn, that no *British* Subject can be legally Taxed, but by the Authority of the *British Parliament,* against the Spirit and Principle of the Declaration, which was aimed only to check and restrain the *Prerogative,* and to establish the Necessity of obtaining *the Consent* of those on whom Taxes were to be levied. Is not this a new Kind of Logic, to infer from Declarations and Claims, founded upon the necessary and essential Principle of a Free Government, that the People ought not to be Taxed without their Consent, that therefore the Colonies ought to be Taxed by an Authority, in which their Consent is not, nor can be concerned; or, in other Words, to draw an Inference from a Declaration or Claim of Privilege, subversive of the very Principle upon which the Privilege is founded? How aukwardly are the Principles of the Revolution applied by some Men! What Astonishment would the Promoters of that glorious Measure, those Patrons and Friends of Liberty, did they now tread the Stage of this World, express, that a *Word,* by which they meant to assert the Privileges of the Subject, and restrain despotic Power, should be relied upon to demolish the very Principle by which themselves were animated, and after all their Pains and Hazards to establish the generous Sentiments of Liberty, that those who feel and enjoy the Blessings of their successful Struggles, should, not be able to raise a Thought beyond the Ideas affixed to systematic Terms.

It was declared also by the *Bill of Rights,* that the Elections of *Members of Parliament* ought to be Free, and the Common Law laid down the same Rule before, which is as applicable to the Election of the Representatives of the Colonies, as of the Commons of *Great-Britain.* But with the Help of the Examiner's Logic, it might be proved from the *Letter* of the *Bill of Rights,* that the Elections *only* of *Members of Parliament* ought to be free; for the Freedom expressed in the Bill of Rights, is as much attached to Elections of Members of Parliament, as the Authority to grant Money is to *the* British *Parliament,* and if the Declaration in the one Case implies a Negative, there is the like Implication in the other. If, moreover, the Common Law, the Great Charter, and the Bill of Rights, do really, as the Examiner asserts, with one Voice declare, that the Inhabitants of the Colonies ought to be Taxed *only* by the *British* Parliament, it is not consistent with that Character of Vigilance, and Jealousy of their Power, commonly ascribed to the *British Parliament*, that, from their first regular Settlement to the Reign of *Geo.* III, the *American* Assemblies should not only have been suffered, without any Animadversion, without one Resolve, or even a single Motion, to restrain them, to encroach upon the Jurisdiction and Authority of the *British Parliament;* but that the Parliament should never before the late *Stamp-Act,* in one Instance, have imposed an internal Tax upon the Colonies for *the single Purpose of Revenue,* and that, even when Acts of Assembly passed in Consequence of Ministerial, enforced by Royal Requisitions, have been laid before them, they should be so far from objecting to their Validity, as actually to recognize the Authority of the Provincial Legislatures, and upon that Foundation superstruct their own Resolves and Acts.

But tho' it hath been admitted, that the *Stamp-Act* is the first Statute that hath imposed an internal Tax upon the Colonies *for the single Purpose of Revenue,* yet the Advocates for that Law contend, that there are many Instances of the Parliament's exercising a supreme legislative Authority over the Colonies, and actually imposing *internal Taxes* upon their Properties—that the Duties upon any Exports or Imports are internal Taxes—That an Impost on a foreign Commodity is as much an internal Tax, as a Duty upon any Production of the Plantations—That no Distinction can be supported between one Kind of Tax and another, an Authority to impose the one extending to the other.

If these Things are really as represented by the Advocates for the *Stamp-Act,* why did the *Chancellor of the Exchequer* make it a Question for the Consideration of the House of Commons, whether the Parliament could impose an *internal Tax* in the Colonies or not, for the *single Purpose of Revenue?*

It appears to me, that there is a clear and necessary Distinction between an Act imposing a Tax for *the single Purpose of Revenue,* and those Acts which have been made for the Regulation of Trade, and have produced some Revenue *in Consequence of their Effect* and Operation as *Regulations of Trade.*

The Colonies claim the Privileges of *British* Subjects—It has been proved to be inconsistent with those Privileges, to Tax them *without their own Consent,* and it hath been demonstrated, that a Tax imposed by Parliament, is a Tax *without their Consent.*

The Subordination of the Colonies, and the Authority of the Parliament to preserve it, have been fully acknowledged. Not only the Welfare, but perhaps the Existence of the Mother-Country, as an independent Kingdom, may rest upon her Trade and Navigation, and these so far upon her Intercourse with the Colonies, that, if this should be neglected, there would soon be an End to that Commerce, whence her greatest Wealth is derived, and upon which her Maritime Power is principally founded. From these Considerations, the Right of the *British Parliament* to regulate the Trade of the Colonies, may be justly deduced; a Denial of it would contradict the Admission of the Subordination, and of the Authority to preserve it, resulting from the Nature of the Relation between the Mother-Country and her Colonies. It is a common, and frequently the most proper Method to regulate Trade by Duties on Imports and Exports. The Authority of the Mother-Country to regulate the Trade of the Colonies, being unquestionable, what Regulations are the most proper, are to be of Course submitted to the Determination of the Parliament; and, if an *incidental Revenue,* should be produced by such Regulations; these are not therefore unwarrantable.

A Right to impose an internal Tax on the Colonies, without their Consent *for the single Purpose of Revenue,* is denied; a Right to regulate their Trade without their Consent is admitted. The Imposition of a Duty, may, in some Instances, be the proper Regulation. If the Claims of the Mother-Country and the Colonies should seem on such an Occasion to interfere, and the Point of Right to be doubtful, (which I take to be otherwise) it is easy to guess that the Determination will be on the Side of Power, and that the Inferior will be constrained to submit.

The Writer on the Regulations lately made with respect to the Colonies, who is said to have been *well informed,* asserts a Fact, which indisputably proves, that the Impositions mentioned, were *only* Regulations of Trade, and can, with no kind of Propriety, be considered in any other Light. The Fact he asserts, is, that "the whole Remittance from all the Taxes in the Colonies, at an Average of Thirty Years, has not amounted to 1900 *1.* a Year, and in that Sum, 7 or 800 *1. per Annum* only, have been remitted from *North-America;* and, to make it still more ridiculous, the Establishment of Officers necessary to collect that Revenue of 1900 *1.* amounts to 7600 *1. per Annum.*

It would be ridiculous indeed to suppose, that the Parliament would raise a Revenue by Taxes in the Colonies to defray Part of the National Expence, the Collection of which Taxes would increase that Expence to a Sum more than three Times the Amount of the Reveune; but, the Impositions being considered in their true Light, as Regulations of Trade, the Expence arising from an Establishment necessary to carry them into Execution, is so far from being ridiculous, that it may be wisely incurred.

The Author of the Claim of the Colonies, &c. gives (as hath been observed,) the Epithets of *unjust* and *partial,* to a Tax which should be imposed upon the Non-Electors, only in *Britain;* and, in that very Instance, proves, that a Tax upon the Non-Electors in the Colonies, is more unjust and partial, and yet undertakes to defend the Justice of it; and the Writer on the Regulations of the Colonies declares, that it is in vain to call the Acts he has cited as Precedents, by the Name of mere Regulations, notwithstanding he hath irrefragably proved, that they are ridiculous, if considered in any other Light. *(See The Regulation of the Colonies,* &c. Page 105-57, and *The Claim of the Colonies,* &c. Page 28, 29, 30.)

29. The Objection to American Representation in Parliament

[*Pennsylvania Journal,* March 13, 1766.]

To the Printer.

We have had lately several hints among the articles of intelligence from Great-Britain, that a proposal was likely to be made, to allow the colonies *Representatives* in *Parliament;* with a view to quiet our uneasiness, and remove our principal objection against the Stamp Act. Some of their political writers have warmly recommended it, as the only way to set us on equal footing with themselves, and secure to the parliament the right they

claim to tax us; others have espoused it as the means to annihilate effectually the power of our assemblies, which it seems they will gladly do if they can. A proposal so insidious as this, ought to be maturely considered, and its baneful tendency exposed to public view, that if they attempt to insnare us this way, we may be sufficiently guarded against it. Some of our writers have just mentioned it as what would be very mischievous, should it take place; but none that I remember have employed that attention about it, which its importance deserves.

It is easy to see that this proposal, if adopted by the colonies, will involve them in a very burdensome expence—can do them no service—will expose them to great and irreparable evils, and therefore that it would be the height of infatuation to comply with it if offered. It will involve them in a very burdensome expence—We have few gentlemen in the colonies, who have fortunes sufficient to enable them, and fewer still I fear who have public spirit enough to be willing to reside at the court of Great Britain at their own expence. To send them there without handsome appointments for their support, would be throwing them into the very jaws of temptation; it would be to make it in some sort necessary for many of them at least to betray their trust. They must then be reputably supported by their respective colonies. But it is well known that a gentleman cannot live at court reputably, or even decently in a public character, for less than £ 500 *per annum;* and if the damage arising from their abscence from their private affairs be estimated (which in common justice ought to be done) in most cases the above-mentioned sum must be doubled. If then, upon an average, each of the colonies be admitted to send four members to parliament (which number will give them no great weight in the house of commons, which consists of 558 members) the charge of supporting them will amount of £ 4000 sterling *per annum* to each colony; which vastly exceeds the current expences of government in most of them, and would be an extremely grievous addition to the other burdens they at present labour under.

Again, this scheme, if adopted, would not only be grievously expensive to the colonies, but can do them no service. For we may take it for granted that Great Britain will never offer us such a number of representatives in the house, as would give us any considerable weight or influence there. To allow the colonies such a number of members in the house of commons, as would enable them to carry points against the mother country, when a competition of interests arises, would be in effect to resign her own independency, which we may be assured she never will do. It would be unsafe to allow even such a number, as to be able to turn the scale for, or against the ministry; which a few might often do if they took care to be united. For if they have weight enough to render a ministry secure against the attacks of their enemies, or overthrow them by joining in the opposition, that very circumstance will render them considerable; and they will seldom want opportunities to encrease their strength, if they are watchful to improve them. For the colonies are growing fast in population and wealth, and consequently in influence; as these increase it will be natural to suppose their number of representatives ought to increase. Vast tracts of land remain to be settled, which will afford ample room for at least as many new colonies, as we now possess on the coast: these when settled, will have as good a claim to a representation in the house, as we now have. Our members already there will have it easily in their power, if they are only united, to introduce any reasonable number of new ones, by seizing such favourable conjunctures as often will occur; as for instance, when the ministry cannot stand their ground without their assistance. Thus the strength of the Americans in the house will be continually increasing, and that of the Britons as distinguished from it, will be at a stand: and it is easy to see that the former must in time overtop the latter.

Whenever the American interest obtains the ascendency in the house, it will be in the power of our representatives to remove the seat of government to their native country, (which is to be supposed they will be forward enough to do, as their own interest would be eminently promoted by it) and then Great-Britain, from being the head of a vast empire, will dwindle away to an American province. Nor is this event to be regarded as a remote contingency; in one century such a revolution might easily be effected. This will in all probability be the issue, if any considerable number of members of parliament are introduced from America. It requires no large share of penetration to foresee it: Great-Britain will certainly foresee and prevent it, as her own dignity and importance are ruined if it be not prevented. Therefore if a representation in parliament is offered us, it will be limited to so small a number of members, as will effectually prevent our having any weight or influence there. But what imaginable service can such a representation do us? It is only when a supposed collision of interest between Great Britain and the Colonies arises, that having members in parliament can be of any importance. But in an assembly, where for [far?] the greater part of the members have their residence and whole interest in Britain, and where every thing is decided by a majority of votes, to expect the interest of America, when supposed to be opposite to theirs, would be generally considered, is as absurd as to expect a steady and inviolable distribution of justice from men when admitted to be judges in their own cause. It would be to suppose men are not generally to be swayed by their own interests, contrary to the universal experience of all ages. The power of determining all matters brought before them respecting the whole empire, will entirely reside in the *British* members: for *us* to have a few members cannot be of any consequence.

Besides, the house of Lords is an essential part of the legislature, as well as the house of Commons; *they* have an equal voice in framing and repealing all laws; and their consent is necessary in all supply bills. But we have no American Peers, and are not like to have any soon: a representation in that house will be impracticable. This will be an additional reason,

why no benefit can be derived from such a representation in the house of Commons, as they will ever allow us.

But if this scheme on the one hand, promises no advantage, it affords a prospect of infinite damage on the other. When venality and corruption reign with such unlimited sway, as it is known they have done in Britain for many years past, excepting one or two short intervals, it requires no ordinary stock of virtue to resist the torrent. Though I have the most honourable sentiments of my countrymen, yet I may suppose they have the same passions with other men. They will be liable to the artful attacks of bribery in some form or other, and we never can have any assurance they will not fall before them. Their living at such a distance from their native country, without any private emolument from their faithful discharge of their trust, may in many instances increase the temptation; especially when the prevalency of universal example is known to be sufficient to make almost any practice appear reputable, or at least to take of the shame and disgrace, that would otherwise attend it, and which is one of our strongest guards against all base actions. It may be viewed then as a probable event, that American Representations would be more or less infected with the common contagion. If in some unfortunate period they should be induced to betray their trust, by concurring in some iniquitous scheme to ruin us, either by passing injurious and oppressive laws, or levying burthensome and oppressive taxes, such as we should not be able to bear, what regular method should we have to rid ourselves of them? We could not pretend to say they were unconstitutional, for they are supposed to be enacted by an assembly, where we are duly represented: and what could hinder our having all our liberties sold one after another, if our representatives were villanous enough to sell, and the ministry disposed to buy them; It is plain they will be in a state of great insecurity, if they depend on the fidelity of a few individuals at such a distance from us. There is no kind of oppression that can be thought of, which might not be obtruded upon us, under the sanction of a law, and we should have no regular way to shake it off.

But the disadvantages attending this scheme, if ever adopted, are not barely such as may happen, if our members of Parliament should be corrupted; a subversion of our fundamental liberties, will be implied in the very nature of it. We have now a right to claim full and compleat legislation in every province; but if the scheme, I am considering takes place, this claim must be at an end. Though it would be necessary for various purposes, that our provincial assemblies should continue, yet their powers of Legislation must be subordinate to the general legislature of the whole empire. For a colony to be represented in two distinct legislative bodies, equal and independent of each other, and the laws of each to be equally binding at the same time, would be a perfect solecism in any system of government; for it is plain such equal and independent powers would frequently clash, which can issue in nothing but anarchy and confusion. Supreme and independent legislation must subsist somewhere in every state; but on the supposition before us, it can subsist no where but in the parliament of Great-Britain, which would be considered as the general legislature of the whole empire. Britain, though but a part would have the whole influence, and govern every thing as her own interests directed. In a confederacy of states, independent of each other, yet united under one head, such as I conceive the British empire at present to be, all the powers of legislation may subsist full and compleat in each part, and their respective legislatures be absolutely independent of each other; at least so far that the acts of one may not be liable to be repealed by another. In this case there is no proper subordination of one part to

another, though the power and influence of one of these confederate states may be vastly superior to any of the rest, or indeed to all of them united. If then the lesser states surrender their powers of free and independent legislation to a general diet, or parliament made up of representatives from every part, but where the proportion of members deligated by each are so adjusted, that the larger and more important state secures to herself the whole influence; and will always be able to direct every determination as she pleases, it is plain that the powers of legislation are lodged in her alone, and the lesser states are no longer confederates belonging to the same body, but are as really subjected to the larger, as if they had been conquered by her arms. Thus in the case before us, if we accept of a representation in parliament, we do from the very nature of the thing, by our own act and deed surrender our powers of legislation to the parliament, and no such thing as any compleat legislative authority can subsist any longer in America. Our provincial assemblies would be little more than petty corporations, having power to make a few by-laws for present conveniency.

If a general legislature was erected for the whole British empire in America, composed of delegates from each colony, (which indeed would be a very desirable event) the several provincial legislatures would be necessarily subordinated to it; and though their powers of legislation would be still independent of each other, yet the exercise of them would be subject to such limitations as arise from the nature of their subordination. But this would be subjecting each part regularly to the whole; not subjecting the whole to *one part*. There is a very wide difference between subordinating the provincial legislatures to a general legislature, where each province has its due share of influence, and where no collision of interests between the members of such general and provincial legislatures is supposable; and subordinating them all to an assembly, where none of them will have any influence, and where a collision of interest between the members of said assembly, and the several parts subjected to them, is frequently supposable. It is indeed hard to conceive of a worse system of government than that to which we shall subject ourselves, if we accept of a representation in parliament. It will be in vain to clamour about oppressive taxes, injurious restrictions on trade, manufactures, &c we must submit to whatever impositions they see fit to lay upon us; for all will be perfectly agreeable to the genius and spirit of the constitution we shall have expressly adopted. Our dependence on Britain, instead of being lessened, will be vastly increased. We shall have indeed the shadow of liberty, but be destitute of the substance. Our influence in the British legislature will in reality be no more than it is now, but instead of being free from its jurisdiction, we shall be regularly and properly subject to it. They will have a right by the very constitution, to command our purses and persons at pleasure. Our liberties, our lives, and every thing that is dear, will be at their mercy. They may indeed for a while be *gentle masters*, but

they will be our *masters* still, though they permit us the enjoyment of our privileges during pleasure. We may as well admit, without further dispute, the present extravagant claims of the parliament to take our property without our consent, as admit this.

This is I think a fair, but imperfect delineation of the horrid consequences of our accepting a representation in parliament. Surely nothing but compleat infatuation can ever induce the colonies to embrace a scheme so fraught with ruin. It will be virtually to surrender our liberty and property to be held by the meer will and pleasure of a body of men in Britain; it will be to put it in their power to enslave us whenever they please. If such a proposal is made, let it be treated as it deserves; let it be considered as a base crafty device to ensnare us; let it be rejected universally with scorn and indignation. Let those that urge its acceptance, if any such villains be found, be considered as enemies to their country. Let us steadily persist in maintaining our freedom, and though the struggle may be hard, let us not doubt of coming off victorious at last.

F. L.

30. "Cato" Denounces a "vile Miscreant"

[*Connecticut Courant*, Aug. 26, 1765.]

NEW HAVEN

—*Quid non Mortalia Pectora cogis
Auri sacra Fames*   Virgil

Since the late Impositions on the American Colonies by the Parliament of Great-Britain, our Papers have been filled with Exclamations against Slavery and arbitrary Power. One would have thought, by this mighty outcry, that all America, to a Man, had a noble Sense of Freedom, and would risque their Lives and Fortunes in the Defence of it. Had this been really the Spirit of the Colonies, they would have deserved Commisseration and Relief.

Nothing can fill a generous Breast with greater Indignation than to see a free, brave and virtuous People unjustly sunk and debased by Tyranny and Oppression. But who can pity the heartless Wretches whose only Fortitude is in their Tongue and Pen? If we may judge of the Whole by those who have been already tampered with, the Colonies are now ripe for Slavery, and incapable of Freedom.

Have three hundred Pounds a Year, or even a more trifling Consideration, been found sufficient to debauch from their Interest those who have been entrusted with the most important Concerns by the Colonies? If so, O Britain! heap on your Burdens without fear of Disturbance. We shall bear your Yoke as tamely as the overloaded Ass. If we bray with the Pain, we shall not have the Heart to throw off the Load, or spurn the Rider. Have many already become the Tools of your Oppression? and are numbers now cringing to become the Tools of those Tools, to slay his wretched Brethren? 'Tis impossible! But alas! if so, who could have tho't it!— Those who lately set themselves up for Patriots and boasted a generous Love for their Country, are they now saying (O Disgrace to Humanity!) are THEY now creeping after the Profits of collecting the unrighteous *American* Stamp-Duty! If THIS is credible, what may we not believe? Where are the mercenary Publicans who delight in Nothing so much as the dearest Blood of their Country? Will the Cries of your despairing, dying Brethren be Musick pleasing to your Ears? If so, go on! bend the Knee to your Master Horseleach, and beg a Share in the Pillage of your Country —*No*, you'll say, *I don't delight in the Ruin of my Country, but, since 'tis decreed she must fall, who can blame me for taking a Part in the Plunder?* Tenderly said! why did you not rather say—*If my Father must die, who can accuse me as defective in filial Duty, in becoming his Executioner, that so much of the Estate, at least, as goes to the Hangman, may be retained in the Family?*

Never pretend, whoever you are, that freely undertake to put in Execution a Law prejudicial to your Country, that you have the least Spark of affection for her. Rather own you would gladly see her in Flames, if you might be allowed to pillage with Impunity.

But had you not rather these Duties should be collected by your Brethren, than by Foreigners? No! vile Miscreant! indeed we had not. That same rapacious and base Spirit which prompted you to undertake the ignominious Task, will urge you on to every cruel and oppressive Measure. You will serve to put us continually in Mind of our abject Condition. A Foreigner we could more chearfully endure, because he might be supposed not to feel our Distresses; but for one of our *Fellow Slaves* who equally shares in our Pains, to rise up and beg the Favour of inflicting them, is intolerable. The only Advantage that can be hoped for from this is that it will rouse the most indolent of us to a Sense of our Slavery, and make us use our strongest Efforts to be free. Some, I hope, there are, notwithstanding your base Defection, that feel the patriotic Flame glowing in their Bosoms, and would esteem it glorious to die for their Country! From such as these you are to expect perpetual Opposition. These are Men whose Existence and Importance does not depend on Gold. When, therefore, you have pillaged from them their Estates, they will still live and blast your wicked Designs, by all *lawful* Means. You are to look for Nothing but the Hatred and Detestation of all the Good and Virtuous. And as you live on the Distresses, you will inherit the Curses of Widows and Orphans. The present Generation will treat you as the Authors of their Misery, and Posterity will pursue your Memory with the most terrible Imprecations.

CATO

31. An Attack on "designing parricides"

[*New York Mercury*, Oct. 21, 1765.]

It is enough to melt a stone, or even the harder heart of a villain, when he views this wretched land, sinking under the merciless and ill-timed persecutions of those who should have been its upholders and protectors.

It is enough to break the heart of the Patriot, who would joyfully pour out his blood, to extricate his beloved country from destruction, to find her fainting and despairing, hourly expecting to be utterly crush'd by the iron rod of power.

At this most critical conjuncture of affairs; while we are exerting every nerve, to free ourselves from the wretched condition, to which our debts to Great-Britain have reduc'd us; and reasonably fearing that our utmost endeavours will be ineffectual;—to what can we impute the infatuation of our mother country; by whose baneful advice has she been deluded, encouraged, advised! to overwhelm a numerous and well-affected people, to plunge them deep in ruin,—never to rise again.—Ye ruthless crew! Ye infernal, corrupted, detested incendiaries! who hid from the public eye, have invited despotism to cross the ocean, and fix her abode in this once happy land—to you do we owe our misery;—never wou'd Great-Britain so far have forgot her own interest, and ours, as to ruin a country, which, properly supported and encouraged, would have been an inexhaustible source of wealth, had she not been deluded by your false and insiduous insinuations; and had you not assured her, that we were a rich and flourishing people, able to bear any taxes she thought proper to impose on us.— Come and see how well we are able to bear additional taxes! See our poor starving! our liberties expiring! our trade declining! our countrymen dispairing! and if impartial conscience does not petrify you with horror and remorse, when her awful voice declares you have been the execrable cause!—Write again to your former correspondents; congratulate them on the good effects of their severity; bid them lay on new taxes, and spare not, for we cannot be rendered more wretched than we are. —Who that has the least spark of affection left for his native clime, can calmly think of its destroyers? Methinks the guardian angel of America, rises to my view! Indignation and the most poignant grief clouds his lovely face.—How art thou

fallen! thou envy of Europe! he cries. How art thou fallen, murder'd America! murder'd by those for whom thou hast incessantly toil'd, dismember'd, mangled and torn! Even thy own sons have joined to *stamp* on thy bowels.—Think not, whoever you are, that have been instrumental in ruining your country, that you will escape with impunity.—Misery, even in this life, shall be your portion.—The present generation shall never mention your names, but with the most bitter execrations; succeeding ages, inform'd by the faithful historian, to whom they owe their shackles, shall load your accursed memory with everlasting infamy.—How fondly did we hope that Great-Britain would have turn'd a deaf ear to the representations of these designing parricides! Even when she was so far deceived by them, as to enact laws, the execution of which would involve us in immediate ruin, sensible of the justice of our cause, we boldly preferred our complaints, we urged, we humbly pleaded, what we thought our irresistible argument—the exclusive right granted to us, to be solely taxed by our own representatives—that barrier of our defence, which we knew could not be legally surmounted.—But language cannot describe the mingled surprise and indignation, that glowed in the breast of every friend of his country; when fatal experience convinced us, how weak and indefensible was our boasted defence, against the assaults of those, who were as unmoved by our distress, as they were unconfined by their most voluntary and sacred engagements.

* * * * *

Ah! my dear country, curst in peace,
Why did you wish the war to cease;
The war in which you strew'd the plain,
With thousands of your heroes slain.
When Britain to your bleeding shore
Impetuous pour'd her squadrons o'er;
And snatch you from the Gallic Brood,
To drink herself your vital blood!

CHAPTER V

THE BRITISH PRESS

ENGLISHMEN REACTED variously to the colonial arguments against taxation and to the mob violence which accompanied the arguments. Many favored the Americans, and the views stated in the preceding section also found expression in British newspapers and pamphlets. The selections in this section are designed to show the opposite point of view, that of Englishmen who felt that the Stamp Act was both constitutional and equitable.

William Knox, agent for the colony of Georgia, was a participant in the conference of May 17, which he described in *The Claim of the Colonies . . . Considered* (London, 1765) in order to discredit the colonies (No. 32). The piece signed "William Pym" (No. 33), carried originally in the *General Evening Post* of London, attracted wide attention in America, perhaps because it raised a constitutional question which the colonists were prepared to argue. "Anti-Sejanus" was the pen name of the Reverend James Scott, Chaplain to the Earl of Sandwich. He was the most deadly critic of the Rockingham ministry, which replaced that of Grenville in the summer of 1765. In attacking the new ministers, who were known to be friendly to the colonists, Anti-Sejanus found occasion to praise the Stamp Act. The letter included here is only one of many that appeared over this signature in the *London Chronicle* in the winter of 1765-66 (No. 34).

Probably the most extreme critic of the colonists was the one who signed himself "Pacificus" (No. 35). His article provoked a strong reaction in the English press as well as the American. The piece by "John Ploughshare" purports to represent the reaction of the common man in England to America's resistance against taxation (No. 36).

QUESTIONS

1. To what extent do the English writers answer the Americans?

2. In what ways did the English view of the imperial constitution differ from that exhibited in the colonial resolutions and in the colonial press?

3. How accurate a knowledge of events in America or of the American position do the English writers show?

4. How does William Knox's account of the conference of May 17, 1765, compare with those by Garth and Mauduit?

5. Do the British writers make a good case, either in equity or in law, for parliamentary taxation of the colonies?

32. William Knox on the Claim of the Colonies

[Knox, *The Claim of the Colonies . . . Considered* (London, 1765), 31-36.]

When the house of commons had last year come to the resolution, *That it might be proper to charge certain stamp-duties upon the colonies;* the agents for the colonies on the Continent understanding that the resolution was conceived in such terms, and the further proceedings thereon suspended till the next session, in order to give the colonies an opportunity of making propositions in compensation for the revenue that such a tax might be expected to produce; and understanding also, that not a single member of parliament doubted of the right of parliament to impose a stamp-duty, or any other tax upon the colonies; thought it their duty to wait upon the chancellor of the Exchequer, to thank him for his candor and tenderness to the colonies; and to ask his opinion of the sort of proposition, which would probably be accepted from them to parliament. That gentleman, with great openness and affability, told them, He had proposed the resolution in the terms the parliament had adopted, from a real regard and tenderness for the subjects in the colonies; that it was highly reasonable they should contribute something towards the charge of protecting themselves, and in aid of the great expence Great Britain put herself to on their account; that no tax appeared to him so easy and equitable as a stamp-duty; and what ought particularly to recommend it to the colonies, was the mode of collecting it, which did not require any number of officers vested with extraordinary powers of entering houses, or in any respect served to extend a sort of influence which he never wished to encrease. He hinted that the colonies would now have it in their power, by agreeing to this tax, to establish a precedent for their being consulted before any tax was imposed on them by parliament; and he recommended it to the agents to represent it properly to their several colonies, and to advise their respective councils and assemblies to take it under their consideration; and if, upon deliberation, a stamp-duty appeared to them an eligible tax, to authorize their agents to declare their approbation of it, which being signified to parliament next year, when the tax came to be imposed, would afford a forcible argument for the like proceeding in all such cases. He told them further, that if the colonies thought any other mode of taxation more convenient to them, and made any proposition which should carry the appearance of equal efficacy with a stamp-duty, he would give it all due consideration.

The agents writ immediately to their respective colonies, and desired instructions for their direction against the next meeting of parliament. Some of the colony assemblies thought the advice their agents gave them impertinent, and supposing that obstinacy and strong expressions would have the same effect on the British parliament that they found them to have on some American governors, instead of sending over to their agents discretionary instructions, they framed petitions themselves, positively and directly questioning the authority and jurisdiction of parliament over the properties of the people in the colonies; and directed their agents to present them to king, lords, and commons. Others (not all) of the assemblies, less violent, gave instructions to their agents to petition parliament against the tax, and above all things to insist in their petitions on the right and privilege of the colonies to be exempt from internal taxes imposed by parliament; so that of the whole number, not a single colony authorized its agent either to consent to a stamp-duty, or to offer any precise compensation. Indeed, two of the colonies desired their agents to signify their readiness to contribute *their proportion* of that duty by methods of their own; but when the other agents asked those gentlemen if they could undertake for any particular sum, they confessed they had no authority to do so.

Such of the agents as were left by their constituents to act as their discretion should direct them in opposing this tax, thought the best that could be done for the subjects in America was, for the agents to endeavour at obtaining a precedent for their being heard in behalf of their respective colonies against the tax, since their instructions would not permit them to endeavour at establishing one for their consent being obtained. A petition for this purpose was accordingly prepared, in which no expressions tending to question the jurisdiction of parliament were inserted. But the agents who had petitions transmitted by their assemblies, did not think themselves at liberty to sign or present any other petition than those of their colonies; and accordingly they had them offered to the house of commons, which would not suffer them to be read, as upon the opening of them by the gentlemen who offered them, they were found to contain expressions questioning the jurisdiction of parliament. The petition transmitted by one colony was not indeed offered, for it was conceived in such offensive terms, that no member of parliament would carry it in.

From this candid account, every impartial man must lay it to the charge of the colonies, that a precedent in favour of the subjects in America was not obtained upon this occasion; and should a tax upon the colonies be proposed hereafter, and carried into effect the same session, the colonies could scarcely complain of a hardship, as it might with justice be said to them, when the parliament did give them an opportunity of transmitting their sentiments, instead of receiving from them any information of their circumstances, they had heard nothing but impeachments of the jurisdiction of parliament over them.

33. "William Pym": "The British parliament can at any time set aside all the charters"

[*London General Evening Post*, Aug. 20, 1765, reprinted in the *Newport Mercury*, Oct. 28, 1765.]

The people in our American colonies lay a very great stress upon the importance of their charters, and imagine that the privileges granted to their ancestors, at the time of their original establishment, must infallibly exempt them from participating in the least inconvenience of the Mother country, though the Mother country must share in every inconvenience of theirs. This mode of reasoning is however no less new than it is extraordinary: and one would almost be tempted to imagine that the persons, who argue in this manner, were alike unacquainted with the nature of the colonies and the constitution of this kingdom.

I shall very readily grant, that the colonies at the time of their first settling might receive particular indulgences from the Crown, to encourage adventurers to go over; and I will also grant, that these charters should be as inviolably adhered to as the nature of public contingencies will admit. But at the same time let me inform my fellow subjects of America, that a resolution of the British parliament can at any time set aside all the charters that have ever been granted by our monarchs; and that consequently nothing can be more idle than this pompous exclamation about their charter exemptions, whenever such a resolution has actually passed.

The great business of the British Legislative power is, to consult upon what new laws may be necessary for the general good of the British dominions, and to remove any casual inconveniencies which may arise from the existence of their former acts. In the prosecution of this important end, they cannot expect but what the most salutary laws will prove oppressive to some part of the people. However no injury, which may be sustained by individuals, is to prevent them from promoting the welfare of the community; for if they debated till they framed an ordinance agreeable to the wishes of every body, 'twould be utterly impossible for them ever to frame any ordinance at all.

If then the Legislative power of this country have a right to alter or annul those public acts which were solemnly passed by former princes and former parliaments; it must be a necessary consequence that they have an equal right to annul the private charters of former princes also; and that these charters, which are by no means to be set in the same degree of importance with our laws, are at least every whit as subject to their jurisdiction and authority. This is a circumstance which the assembly of Virginia in particular should have attended to before their late unaccountable resolutions; and

'tis what I hope the assemblies of our other settlements will judiciously attend to, if they find the least propensity to follow the extraordinary example of their Sistercolony.

The people of Ireland, though they have a parliament of their own (and a parliament, I will take the liberty of saying, composed of people to the full as eminent for their fortune and abilities, as any of our American assemblies) are nevertheless under the immediate subjection of the British Legislature. The vote of an English Senate can in an instant abrogate all the laws of that kingdom; and surely none of the plantations can possibly plead a greater share either of merit or privileges than our Irish fellow subjects; who nevertheless behave with an uncommon degree of respect to our decisions; and never presume to blame the hand which increases their burdens, however they may groan beneath the heaviness of the load.

I am very well aware that the present impatience, which the whole kingdom feels at the least increase of taxes, will naturally create a number of friends for the colonies: but at the same time let us consider that the propriety of the tax, which has excited such a ferment among our American fellow-subjects, is not now the foundation of dispute. The question now is, Whether those American subjects are, or are not, bound by the resolutions of a British parliament? If they are *not,* they are entirely a separate people from us, and the mere reception of officers appointed in this kingdom, is nothing but an idle farce of government, which it is by no means our interest to keep up, if it is to produce us no benefit but the honour of protecting them whenever they are attacked by their enemies. On the other hand, if the people of America *are* bound by the proceedings of the English legislature, what excuse can the Virginians possibly make for the late indecent vote (to give it no harsher appellation) of their assembly. The present crisis, Sir, is really an alarming one; and after all the blood and treasure which we have expended in defence of the colonies, it is now questioned, whether we have any interest in those colonies at all.

If the people of Virginia were offended either with the tax itself, or with the mode of taxation, the proper method of proceeding would have been to petition the parliament, to point out the grievances arising from it, and to solicit the necessary redress. This is the invariable manner in which all the rest of their fellow-subjects (at least the European part of their fellow subjects) have acted in cases of a like nature. But to think of bullying their King, and the august Council of the Mother country, into an acquiescence with their sentiments, by a rash and hot headed vote; not only must expose them to the ridicule, but to the resentment of every considerate man who wishes well either to their interest or to the prosperity of this kingdom.

The people of the colonies know very well that the taxes of the Mother country are every day increasing; and can they expect that no addition whatsoever will be made to theirs? They know very well that a great part of our national debt was contracted in establishing them on a firm foundation, and protecting them from the arbitrary attempts of their implacable enemies. —Can anything then be so unreasonable, as a refusal of their assistance to wipe a little of it off? For my own part I am as much astonished at their want of justice, as I am surprized at their want of gratitude; and cannot help declaring it as my opinion, that we ought to shew but a very small share of sensibility for the circumstances of those people who are so utterly regardless of ours. To be sure, Sir, in assisting the colonies we had an eye to our own interest. It would be ridiculous otherwise to squander away our blood and our treasure in their defence. But certainly the benefit was mutual; and consequently the disadvantage should be mutual too. If we reap emoluments from the existence of the colonies, the colonies owe every thing to our encouragement and protection. As therefore we share in the same prosperity, we ought to participate of the same distress; and nothing can be more inequitable, than the least disinclination to bear a regular portion of those disbursements, which were applied to support the general interest both of the mother-country and themselves.

WILLIAM PYM.

34. Anti-Sejanus: "The whole Stamp Act appears to be unexceptionable"

[*London Chronicle,* XVIII, 523 (Nov. 28-30, 1765).]

To the PRINTER.

THE Mother-Country may endue the colonies with peculiar grants and privileges; may invest them with a power of enacting laws, levying supplies, punishing malefactors, and determining all matters of property. Yet these charters are held under her; and the several different governments, that are established in different colonies, are not independent and absolute, but *tanquam imperia in imperio.* Indeed it implies an absurdity, to suppose only the contrary: For if the colonies are to be considered as distinct from the Mother-Country; to what purpose did she lavish away her blood or treasures, in securing to herself only an *ideal* right to a barren territory? And why did she afterwards part with her own natural vigour, to feed and cherish an Alien? For if the strength and riches of a State depend upon the number of inhabitants, it is manifest that by every *Emigration,* it must suffer in both these respects, unless it derives an equivalent from the country, to which such an Emigration is made.

That the Mother-country is entitled to the support of her colonies, as a parent to the obedience of her children, is not only demonstrable from reason, and the law of nations, but from history and experience. The Romans, who were the most generous of all other people, and cared for little more than the *bare* extension of the majesty of the Roman name, asserted the right of tribute over their colonies, which they diminished or augmented at pleasure; though they would sometimes entirely remit it, as towards the Ilienses, whom they regarded as the original fathers of their empire. But I shall not insist any longer upon this subject, as it will not, I imagine, be disputed even by the Colonists themselves. Nor will any reasonable person object to the tax, which has occasioned so much disturbance among a set of people who want to throw off all dependance and subjection, if he considers it in the following light; as a tax, that does not oppress the manufacturer, does not impede trade, does not fall upon any of the common necessaries of life, nor affect the poorer class of people, who should be exempted as much as possible from every burden and grievance. It is levied upon men of property and opulence; and that too at such convenient seasons, and in so gentle a degree, as cannot fail to render the weight of it almost imperceptible.

Who for instance would grumble at a trifling expence, in securing, recovering, or encreasing his property? Who would refuse to pay a small fine, upon entering upon any preferment civil or military; or upon taking possession of lands, transferred over to him by grants or conveyances? What father would object to part with an inconsiderable sum, in providing a guardian for his child, or putting him out apprentice to a trade? I do not mention the tax that is laid upon amusements, pleasures, and vices, in the duties payable upon news-papers, licences for retailing wine, and spirituous liquors, together with those upon cards and dice; as such a tax is too fit and reasonable to require any vindication. Indeed the whole Stamp Act appears to be unexceptionable, unless perhaps there be one particular clause, which might have been amended: I mean that, which requires that the duties and impositions be paid in Specie (which is not in the plantations sufficient for the currency of the country) rather than in goods and merchandize. To take out of the several colonies so much silver yearly, as the above-mentioned Act was intended to raise, would undoubtedly drain them in a great measure of their ready money, and subject them to far greater inconveniences from a Paper-Currency, than what they already experience. I am,

Your's, &c.

ANTI-SEJANUS

35. "Pacificus" Lectures the "Libertines" of Virginia and the "Pumkins" of New England

[Reprinted in the *Maryland Gazette*, March 20, 1766.]

Our numerous and rich Islands give no Evidences of an ungovernable Temper; nor have the ceded Provinces afforded us any Cause to suspect their Loyalty. Georgia, the two Carolinas, and Maryland, are quiet: As are also the two Jersies, Nova

Scotia, and Newfoundland. As to New York, they are too honest and industrious a People to encourage Insurrections: Some of the lowest of the Inhabitants of that Colony are, as they are every where, somewhat inclined to disorderly Practices;

But Irregularities of the atrocious Nature of Insurrections, will find no Encouragement in that Province, either among the middling Planters, or from Persons in higher Stations: They are too regular Livers, too pious and too industrious, to entertain Sentiments of that black Dye: Nor need we be jealous of Pennsylvania, where industrious Propensities are better rewarded by bountiful Nature than in New-York.

The Virginians indeed are immersed in Libertinism; and the New-Englanders swell with the stiff Tenets of Independency. The latter are a crabbed Race, not very unlike their Half Brothers, the Indians, for unsocial Principles, and an unrelenting Cruelty. Their sanguinary Laws against that harmless Sect the Quakers, are a full Proof of their unmerciful Dispositions.

But shall Britain yield up her Birth Rights, for the Sake of pleasing the Whim of Virginians, whose emaciated Bodies and pale Faces, prove at first Sight the Degeneracy of their Morals, and the consumptive State of their natural Constitutions? These yellow Shadows of Men are by no Means fit for a Conflict with our Troops: Nor will ever such romantic Adventures of Chivalry enter into their trembling Hearts. Such Combatants would be far fitter for an Engagement with our Covent Garden Ladies, than with our embattled Squadrons. So soon as these doughty Champions found Matters growing serious, they might probably then look for Caverns where they could hide their shaking Limbs amongst those extensive Woods which they are too lazy or too feeble to cut down; but they would never think of marching up in the view of our pointed Cannon, or bear to look at the martial Appearance of our advancing Armies. When no Danger is near, they may probably Vapour in their Provincial Assemblies; but I am certain, that in Virginia that Proverb will always maintain its Truth, *That empty Barrels make most Noise when touched even with a Tap of our Knuckle*. He must be very tender of human Blood indeed, who can dread the Consequences of a League between Virginia and New-England against Great-Britain. The Virginians, to give them their due, are too wise to be caught in such a Mouse Trap. In Case an Engagement offered, before the first Onset they would get off as fast as they could from the intended Field of Battle, leaving the Pumkin Gentry whom they hold in most sovereign Contempt, to fight it out as they might, and then Snigger at the Trick they had played the Non Cons, who are also, by the Bye, too cautious to trust such Libertines in an Affair of too great Moment.

As for the New-Englanders, I have given their Characters already. They are the Joke of America. I cannot reasonably imagine that such a Hated and sour tempered Province can find any Allies. Their Valour arising from the Stems [steams?] of their poisonous Rum, will quickly evaporate in sudden Tumults; which, like April Showers, will be almost as soon over as begun. They are not so distracted as to spend much of their Blood in so idle a Cause; in which indeed no Man, above the Degree of an Ideot, would risque his Life, Property, and all that he holds dear in this World. He must have little Sense, who would become liable to be treated as a Rebel for the Sake of shunning Payment of a Shilling or Eighteen Pence for a Sheet of stamped Paper. Our Colonies must be the veriest Beggars in the World, if such inconsiderable Duties appear to be intolerable Burthens in their Eyes: And if they are in such a State of Poverty, where can they find Cannon, Ammunition, and all the other Implements of War, together with MONEY, the Sinews of Mars.—It is impossible.

The Idea of a Rebellion in America, in Consequence of such an unimportant Subject of Dispute, is merely Chimerical. It is a silly Utopian Fancy, which never can be midwifed into Existence; a Bugbear that can frighten none but Persons entirely ignorant of American Affairs. And since there are such great Numbers who harbour mistaken Notions of our Plantations, I have thus copiously laid the whole Affair before the Public, that every Subject of Britain may hereafter be entirely easy as to that Point, and chearfully concur with the Legislature in maintaining our national Dignity in this Dispute, without making any Concessions to the Libertines of Virginia, or the Puritans of New-England.

What Subject of this great Republic, in his right Senses, would agree that our Constitution, so vigorous and so well proportioned, should be broke up at the Pleasure of such Opponents, by the Introduction of Representatives from Virginia or New-England in our House of Commons? Would our Morals be safe under Virginian Legislatures, or would our Church be in no Danger from Pumkin Senators? Shall we live to see the Spawn of our Transports occupy the highest Seats in our Common Wealth? Degenerate Britons! how can ye entertain the humiliating Thought! Remember that Mr. Pitt, and all our real Patriots, have approved of this Tax. After mentioning these great Names, all further Arguments ought to cease: So here I drop my Pen, and leave the Disapprovers of this Law to Blush for their ill-timed Disapprobation.

PACIFICUS

36.   "John Ploughshare": "I am for Old England"

[*London Chronicle*, Feb. 20, 1766.]

To the PRINTER.

I AM a Farmer in Hertfordshire; I rent four-score pounds a year, and pay the taxes (tho' I wish they were not so many) without murmuring. I was glad at my heart whenever I heard that we had thrashed the French and Spaniards during the war. When the peace came, and I understood that we had got all America to ourselves, I thought it would be a great thing for old England; and that our fellow-subjects in that part of the world would trade with us more extensively than ever, and be ready to contribute, according to their abilities, to the payment of our debts and taxes, especially as a great part of the debt (I do not know how much) had been contracted in the late war, undertaken upon their account, and ending to their advantage. When I heard that they were mobbing the King's Officers, and declaring openly that the Parliament of England had no right to tax them, I was as much astonished as if a field where I had sowed barley should turn up pease. Surely they do not pretend to be subjects of England, for the King and Parliament can undoubtedly tax them if they be subjects.— I hear that a very great Man takes their part, and says, that the Parliament of England has no right to tax them, for they are not represented. Mr. Printer, I am not represented, and there are millions of Englishmen, as well as I, who have no more share in the elections of Members of Parliament than the Man of the Moon, and I believe that we notwithstanding pay the greatest part of the taxes. I, for my part, don't desire that it should be otherwise. We are very well in this Country, if we could but think so. But I fear our folly and restlesness will not suffer us to remain long in our present condition:— If these new-fashioned doctrines get once into the people's heads, they won't be easily got out again.

It is a pity to see human creatures like so many sheep follow a great bell-weather, who leads them into all manner of mischief. Every body, forsooth, to vote for

Members of parliament! All the Americans, all the people of the West-Indies and the East-Indies to have representatives! What sort of parliament must that be? I have heard of a Polish Diet, where they fight constantly whenever they meet; I am afraid that the parliament of England, if the Reformers of the constitution prevail, will be like the Polish Diet. It is good encouragement for the Americans to rebel, when some of our great Men at home tell them they are in the right, and the Parliament in the wrong. These are rare times indeed, Mr. Printer. If we were all of one mind, which common sense and common honesty should make us to be, upon such an occasion as this, the Americans durst not rebel. I believe, that if the Americans did not expect to be protected by some people here, they would submit patiently to the just authority of the English Parliament. In my poor opinion, some of our great Men do not believe in a future judgment, or else they would never act such a wicked part in this world. If the Americans throw off their subjection and become a separate people, their condition will be much better than ours, and we shall have reason to rue the day that we conquered America for them, at the expence of so much blood and treasure.

England labours under a great load of debt, and heavy taxes; England has a very expensive government to maintain; the Americans have a government of very little expence; and consequently we must dwindle and decline every day in our trade, whilst they thrive and prosper exceedingly. The consequence of this will certainly be, that the inhabitants will run away as fast as they can from this country to that, and Old England will become a poor, deserted, deplorable kingdom—like a farm that has been over-cropped, and the manure carried away to another man's grounds. I think it no shame to say, that I am for Old England; and I hold it neither fair nor honest in the Americans and their advocates to say, that they will not pay any part of the expence even of that army which defends them against the savages.

I am no politician nor party-man, but I am against all innovations and disturbances, though the pretence be liberty. God help us! we have as much liberty in England as ever any nation had in this world;—more, I fear, than we make a good use of; and if we continue to abuse it, as we are now doing, we shall lose it altogether, and overthrow this excellent government of King, Lords, and Commons. —I wish our great folks themselves may consider of that:—And so, Mr. Printer, I remain your's &c.

Hertfordshire. JOHN PLOUGHSHARE

CHAPTER VI

THE PATTERN OF REBELLION

POPULAR RESISTANCE to the Stamp Act, as distinct from the official action of the colonial assemblies, took two forms. Probably the most effective form in the long run was a boycott of English importations. New York merchants led the way on October 31, 1765 (No. 37). Philadelphia and Boston followed with similar agreements on November 7 and December 9, respectively.

The second form of resistance was to force the resignation of men appointed to distribute the stamped paper. The first violence of this kind occurred in Boston on the night of August 14. Governor Bernard described the event in a letter (No. 38) to Lord Halifax (whose replacement as Secretary of State for the Southern Department was not yet known in America). Twelve days later another riot occurred, directed against the customs officers and also against Lieutenant-Governor Thomas Hutchinson, who was popularly but erroneously supposed to have supported the passage of the Stamp Act. Hutchinson described his experiences in a letter to Richard Jackson (No. 39).

The riot in Newport on August 29 was probably touched off by news of the one in Boston. Dr. Thomas Moffat, who describes it (No. 40), had been a physician in Newport for some thirty-five years. Martin Howard, Jr., who suffered with Moffat in the riot, was an attorney and author of a tract defending parliamentary authority. He and Moffat had contributed a number of anonymous letters to the *Newport Mercury,* urging industry and submission upon their countrymen. They were also suspected, correctly, of petitioning the King to replace Rhode Island's popularly elected government by a royal government. These two men seem to have been more hated than the third victim, Augustus Johnston, the stamp distributor. Joseph Harrison, to whom Moffat's letter is addressed, was a former Newporter who shared Moffat's and Howard's political views and who had brought the petition for royal government to London.

The attacks on Hutchinson, Moffat, and Howard suggest that Americans extended popular resentment against the Stamp Act to help pay off grudges formed on other grounds.   There were similar riots in most of the other colonies; and after November 1, when the act was supposed to take effect, friends of British authority scarcely dared to speak their views.

The colonies for the most part ignored the act, transacting business without stamps as though it had never been passed.   They realized that their actions might provoke a show of force by the mother country.   How serious they were in their resistance may perhaps be perceived by the appearance in every colony of a group calling itself the Sons of Liberty, a name perhaps taken from Colonel Barré's speech.   The Sons of Liberty were, in effect, incipient revolutionary assemblies, and the resolutions they adopted (Nos. 41-46) may be compared and contrasted with those of the regular colonial legislative assemblies.

The Sons of Liberty, though apparently formed spontaneously in different colonies, were ready by the end of 1765 to form an inter-colonial union for the purpose of resisting enforcement of the Stamp Act.   William Gordon, an English minister who came to America in 1770 and later wrote a history of the Revolution, included in it a unique document describing the beginnings of this union (No. 47).

The resolutions and agreements of the Sons of Liberty might perhaps be dismissed as big talk that would have grown smaller in the presence of a British Army.   But two reliable observers with a reputation for sobriety were alarmed at the revolutionary situation that developed in the winter of 1765-66.   Neither man wished for independence; but John Dickinson, writing from Philadelphia to William Pitt, hinted that independence might be the ultimate outcome of Parliament's attempt to tax the colonies (No. 48); and Thomas Hutchinson, who knew the temper of the Boston mob at first hand, described to former Governor Thomas Pownall the collapse of authority in Massachusetts (No. 49).

QUESTIONS

1. On what grounds did the Sons of Liberty justify resistance to the Stamp Act?

2. Do the resolutions propose independence?

3. Can the activities of the Sons of Liberty be considered legal or constitutional?

4. What did John Dickinson mean by "my country"?

5. In your opinion, what would have been the consequences of a determined British effort to enforce the Stamp Act?

Boycotts and Riots

37. The New York Agreement, October 31, 1765

[Pennsylvania Gazette, Nov. 7, 1765.]

At a general Meeting of the Merchants of the City of New-York, trading to Great-Britain, at the House of Mr. George Burns, of the said City, Innholder, to consider what was necessary to be done in the present Situation of Affairs, with respect to the STAMP ACT, and the melancholy State of the North-American Commerce, so greatly restricted by the Impositions and Duties established by the late Acts of Trade: They came to the following Resolutions, viz.

FIRST, That in all Orders they send out to Great-Britain, for Goods or Merchandize, of any Nature, Kind or Quality whatsoever, usually imported from Great-Britain, they will direct their Correspondents not to ship them, unless the STAMP ACT be repealed: It is nevertheless agreed, that all such Merchants as are Owners of, and have Vessels already gone, and now cleared out for Great-Britain, shall be at Liberty to bring back in them, on their own Accounts, Crates and Casks of Earthen Ware, Grindstones, Pipes, and such other bulky Articles, as Owners usually fill up their Vessels with.

SECONDLY, It is further unanimously agreed, that all Orders already sent Home, shall be countermanded by the very first Conveyance; and the Goods and Merchandize thereby ordered, not to be sent, unless upon the Condition mentioned in the foregoing Resolution.

THIRDLY, It is further unanimously agreed, that no Merchant will vend any Goods or Merchandize sent upon Commission from Great-Britain, that shall be shipped from thence after the first Day of January next, unless upon the Condition mentioned in the first Resolution.

FOURTHLY. It is further unanimously agreed, that the foregoing Resolutions shall be binding until the same are abrogated at a general Meeting hereafter to be held for that Purpose.

In Witness whereof we have hereunto respectively subscribed our Names. [*This was subscribed by upwards of Two Hundred principal Merchants.*]

38.   The Boston Riot of August 14, 1765

[Governor Bernard to Lord Halifax, Aug. 15, 1765, The House of Lords Manuscripts for Jan. 14, 1766 (Photocopy in the Library of Congress).]

Castle William August 15, 1765
My Lords,

I am extremely concerned, that I am obliged to give your Lordships the Relation that is to follow; as it will reflect disgrace upon this Province, and bring the Town of Boston under great difficulties. Two or three months ago, I thought that this People would have submitted to the Stamp Act without actual Opposition.

Murmurs indeed were continually heard, but they seemed to be such as would in time die away; But the publishing the Virginia Resolves proved an Alarm bell to the disaffected. From that time an infamous weekly Paper, which is printed here, has swarmed with libells of the most atrocious kind. These have been urged with so much Vehemence and so industriously repeated, that I have considered them as preludes to Action. But I did not think, that it would have commenced so early, or be carried to such Lengths, as it has been.

Yesterday Morning at break of day was discovered hanging upon a Tree in a Street of the Town an Effigy, with inscriptions, shewing that it was intended to represent Mr. Oliver, the Secretary, who had lately accepted the Office of Stamp Distributor. Some of the Neighbours offered to take it down, but they were given to know, that would not be permitted. Many Gentlemen, especially some of the Council, treated it as a boyish sport, that did not deserve the Notice of the Governor and Council. But I did not think so however I contented myself with the Lt. Governor, as Chief Justice, directing the Sheriff to order his Officers to take down the Effigy; and I appointed a Council to meet in the Afternoon to consider what should be done, if the Sheriff's Officers were obstructed in removing the Effigy.

Before the Council met, the Sheriff reported, that his Officers had endeavoured to take down the Effigy: but could not do it without imminent danger of their lives. The Council met I represented this Transaction to them as the beginning in my Opinion, of much greater Commotions. I desired their Advice, what I should do upon this Occasion. A Majority of the Council spoke in form against doing anything but upon very different Principles: some said, that it was trifling Business, which, if let alone, would subside of itself, but, if taken notice of would become a serious Affair. Others said, that it was a serious Affair already; that it was a preconcerted Business, in which the greatest Part of the Town was engaged; that we had no force to oppose to it, and making an Opposition to it, without a power to support the Opposition, would only inflame the People; and be a means of extending the mischief to persons not at present the Objects of it. Tho' the Council were allmost unanimous in advising, that nothing should be done, they were

averse to having such advice entered upon the Council Book. But I insisted upon their giving me an Answer to my Question, and that it should be entered in the Book; when, after a long altercation, it was avoided by their advising me to order the Sheriff to assemble the Peace Officers and preserve the peace which I immediately ordered, being a matter of form rather than of real Significance.

It now grew dark when the Mob, which had been gathering all the Afternoon, came down to the Town House, bringing the Effigy with them, and knowing we were sitting in the Council Chamber, they gave three Huzzas by way of defiance, and passed on. From thence they went to a new Building, lately erected by Mr Oliver to let out for Shops, and not quite finished: this they called the Stamp Office, and pulled it down to the Ground in five minutes. From thence they went to Mr Oliver's House; before which they beheaded the Effigy; and broke all the Windows next the Street; then they carried the Effigy to Fort hill near Mr Oliver's House, where they burnt the Effigy in a Bonfire made of the Timber they had pulled down from the Building. Mr Oliver had removed his family from his House, and remained himself with a few friends, when the Mob returned to attack the House. Mr Oliver was prevailed upon to retire, and his friends kept Possession of the House. The Mob finding the Doors barricaded, broke down the whole fence of the Garden towards fort hill, and coming on beat in all the doors and Windows of the Garden front, and entered the House, the Gentlemen there retiring. As soon as they had got Possession, they searched about for Mr Oliver, declaring they would kill him; finding that he had left the House, a party set out to search two neighbouring Houses, in one of which Mr Oliver was, but happily they were diverted from this pursuit by a Gentleman telling them, that Mr Oliver was gone with the Governor to the Castle. Other-

wise he would certainly have been mur-
dered. After 11 o'clock the Mob seeming
to grow quiet, the (Lt. Governor) Chief
Justice and the Sheriff ventured to go to
Mr Oliver's House to endeavour to per-
swade them to disperse. As soon as they
began to speak, a Ringleader cried out,
The Governor and the Sheriff! to your
Arms, my boys! Presently after a volley
of Stones followed, and the two Gentlemen
narrowly escaped thro' favour of the Night,
not without some bruises. I should have
mentioned before, that I sent a written
order to the Colonel of the Regiment of
Militia, to beat an Alarm; he answered,
that it would signify nothing, for as soon
as the drum was heard, the drummer
would be knocked down, and the drum
broke; he added, that probably all the
drummers of the Regiment were in the
Mob. Nothing more being to be done, The
Mob were left to disperse at their own
Time, which they did about 12 o'clock.

39.   The Boston Riot of August 26, 1765

[Thomas Hutchinson to Richard Jackson, Aug. 30,
1765, Massachusetts Archives, XXVI, 146-47.]

                                    Boston, August 30, 1765
My Dear Sir
    I came from my house at Milton with
my family the 26th in the morning. After
dinner it was whispered in town there
would be a mob at night and that Paxtons
Hallowell, and the custom-house and admiralty officers houses would be attacked
but my friends assured me the rabble were
satisfied with the insult I had received and
that I was become rather Popular. In
the evening whilst I was at supper and
my children round me somebody ran in
and said the mob were coming. I directed
my children to fly to a secure Place and
shut up my house as I had done before
intending not to quit it but my eldest
daughter repented her leaving me and
hastened back and protested she would not
quit the house unless I did. I could not
stand against this and withdrew with her
to a neighbouring house where I had been
but a few minutes before the hellish crew
fell upon my house with the Rage of devils
and in a moment with axes split down the
doors and entred my son being in the great
entry heard them cry damn him he is
upstairs we'll have him. Some ran immediately as high as the top of the house
others filled the rooms below and cellars
and others Remained without the house
to be employed there. Messages soon
came one after another to the house where
I was to inform me the mob were coming
in Pursuit of me and I was obliged to retire thro yards and gardens to a house
more remote where I remained until 4
o'clock by which time one of the best
finished houses in the Province had nothing remaining but the bare walls and
floors. Not contented with tearing off
all the wainscot and hangings and splitting
the doors to pieces they beat down the
Partition walls and altho that alone cost
them near two hours they cut down the
cupola or lanthern and they began to take
the slate and boards from the roof and
were prevented only by the approaching
daylight from a total demolition of the
building. The garden fence was laid flat
and all my trees &c broke down to the
ground. Such ruins were never seen in
America. Besides my Plate and family
Pictures houshold furniture of every kind
my own my children and servants apparel
they carried off about £ 900 sterling in
money and emptied the house of every
thing whatsoever except a part of the
kitchen furniture not leaving a single book
or paper in it and have scattered or destroyed all the manuscripts and other
papers I had been collecting for 30 years

together besides a great number of Publick Papers in my custody. The evening being warm I had undressed me and slipt on a thin camlet surtout over my wastcoat, the next morning the weather being changed I had not cloaths enough in my possession to defend me from the cold and was obliged to borrow from my host. Many articles of cloathing and good part of my Plate have since been picked up in different quarters of the town but the Furniture in general was cut to pieces before it was thrown out of the house and most of the beds cut open and the feathers thrown out of the windows. The next evening I intended with my children to Milton but meeting two or three small Parties of the Ruffians who I suppose had concealed themselves in the country and my coachman hearing one of them say there he is, my daughters were terrified and said they should never be safe and I was forced to shelter them that night at the castle.

The encouragers of the first mob never intended matters should go this length and the people in general express the utmost detestation of this unparalleled outrage and I wish they could be convinced what infinite hazard there is of the most terrible consequences from such daemons when they are let loose in a government where there is not constant authority at hand sufficient to suppress them.

I am told the government here will make me a compensation for my own and my family's loss which I think cannot be much less than £ 3000 sterling. I am not sure that they will. If they should not it will be too heavy for me and I must humbly apply to his Majesty in whose service I am a sufferer but this and a much greater sum would be an insufficient compensation for the constant distress and anxiety of mind I have felt for some time past and must feel for months to come. You cannot conceive the wretched state we are in. Such is the resentment of the people against the stamp duty that there can be no dependence upon the general court to take any steps to enforce or rather advise the payment of it. On the other hand, such will be the effects of not submitting to it that all trade must cease all courts fall and all authority be at an end. Must not the ministry be extremely embarrassed. On the one hand it will be said if concessions be made the Parliament endanger the loss of their authority over the colonies on the other hand if external force should be used there seems to be danger of a total lasting alienation of affection. Is there no alternative? May the infinitely wise God direct you. I am with the greatest esteem

Sir Your most faithful humble servant

40. The Newport Riot, August 29, 1765

[Dr. Thomas Moffat to Joseph Harrison, Oct. 16, 1765, Chalmers Papers, New York Public Library. The original manuscript contains no paragraphing.]

Mr. J. Harrison
Sir

I may be very positive in concluding you under some degree of surprize at receiving a letter from me dated at London and that your wonder may not diminish but encrease you are also informd and assurd that Mr Howard passd the atlantick with me, why and wherefore the fol-

lowing will gradually unfold. If by your residence in New England and the very good opportunity you then had of observing the true complexion and temper of the People, their raw and loose opinions concerning the relation connexion and dependency in which Providence has so happily placd them under the protection and Dominion of Great Britain: Or if this very Topick had never been the subject of our early and late conversation. Or if but a slight or ordinary acquaintance had only subsisted between us I should blush or be really afraid that the detail which I am now to give you would require some other seal and sanction besides that of my own averrment. But when I with pleasure well remember the commencment of our Acquaintance gradually improving and cultivated into intimacy confidence and firm Friendship I cannot but depend and trust my testimony alone is sufficient and valid with you and may therefore obtain a currency of credit through your means and influence with your Friends and Acquaintance because (if I err not) it is high time that the disposition and conduct of some parts of North America should be very exactly known or represented to the end that they may be remedied and rectified before they have run into too great a Career of tumult disorder riot and disobedience.

Ever since the Act of Parliament for levying a duty from stampd paper was known in New England a spirit of uneasines and discontent attended with innumerable surmises Jealousies and fears hath been propagated encouraged and blown up among the lower and middling ranks of the people by a few crafty seditious popular malignants who first infusd suspicions apprehensions and then a clear perswasion and faith that the Colonies were now actually subjugated and enslavd by the rigorous injustice of Parliament. It is not very easy either to express or conceive how quickly and universally these absurd and very dangerous tenets were propagated adopted and beleivd. On the contrary the very few Persons here who endeavourd to counteract this seditious temper by cultivating a reverence for supreme Authority and obedience and submission to acts of Parliament or the dutiful method of supplicating or petitioning for redress if aggrievd were by the secret suggestions and insinuations of these popular leaders

represented as Enemies to the liberties of North America or ministerial mercenaries and Expectants by which means they not only lost their proper or usual influence but really were rendred obnoxious.

These seducers of the people sensible of and elated with their success thought fit on the 13th of Agust to try their followers in action and to flush them with certain victory they were led forth to expose the effigy of Secretary Oliver their Stamp Master at Boston hanging up by the neck on a tree; In the evening they burnt the figure and concluded by assaulting and defacing his house after the dusk of Evening. It should not be omitted as an instance and proof of the infirmity of that Provincial Government or if you will of the Majesty and might of that Grave band of Heroes and Patriots that the Committee of the Kings Council sat in the town house of Boston in the forenoon afternoon and Evening of that day without interrupting or trying to disperse the mobility. In the Evening of the 26th of August The Chiefs of the mob of Boston again assembled their followers entred and rifled the Houses of Mr Story admiralty register and Mr Hallowell comptroller of the Kings Custom House, and from thence proceeded to Lieut Govr. Hutchisons house, which they compleatly plunderd and sackd.

The same factious tumultuary and riotous disposition having been communicated and widely spread in the Colony of Rhode Island Mr Howard on the 20th of Agust intimated to me a design being a foot of exposing the Effigial figures of Mr Johnson Him and me as on the 27th that day being in course a Quarterly meeting of the Newport Freeholders. We summond our Friends collected intelligence and tryd all measures to divert defeat or suppress this intended Spectacle. On the 24th Mr Howard waited upon Governor Ward told Him every circumstance He knew of this affair, and namd to Him some of the most active Ringleaders. The

Governor replied to Mr Howard that He was informd of the design but did not think or understand that any thing more or farther would be done besides the exposing of the Effigys.

Early next morning (the Governor being then my Patient) I waited on him also circumstantially related the rise progress and probable event of this exhibition I told him that as his nearest Friends were the most Zealous abettors of this unwarrantable and very daring undertaking He should the rather interest Himself in preventing or suppressing it I represented to Him that the bare presuming at such a spectacle with an intention to draw the rabble together was a manifest insult upon Himself and a defiance of all the Authority of the Colony I mentiond to him many particulars of Mr Howards principles and conduct in life that should induce and animate Him to a vigorous exertion of his utmost influence and power to prevent it and concluded with intimating that if this spectacle was exhibited it might create or kindle a suspicion that some in power were accessory privy to or silently approving of this detestable enterprize. The Governor answerd me that this affair gave him much uneasines He wishd to suppress it Mr Ayrault and others had been yesterday with Him advising Him to exert all the Authority of Government to hinder its taking place. The Governor told me He would instantly send for the secretary who should summon his best Friends and that He would concert effectual measures to stop it. We were attentive to the steps taken by the Governor but heard of none except in the Evening his sending for two of the Principal Ringleaders Samuel Vernon and William Ellery whom he exhorted to desist and entreated as a favour of them to prevail with their accomplices to forbear proceeding farther in that affair then dismissing them both He only requested their appearance before Him next morning to give an account of their mediations.

Early on the 26th I met Samuel Vernon and askd him if they were ready to exhibit tomorrow; at first he pretended not to understand me but soon very deliberately told me they were unalterably fixd upon it. On my asking How He or any other Person could think of using me in that contemptuous shocking manner? He replied that He lovd and respected me was under many and singular obligations to me but that He and his Confederates proceeded upon just principles drawn from the absolute necessity of some proper sacrifices at this dangerous and very critical conjuncture when the shackles and chains of North America were not only forgd but on the very point of being fastned on and clinchd for ever. I askd Him how he or any of his consociates could think of me as a victim who had neither interest influence or expectation from the Events he alluded to. He said it was notorious in New England that I had on many occasions and even to Himself asserted and maintaind the uncontroulable authority and jurisdiction of Parliament over America and that I had perswaded others to embrace and profess the same opinion. He told me that your Friend Howard insists too upon the Justice and validity of the acts of trade and has publickly Justifyd all the parliamentary restraints upon the commerce of America and in his Halifax letter has branded the merchants of Rhode Island as smugglers which accusation alone Justly deserves death. I answered him that admitting all and much more than He had said as strict truth yet they were proceeding very foolishly to say no worse of their intended spectacle. He urgd me much to explain how that appeard I told him although the opposition and defiance of supreme authority is now indeed very prevalent yet as it would most certainly be crushd into obedience the only good plea for the Colony would be these very writings which He now so hotly condemnd because they would serve to shew that the defection was not universal. I affirmd to him that if by the exhibition of these effigial figures they should be capable of drawing the rabble or if by means of strong drink promises of money or the hope or expectation of plunder they should really enflame and excite them to acts of violence pillage and blood they might when too late discover that they had offerd up two of the best Friends the Colony ever had. I then insisted much and long with him that He was the Prime director and that hereafter He might claim much merit in being the Chief instrument of preventing this foul and perhaps very disastrous scene and that the desisting from or stopping it would yield him and all concernd in it much more pleasure than ever the execution of it would. On this we parted.

Early on the morning of the 27th a few persons without any interruption on the south side of the Colony house and within forty paces of it erected a Gallows thereon placing the effigys of Mr Howard Mr Johnson and me with very scurrilous scandalous and defamatory labels fixed in the hands and upon the breast of the figures. At Eleven in the forenoon when the Governor and others of authority with the freeholders went into the Court house there was no concourse of people or acclamation and this Theatre and figures were guarded only by Samuel Vernon William Ellery and Robert Crook who walkd under and before it in muffled big coats flappd hats and bludgeons. Towards five in the afternoon the chief contrivers shewd some uneasines Jealousie and fear least the rabble should not assemble therefore they sent into the street strong Drink in plenty with Cheshire cheese and other provocatives to intemperance and riot. By these means the mob was collected and after sunset the figures were cut down and burnt on the spot.

Next day it was the general opinion that this extraordinary Tribunal of Justice was fully satisfied but a little past eight o'clock in the evening the chief ring leaders of yesterdays spectacle rushd into the streets with a chosen band of Ruffians at their heels having their faces painted and being prepard and furnishd with broad axes and other tools of desolation proceeded huzzaing to the house of Mr Howard which they forcibly entred destroying and demolishing all his furniture instantly dashing into pieces all his china looking glasses &c then stripping and plundering every apartment of every article carrying off all his wearing apparell bed and table Linnen in the most open daring and unrestraind manner, then breaking into his Cellars drank wasted and carried away all his wines and other liquors. From Mr Howards they repaird to my house splitt open the doors committing the same acts of violence pillage and rage in every point and instance and were even so brutal after hewing down the mahogany cases as to throw what books they could not carry off or otherwise destroy into the well with all my writings Physical instruments and many other articles which I highly valued. Towards eleven at night they entred Mr. Howards house again cleaving to bits all the doors and casements tore up all the floors hearths and chimneys leaving the house a miserable shell only. From thence they roard up to my house where the same scene of ruin was repeated and committed exactly. Now the Ringleaders and their adherents were intoxicated and heated even to a thirst of blood and a parole for discovering us was now given out in form but they could by no means learn where we were. The rabble also surrounded Mr Johnsons house but were diverted from destroying it by an assurance solemnly given that He should renounce the stamp office to morrow for ever. The mob also surrounded the house where Mr Robinson the Collector lodges and keeps the custom house entred at the windows of the house peremptorily demanded a surrender of the Collectors Person but on being well assurd and satisfyd that He was aboard His Majesties Ship Cygnet they dispersd. At two in the morning they again visited Mr Howards house still farther spoiling and destroying it and concluded their triumphal victory by cutting down the locust trees which you may remember were planted on a line in front of his house. Next day after this Riot in the forenoon Governor Ward went to his country seat at Westerly. From many of my friends I learned that neither Mr Howards nor my person was safe in Newport therefore at noon went down to your Brothers in a chaise together and from thence aboard the Cygnet where we were receivd and entertaind by your Friend Captain Leslie with the greatest humanity kindnes and civility. Aboard the Cygnet we learnd that Mr Johnson had appeasd the wrath of the populace by a written instrument resigning the office of Stamp master. Agust 30th Mr Johnson came aboard the Cygnet told us that the mob were again tumultuary and noisy on his account, that yesterday he had lulld and entirely quieted them by an ambiguous ineffectual declaration in writing which implyd a resignation of the stamp office but as it had been extorted under the threatnings of ruin and destruction He never intended to observe or regard it but had given it to the Ringleaders only to sooth them into Quiet and very happily it had the effect untill this morning Mr Stiles the minister (from Yale or New Haven college) came into the street declard the instrument of resignation artful base insufficient and harrangued upon its defects in form and method pointed out that there was no clause obligatory that it was not avouchd and that notwithstanding of it Mr Johnson might execute the office. This has so incensd the people that Mr Johnson says He will retire immediately to Boston and be incognito. After deliberating upon the indignity that has been offerd to us and the very great loss and damage that we have sustaind and the hair breadth escape with limb or life from an enragd and desperate mob led and instigated by a few implacable enemies to the subordination of North America to a British parliament what remaind for us to resolve upon or what course should we prosecute? we had respectfully applied and informd the Governor early of all the steps of this design we have seen and felt its execution deeply with the additional mortification of not a single measure taken to prevent it, and to crown our despair of either releif or protection here we saw on the morning of the day after our disaster and danger the Governor withdraw himself from Newport. Under all these unhappy Circumstances we concluded upon embracing an oportunity of ship for Bristol then lying under Conanicut and accordingly embarked on the 31st of Agust happily arriving there the ninth of [October] and came to London this very Day in some hopes and confidence that our Sufferings and the Cause thereof will recommend us to a publick notice and retrebution. We thought it best to give you this very particular and circumstantial account that we may have the benefit and advantage of your counsel and all your influence and interest in town and Country. For this purpose and end I request and entreat of you to write me under cover of Naphtali Hart Myers your opinion and Judgment of this matter and that you would try to know the opinion of your Friends and acquaintance in the country concerning it. I desire much to see you and next to that to hear largely and freely from you and I pray you to condescend on the time when you will be at London Mr Howard and I have some thousand articles to communicate to you. I propose consulting Dr Pringle immediately about inoculating Him so that He may be safe free and well before the time of publick busines comes on. We both join in wishing you and yours every felicity. I am Sir

Your most obedient Humble Servant

Thomas Moffat

London October 16th 1765

The Sons of Liberty

41.   Wallingford, Connecticut, January 13, 1766

[*Connecticut Courant*, Feb. 3, 1766.]

At a Meeting of a Number of the Sons of Liberty in Wallingford, in New-Haven county, on the evening of the 13th day of January 1766. After duly form'd by chosing a moderator and clerk the following Resolves were come into, viz.

Resol. 1. That the late act of Parliament called the Stamp-Act, is unconstitutional, and intended to enslave the true subjects of America.

Resol. 2. That we will oppose the same to the last extremity, even to take the field.

Resol. 3. That we will meet at the Court House in New-Haven on the third Tuesday of February next; and we desire all the Sons of Liberty in each Town in the County would meet themselves or representatives. There to consult what is best to be done in order to defend our liberties and properties, and break up the stop to publick affairs.

Resol. 4. That this Meeting be adjourned to the first Tuesday of February next, then to choose our representatives to attend the said Meeting.

42.   New London, Connecticut, December 10, 1765

[*Connecticut Courant*, Dec. 30, 1765.]

At a Meeting of a large Assembly of the respectable Populace in New-London, the 10th of Dec. 1765, the following Resolves were unanimously come into.

Resolved 1st. That every Form of Government rightfully founded, originates from the Consent of the People.

2d. That the Boundaries set by the People in all Constitutions, are the only Limits within which any Officer can lawfully exercise Authority.

3d. That whenever those Bounds are exceeded, the People have a Right to reassume the exercise of that Authority which by Nature they had, before they delegated it to Individuals.

4th. That every Tax imposed upon English Subjects without Consent, is against the natural Rights and the Bounds prescribed by the English Constitution.

5th. That the Stamp-Act in special, is a Tax imposed on the Colonies without their Consent.

6th. That it is the Duty of every Person in the Colonies, to oppose by every lawful Means, the Execution of those Acts imposed on them,—and if they can in no other Way be relieved to reassume their natural Rights, and the Authority the Laws of Nature and of God have vested them with.

And in order effectually to prevent the Execution thereof it is recommended,

1st. That every Officer in this Colony duly execute the Trust reposed in him, agreeable to the true Spirit of the English Constitution and the Laws of this Colony.

2d. That every Officer neglecting the Exercise of his Office, may justly expect the Resentment of the People; and those who proceed may depend on their Protection.

3d. It is presumed no Person will publickly, in the Pulpit or otherwise, inculcate the Doctrine of passive Obedience, or any other Doctrine tending to quiet the Minds of the People in a tame Submission to any unjust Impositions.

4th. We fully concur with the respectable Body of the Populace in all their Resolves made at Windham the 26th November, 1765, and published in the New-London Gazette.

43.   New York, January 11, 1766

[New York Mercury, Jan. 13, 1766.]

On Tuesday Evening last, a great Number of Gentlemen, Sons of Liberty, assembled at the House of Mr. William Howard, in this City, in Consequence of an Invitation from some of the Members of their Society. . . . the following Resolutions were proposed and agreed to by a great Majority of the Company, and order'd to be printed, viz.

Resolved, That we will go to the last Extremity, and venture our Lives and Fortunes, effectually to prevent the said Stamp-Act from ever taking Place in this City and Province.

Resolved, That any Person who shall deliver out or receive any Instrument of Writing upon Stamped Paper or Parchment, agreeable to the said Act, shall incur the highest Resentment of this Society, and be branded with everlasting Infamy.

Resolved, That the Persons who carry on Business as formerly, on unstamped Paper, without Regard to the Stamp-Act, shall be protected to the utmost Power of this Society.

Resolved, That as we have not been concerned in publishing or propagating any Thing tending to cast an Odium on any Society or Body of Men, or on the private Character of any Person, farther than as he was a Promoter or Abettor of the Stamp-Act, so neither will we be concern'd in reporting, publishing or propagating any Thing that may affect the Reputation of any Individual, or Body of Men, otherwise than as he or they may be Promoters of the said Act.

Resolved, That we will to the utmost of our Power maintain the Peace and good Order of this City, so far as it can be done consistently with the Preservation and Security of our Rights and Privileges.

44.   New Brunswick, New Jersey, February 25, 1766

[Pennsylvania Journal, March 6, 1766.]

At a meeting of the Sons of Liberty of the city of New-Brunswick, in the county of Middlesex, and province of New-Jersey, the 25th of February, 1766, it was resolved;

1. That we will chearfully embark our lives and fortunes in the defence of our liberties and privileges.

2. That we will resist, as far as in us lies, all illegal attempts to deprive us of our indubitable rights; and for that reason, will, to the last extremity, oppose the exercise of the Stamp Act in the colony.

3. That we will contribute all in our power to preserve the public tranquility, so far as it may be preserved, consistent with the principles already professed.

4. That we will do our utmost to support and defend the officers of government in this colony, who shall act agreeable to the above resolves.

5. That we shall always be ready with

hearts and hands, to assist the neighbour-ing provinces, in opposing every attempt that may be made to deprive them and us, of those privileges and immunities, which God and Nature seem to have intended us.

And lastly, That we do bear his Maj-esty King George the Third, true Alle-giance, and will at all times faithfully adhere to his royal Person, and just government, and heartily defend him from every attempt to injure his person, crown or dignity.

45.　Norfolk, Virginia, March 31, 1766

[*Pennsylvania Journal,* April 17, 1766.]

At a meeting of a considerable number of inhabitants of the town and county of Norfolk, *and others,* SONS OF LIBERTY, *at the Court House of the said county, in the colony of* Virginia, *on* Monday *the 31st of* March, 1766.

Having taken into consideration the evil tendency of that oppressive and un-constitutional act of parliament commonly called the Stamp Act, and being desirous that our sentiments should be known to posterity, and recollecting that we are a part of that colony, who first, in General Assembly, openly expressed there [sic] detestation to the said act, which is pregnant with ruin, and productive of the most pernicious consequences; and unwill-ing to rivet the shackles of slavery and op-pression on ourselves, and millions yet un-born, have unanimously come to the fol-lowing resolutions:

I. Resolved, That we acknowledge our sovereign Lord King George III to be our rightful and lawful King, and that we will at all times, to the utmost of our power and ability, support and defend his most sacred person, crown, and dignity; and will be always ready, when constitu-tionally called upon, to assist his Majesty with our lives and fortunes, and defend all his just rights and prerogatives.

II. Resolved, That we will by all law-ful ways and means, which divine provi-dence hath put into our hands, defend ourselves in the full enjoyment of, and preserve inviolate to posterity, those in-estimable privileges of all free-born British subjects, of being taxed by none but representatives of their own choosing, and of being tried only by a jury of their own Peers; for, if we quietly submit to the exe-cution of the said Stamp Act, all our claims to civil liberty will be lost, and we and our posterity become absolute slaves.

III. Resolved, That we will, on any future occasion, sacrifice our lives and fortunes, in concurrence with the other Sons of Liberty in the American prov-inces, to defend and preserve those invalu-able blessings transmitted us by our an-cestors.

IV. Resolved, That whoever is con-cerned, directly or indirectly, in using, or causing to be used, in any way or manner whatever, within this colony, un-less authorized by the General Assembly thereof, those detestable papers called the Stamps, shall be deemed, to all intents and purposes, an enemy to his country, and by the Sons of Liberty treated accordingly.

V. Resolved, That a committee be appointed to present the thanks of the Sons of Liberty to Colonel Richard Bland, for his treatise entitled "An Inquiry into the Rights of the British Colonies."

VI. Resolved, That a committee be appointed, who shall make public the above resolutions, and correspond as they shall see occasion, with the associated Sons and Friends of Liberty in the other British colonies in America.

46. North Carolina, February 18, 1766

[*Maryland Gazette*, April 10, 1766.]

We the Subscribers, free and natural-born Subjects of George the Third, true and lawful King of Great-Britain, and all its Dependencies, (whom God preserve) whose sacred Person, Crown, and Dignity, we are ready and willing, at the Expence of our Lives and Fortunes, to defend, being fully convinced of the oppressive and arbitrary Tendency of a late Act of Parliament, imposing Stamp Duties on the Inhabitants of this Province, and fundamentally subversive of the Liberties and Charters of North-America; truly sensible of the inestimable Blessings of a free Constitution, gloriously handed down to us by our brave Forefathers, detesting Rebellion, yet preferring Death to Slavery, do with all Loyalty to our most gracious Sovereign, with all deference to the just Laws of our Country, and with a proper and necessary Regard to Ourselves and Posterity, hereby mutually and solemnly plight our Faith and Honour that we will, at any Risk whatever, and whenever called upon, unite, and truly and faithfully assist each other, to the best of our Power, in preventing entirely the Operation of the Stamp-Act.

Witness our Hands this 18th Day of Feb. 1766.

47. Union in Arms

[Sons of Liberty Agreement, New London, Conn., Dec. 25, 1765, William Gordon, *The History of the Rise, Progress, and Establishment of the Independence of the United States of America* (London, 1788), I, 195-98.]

Certain reciprocal and mutual agreements, concessions and associations made, concluded and agreed upon by and between the sons of liberty of the colony of *New York* of the one part, and the sons of liberty of the colony of *Connecticut* on the other part, this twenty-fifth day of December, in the sixth year of the reign of our sovereign Lord *George* the Third, by the grace of God, of *Great Britain, France* and *Ireland* king, defender of the faith, and in the year of our Lord one thousand seven hundred and sixty-five.

The aforesaid parties taking into their most serious consideration the melancholy and unsettled state of *Great Britain* and her *North American colonies,* proceeding as they are fully persuaded, from a design in her most insidious and inveterate enemies, to alienate the affections of his majesty's most loyal and faithful subjects of *North America* from his person and government—Therefore to prevent as much as in us lies the dissolution of so inestimable an union, they do, in the presence of *Almighty God,* declare that they bear the most unshaken faith and true allegiance to his majesty King *George* the Third—that they are most affectionately and zealously attached to his royal person and family, and are fully determined to the utmost of their power, to maintain and support his crown and dignity, and the succession as by law established; and with the greatest cheerfulness they submit to his government, according to the known and just principles of the BRITISH CONSTITUTION, which they conceive to be founded on the eternal and immutable principles of justice and equity, and that every attempt to violate or wrest it, or any part of it from them, under whatever pretence, colour or authority, is an heinous sin against God, and the most daring contempt of the people, from whom (under God) all just government springs. From a sacred regard to all which, and a just sense of the impending evils that might befal them, in consequence of such a dreadful dissolution, They do hereby voluntarily, and of their own free will, as well for the support of his majesty's just prerogative and the British constitution as their own mutual security and preservation, agree and concede to associate, advise, protect, and defend each other in the peaceable, full and just enjoyment of their inherent and accustomed rights as British subjects of their respective *colonies,* not in the least desiring any alteration or innovation in the grand bulwark of their liberties and the wisdom of ages, but only to preserve it inviolate from the corrupt hands of its implacable enemies—And whereas a certain pamphlet has appeared in America in the form of an act of parliament, called and known by the name of the *Stamp-Act,* but has never been legally published or introduced, neither can it, as it would immediately deprive them of the most invaluable part of the British constitution, viz. the trial by juries, and the most just mode of taxation in the world, that is, of taxing themselves, rights that every British subject becomes heir to as soon as born. For the preservation of which, and every part of the British constitution, they do reciprocally resolve and determine to march with the utmost dispatch, at their own proper costs and expence, on the first proper notice, (which must be signified to them by at least six of the sons of liberty) with their whole force if re-

quired, and it can be spared, to the **relief** of those that shall, are, or **may be in** danger from the *stamp-act,* or its **pro**-moters and abettors, or any thing **relative** to it, on account of any thing that **may have** been done in opposition to its obtaining—And they do mutually and most fervently recommend it to each other to be vigilant in watching all those who, from the nature of their offices, vocations or dispositions, may be the most likely to introduce **the** use of stamped papers, to the total subversion of the British constitution and American liberty; and the same, when discovered, immediately to advise each other of, let them be of what rank or condition soever; and they do agree, that they will **mutually,** and to the utmost of their power, by all just ways and means, endeavour to bring all such betrayers of their country to the most condign punishment—And further, they do mutually resolve to defend **the** liberty of the press in their respective colonies from all unlawful violations and impediments whatever, on account of **the** said act, as the only means (under divine Providence) of preserving their lives, liberties and fortunes, and the same in regard to the judges, clerks, attornies, &c. that shall proceed without any regard to the *stamp-act,* from all pains, fines, mulcts, penalties, or any molestation whatever—And finally, that they will, to the utmost of their power, endeavour to bring about, accomplish, and perfect the like *association* with all the *colonies* on the continent for the like salutary purposes and no other."

The Collapse of Authority

48.   John Dickinson Appeals to William Pitt

[Dickinson to Pitt, Dec. 21, 1765, Dickinson Papers, Historical Society of Pennsylvania.]

Honourd Sir,

If a sincere Desire to promote the public good may excuse actions that otherwise would appear presumptuous, I hope

the motive that now perswades me to address You will procure me your pardon for the Liberty I take.

Several Reflections have occurrd to me

respecting the present Situation of Affairs in America, that being dictated by what I hear and see may perhaps have escapd in some measure the observation of persons at a greater Distance.

This Consideration has inducd me to think of submitting my sentiments to the judgment of some Gentleman in England, able and willing to improve every hint that can be improvd, for the Benefit of his Country, and generous enough to reject without Contempt the well meant Endeavours of the mistaken. Forgive me sir, if my Reverence for your Character has determined me to trouble you on this occasion.

Intelligence of the Disturbances by the late Act of Parliament imposing Stamp Duties in these Colonies must I imagine before this Time have reachd Great Britain, and I presume produced a general opinion, that opposition here made to the execution of that act is a Matter of the most alarming Importance. It is undoubtedly so: for the Measures that shall be thereupon pursued by Great Britain, must have a strong Influence on points of no less Consequence, than the Dependence, and future Utility of the Colonies.

I mean not, sir, to exaggerate things: but beyond all Question it is certain, that an unexampled and universal Jealousy, Grief and Indignation have been excited in the Colonists by the Conduct of their Mother Country since the Conclusion of the last War.

The sudden and violent Restrictions of their Commerce were extremely disgusting and afflicting; tho a high Veneration for the august Authority that imposed them, might perhaps have supprest their Murmurs on that Head. But no sooner did they hear of the Stamp Act being past, than they felt and acted as Men will do, who love their Liberty and who think it is invaded.

The Storm is now raging, and how it can be laid in the best Manner for the Happiness of Great Britain and her Colonies I pray God may engage the attention of that Wisdom which once saved her from her Enemies, and I hope will now save her from herself.

My Passion, sir, for the Welfare of Great Britain and of my native Country, is the same; because I think their Interests are the same, and that the Prosperity of the one cannot be infected, without the other's catching the Contagion. I therefore ardently wish, that the Connection which has hitherto subsisted between them, may subsist to the latest Posterity; and I regard with inexpressible Detestation and Abhorrence the Notion of the Colonies becoming independent. Not that I doubt in the least, that the Attempt may be executed whenever it is made. The Strength of the Colonies, their Distance, the Wealth that woud pour into them on opening their Ports to all Nations, the Jealousy entertained of Great Britain by some European Powers, and the peculiar Circumstances of that Kingdom, woud insure Success. But what, sir, must be the Consequences of that Success? A Multitude of Commonwealths, Crimes, and Calamities, of mutual Jealousies, Hatreds, Wars and Devastations; till at last the exhausted Provinces shall sink into Slavery under the yoke of some fortunate Conqueror. History seems to prove, that this must be the deplorable Fate of these Colonies whenever they become independent.

However the Temptations above mentiond being immediate and glaring, may have a general Influence over discontented Minds, while the following Evils, being more remote, will be less regarded. The Colonists have that Sense of Freedom and Justice, that becomes the Descendants of Britons and therefore I apprehend it may with Truth be asserted, that their Dependence cannot be retaind but by preserving their Affections; and that these cannot be preservd, but by treating them in such a Manner, as they think consistent with Freedom and Justice.

I will endeavour to explain my sentiments more particularly.

The Colonists at this Time have strong Attachments to their Mother Country. They derive great Advantages from their Relation to her. As long as these Attachments continue, she must encrease in Power, and therefore the same advantages must attend the Continuance of that Relation. It must be, I presume, essentially necessary for regulating her Conduct, to know at what Rate they value these advantages, and how far the Exercise of her Authority may be extended, without appearing in their opinion to overballance them. These Things being duly considered and regarded, it is apprehended, that the Dependence of these Colonies on Great Britain may be perfectly secured, and their mutual Prosperity establishd on the firmest Foundations that can be given to human Designs.

The authority of Great Britain may be exercisd in two Ways. Either, in the internal Government of the Colonies; or in the Regulation of their Commerce.

As to the first—It is humbly conceivd, that The Mother Country cannot be too tender in taking from the Colonies any Priviledges or Immunities which she herself enjoys. Such Treatment must produce odious and inflaming Comparisons; and while they think themselves, as they will always think themselves, entitled to the same Rights with her, they will esteem those Restrictions, insulting Abuses of her Power, and their Condition as a state of slavery. From this they will ever wish, and as soon as there is a probability of effecting their Purpose, they will endeavour to escape—But this may not be, till these Restrictions are generally felt.

Under this head may be rankd the Prohibitions by Great Britain of several Manufactures in the Colonies. They have been submitted to, because the Manufactures being in their Infancy, they affected few persons. But it cannot be imagined, that this is a prudent Method to hinder the Colonies from interfering in her other Manufactures. She may divert the Colonies from such Schemes by indulging their Trade, and Imperceptibly to prevent, is certainly better than positively to prohibit. This kind of Policy is likely without the utmost Caution, to be the Cause of deep Dissatisfaction.

Another source of present Uneasiness, and as it is justly to be dreaded, of future Unhappiness, is the Extension of the Prerogative in these Colonies. It seems to have been the constant Intention of the Administration, except in some short and shining Periods, to establish a Prerogative in America quite different from that in Great Britain. In short, to give the Crown a Power here, that if aimd at there, would rouse the whole Nation in Vindication of its Rights.

These Claims serve only to loosen the Colonies from Great Britain, by discovering an invidious Distinction between her and themselves. Their Dependence can never be secured but may be destroyed by straining the Prerogative.

Nothing, sir, is farther from my Intention than to cast any Reflections in what I now say upon the Conduct of the Crown, or its Ministers. My sole Design is to speak plain and wholesome Truths, in which the future Felicity of my Country is involvd and if this Design inadvertently leads me into too great a License of Expression, I hope, sir, you will be pleased to regard it as an honest Fault.

The last and greatest Cause of Discontent in the Colonies, with respect to their internal Government, is the Imposition of Taxes by Great Britain. What they suffer on this occasion, cannot be described. All other Complaints, all other Distresses are drownd in this. If I could form a Judgment, Honourd sir, what may be the immediate Consequence of Great Britain's insisting on the Execution of the Stamp Act, I would venture to mention it: but I am utterly at a Loss to decide what it will be, though I cannot forbear apprehending very great misfortunes.

On the other Hand it may be said, that Great Britain by repealing that act will tacitly acknowledge, that she has no Right to tax the Colonies.

If the Repeal should be construed as such an Acknowledgment, it will only be renouncing a Right, the Exercise of which can never be repeated without throwing the Colonies into Desperation. This I hope Great Britain will never do; and therefore she cannot lose any thing by such a Renunciation.

But there seems to be no Reason to think that the Repeal will be considered in this Light by the Colonists. The Act was the Measure of a Ministry not at all admired here: and the repealing it will be regarded as the Correction of their Error. The People of Great Britain are universally thought in America to be pleased, that those Ministers have lost their Power: and that an opportunity offers of convincing the Colonists, that the Measure was rather ministerial than national. Indeed to a Person acquainted with these Colonies it is evident, that the Duties imposed by the Stamp Act are by no means suited to their Circumstances, that they must be attended with great Inconveniences, and in the End must be equally injurious to them and to Great Britain. For a proof, sir, of this assertion, I beg Leave to refer to a Pamphlet that has lately been printed here, and I understand will soon be reprinted in London, entituld "The late Regulations respecting the British Colonies on the Continent of America considered."

If this shall be thought by the Parliament too slight a Pretence for the repeal, and that their Authority may be wounded by such a Condescension, I am afraid they cannot hereafter rely on the Affection of the Colonies.

I believe, sir, there are many persons in Great Britain who think these Colonies will throw off their Dependence as soon as they imagine they are able, and therefore that it is useless for her to cultivate their affections. But this I apprehend to be a Mistake, As long as a good Understanding prevails between the Mother Country and her Colonies, they will, as they now do, greatly love and revere her. They will really partake of her Prosperity, and they will think that they partake of her Glory. However powerful these Colonies may grow, her Power will increase proportionably: and the Struggle whenever it should be made, woud be a bloody one; A People is never fond of plunging into the horrors of War without great Temptations or Provocations, and these with prudent Management may be utterly removd from the Colonies—

Another Reason as it is presumd, why the Colonies will not aim at Independence, unless excited by the Treatment they receive from Great Britain is this; That they will not engage in such a Scheme unless they unite in it, and they will not unite, unless it be in a common Cause, that points all their Passions at one Object.

Their different Interests have excited Jealousies of each other among them, that are sufficient to keep them divided, untill some greater Jealousy shall conquer the rest. Nothing is likely to produce this Event but the Conduct of the Mother Country, since Nothing is so inflaming to a People who love their Liberty, as to think it is invaded. No Colony apprehends that any other has Designs upon its Liberty. Their Contests are of an inferior Nature, and will vanish when one more dreadful to them commences.

I now proceed, sir, to mention the Exercise of Great Britain's Authority in regulating the Commerce of the Colonies.

It being indispensably necessary for preserving the Dependence of the Colonies on their Mother Country, that all their European Trade shoud be confined to her, so far as to prevent their using the manufactures of any other Nation. such a Regulation cannot possibly be too strictly adherd to.

It is besides so consistent with the Relation of Colonies, and so extremely just, that I am perswaded this alone will never be regarded by them as a Grievance, unless their Minds are embitterd by other Measures.

But, sir, however easily they may be reconcild to Regulations calculated to preserve their Relation to their Mother Country, they will be filld with Resentment, when they find her Power exerted to advance the Interests of some of her other Dominions at their Expence. In this Light the Restrictions laid on their Trade to the foreign Plantations in the West Indies are regarded, and will be regarded. The natural Consequences of these Restrictions are to impoverish the Continental Colonies, to render them dissatisfied, and gradually to break off their Connection with Great Britain by lessening their Demands for her Manufactures. For some further Observations on this subject, I beg Leave Sir again to referr to the Pamphlet I have before mentioned.

Thus have I venturd, to lay before You, Honourd Sir, those great Causes of Discontent, which if ever these Colonies aim at Independence will in my humble opinion prompt the Attempt—At what Period the dire Disease will subdue all the tender Connections between them and their Mother Country, cannot now be determined; but these are the fatal Leeds, that,

"Grow with their Growth

And strengthen with their strength"

and must at last produce the horrid Victory. My Mind with an affectionate Anxiety looks forward to the future Fortunes of my Country, and therefore I am tempted in too bold and indigested a manner, I fear, to offer my sentiments in such a way, as may if they are worthy of any Notice, most effectually serve her.

You, Honourd sir, are loved and revered here, as the Friend and Preserver not only of Great Britain but of these Colonies; as the Friend of Liberty and Justice. If it is possible to form a Plan of Policy that shall establish for Ages the Union of Great Britain and her Colonies, We think it may be expected from You. We hope, sir, that the same Wisdom and Virtue that taught a disgracd and dispirited People, how to act in War, will also teach that People now glorious and triumphant, how to act in Peace—That from henceforward, the Conduct of Great Britain animated by the spirit of your Administration, may render her as dear to her Friends, as she is dreadful to her Enemies.

My Country, sir, owing her safety to You, I think Myself indebted under the Favour of Divine Providence to You for all the Happiness I now enjoy. I can make no Returns, but by being thankful, and if the Acknowledgments of a person no otherwise to be regarded, than as his Heart is truly sensible of his Obligations to You can give You the slightest Satisfaction, I ought not to repent of the Freedom I assume, since it affords me an Opportunity of expressing the Gratitude and Veneration with which I am,

Honourd Sir,
your most obedient and
most humble servant

[Endorsement: December 21st 1765—]

49. Thomas Hutchinson on the Collapse of Authority in Boston

[Hutchinson to Thomas Pownall, March 8, 1766, Massachusetts Archives, XXVI, 207-14.]

Boston March 8. 1766

Sir

I am very much obliged to you for your favour of December the 3d, under Mr. Hancock's cover. If I had received any letter from you before, since my misfortunes, I should have acknowledged it. Some of my letters from England I have reason to think stop by the way. I wish I could have had your sentiments in what manner those who wish well to America should conduct themselves, those I mean who are in America, for I am sure they never stood so much in need of advice. I have often had occasion to reflect upon your sentiments of the People of America, more justly formed, from the experience of a few years, than my own, from living among them all my days. A thought of independence I could not think it possible should enter into the heart of any man, in his senses, for ages to come. You have more than once hinted to me that I was mistaken and I am now convinced that I was so, and that the united endeavours of the friends to Britain and her colonies, in Europe and America, are necessary to restore the colonists to a true sense of their duty and interest. It would be presumption in me to suggest measures to His Majesty's ministers. If I am capable of doing any service it must be by acquainting you with rise and progress of this taint of principles and the degree to which it prevails.

It is not more than two years since it was the general principle of the colonists, that in all matters of privilege or rights the determination of the Parliament of Great Britain must be decisive. They could not, it is true, alter the nature of things and the natural rights of an english man, to which no precise idea seems to have been affixed, would remain in him, but the exercise of that right, during the continuance of such determination or act, must be suspended. To oppose by an armed force the execution of any act of parliament, grand juries, without offence, have been often instructed was high treason, as well in America as in Europe, and that his Majesty as King of Great Britain had no subjects in any part of the world upon whom an act of the Parliament of Great Britain was not binding.

You will give me leave to mention to you how these principles have gradually changed, for others which approach very near to independence. You are sensible the Parliament had scarce in any instance imposed any tax or duty upon the colonies for the purpose of a revenue. The 18d. sugar duty was considered for the regulation of trade, the Molosses act of the 6th. of George the 2d was professedly designed meerly as a prohibition from the foreign islands, the Greenwich hospital duty was upon seamen who, generally, are rather inhabitants of the world than any colony, and the Post office was supposed to be established for publick convenience; and until the late act which lowered the duties upon molosses and sugar, with a professed design to raise a revenue from them, few people in the colonies had made it a question how far the Parliament, of right, might impose taxes upon them. When this first became a topick for conversation, few or none were willing to admit the right, but the power and, from thence the obligation to submit none would deny. The Massachusets assembly was the first representative body, which took this matter into consideration. Besides the act for raising a revenue from molosses, &c. there had been a resolve of the House of commons, that the parliament had a right to raise money from the colonies by internal taxes. A committee of the council and house were appointed to prepare an address to His Majesty, or the Parliament, for relief. The committee soon determined the latter to be the most proper. I was chairman of the committee, but declined drawing any address. Several were prepared which expressed in strong terms an exclusive right in the assembly to impose taxes. I urged the ill policy, when they had the resolution of the house of commons before them, of sending an address, in express words, asserting the contrary and, after a fortnight spent, at the desire of the committee, I drew an address, which considered the sole Power of taxation as an indulgence which we prayed the continuance of, and this was unanimously agreed to. The proceeding of the general court was also approved and applauded out of doors, until the copy of an address from the assembly of New York was brought to Boston by Mr. Bayard, one of the city members. This was so high, that the heroes for liberty among us were ashamed of their own conduct and would have recalled what had been done here, if it had not been too late. Still this was not the general sense of the people. It was supposed the New York address and any others in the same strain would bring down the resentment of Parliament, but when news came, that the stamp act had passed and that no distinction was made in the addresses, it was then said, that if all the colonies had shewn the like firmness and asserted their rights the act would never have passed, and the promoter of the measure here was charged with treachery and from his dependance on the crown betraying his country.

It had not, however, been suggested that the act would not be executed and several persons, who are now for dying rather than submit to it, were then making interest with the distributor for places for themselves or friends. But soon after, the resolves of the Virginia assembly were sent hither. A new spirit appeared at once. An act of Parliament against our natural rights was ipso facto void and the people were bound to unite against the execution of it. You know the temper of the tradesmen of the town of Boston. They were inflamed, began the first violence against the distributor and then went on to more enormous acts, until they were struck with horror at looking back and thought they had done enough to deter all persons from giving the lest countenance to the act. This flame, by all the art of superior incendiaries, has been spread through this and every other colony upon the continent, and every where, it is the universal voice of all people, that if the stamp act must take place we are absolute slaves. There is no reasoning with them,

you are immediately pronounced an enemy to your country.

It looks doubtful from your letter whether the act will be repealed. The general opinion is, among the most moderate, that nothing but superior force will carry it into execution. If you urge the invalidity of all instruments and law proceedings, it is immediately asked who will dare dispute them. Confusion, and convulsion, will be the inevitable consequence, how great or how durable it is not possible to judge.

If the act should be repealed, we shall still be in a deplorable condition. In the capital towns of several of the colonies and of this in particular, the authority is in the populace, no law can be carried into execution against their mind. I am not sure that the acts of trade will not be considered as grievous as the stamp act. I doubt whether, at present, any custom house officer would venture to make a seizure. In the country towns, in this province, I should hope the people in general would return to reason and be convinced of the necessity of supporting the authority of government. I do not mention this as a sufficient argument against external provision for the future support of government, but it may possibly be a reason for deferring for a short time, at lest in degree, any measures for that purpose, until the minds of the people are somewhat calmed, and the effect of the repeal, if that should be the case, shall appear.

I cannot avoid acquainting you with a further fact the consequence of the disaffected state of mind among the people and which I believe you have not a full conception of. When I first saw the proposals for lessening the consumption of english manufactures I took them to be mere puffs. The scheme for laying aside mourning succeeded to my surprize and scarce any body would now dare to wear black for the nearest relation. In this town, there is yet no very sensible alteration in other articles, but in the country, in general, there is a visible difference and the humour for being cloathed in homespun spreads every day not so much from oeconomy as to convince the people of England how beneficial the colonies have been to them, supposing the worth of any thing to be best known by the want of it.

A general representation of facts is all that is necessary to write to you, who know so perfectly the constitution of every colony, the disposition and temper of all the inhabitants; it is all that in prudence I ought to write to any body, considering the present prevailing jealousy in the minds of people improved, by a much more abandoned man than Clodius to render obnoxious every person who opposes his wicked schemes of popularity. I may safely say, that by some means or other the authority in the colonies first or last must be strengthened, that those are the most eligible which shall evidently appear, to be intended to preserve to them all the rights and liberties, which can consist with their connexion with their mother country. In this way, the present alienation may be removed and, instead of seeking to lessen the profit the mother country may make from trade and commerce with them, they will seek means to increase it, but while this alienation remains, although effectual means should be used to maintain a subordination, it will be impossbile to continue equal advantages from trade as if it was removed.

It will be some amusement to you to have a more circumstantial account of the present model of government among us. I will begin with the lowest branch partly legislative partly executive. This consists of the rabble of the town of Boston headed by one Mackintosh who I imagine you never heard of. He is a bold fellow and as likely for a Massianello as you can well conceive. When there is occasion to hang or burn effigies or pull down houses these are employed, but since government has been brought to a system they are some what

controuled by a superior set consisting of the master masons carpenters &c of the town. When the Secretary was summoned to attend at the tree of liberty he sent to T. Daws to desire him to interpose and at lest procure leave for him to resign at the town house but after two or three consultations nothing more could be obtained than a promise of having no affront offered and a proposal to invite the principal persons of the town to accompany him.

When any thing of more importance is to be determined as opening the custom house or any matters of trade these are under the direction of a committee of merchants. Mr. Rowe at their head then Molyneux Solomon Davis &c. but all affairs of a general nature opening all the courts of law &c. this is proper for a general meeting of the inhabitants of Boston where Otis with his mobbish eloquence prevails in every motion, and the town first determine what is necessary to be done and then apply either to the Governor and council or resolve that it is necessary the general court should meet and it must be a very extraordinary resolve indeed that is not carried into execution. The town applied to the governor in council to desire him to order the executive courts to do business with out stamps. This the council refused to advise to but advised him to recommend to the Justices of the inferior court for Suffolk to meet and determine whether at the court which was to be held in two or three days after they should proceed, but the town who kept their meeting alive by adjournment immediately upon receiving the answer resolved it was unsatisfactory. After this upon the motion of Otis they sent a committee to desire the governor not to prorogue the general court any further. When the court met the House resolved not above half a dozen dissenting that the courts ought to go on with business and sent to the council to concur. I opposed it as taking from the executive courts their right of judgment and moved the resolve should ly that if enquired after the house might be told it was extrajudicial. A day or two after I was charged in the news paper my name at large with declaring in council the vote was impertinent below the notice of the board and by usurping the president's place obtaining an undue influence &c. and the printers were directed to tell the author's name if required. Otis did not deny his being the author. A publication in the same paper had done a great deal towards raising the former storm against me and I expected a second shipwreck, and therefore moved to the council to send for the printers and if they should mention Otis as the author that the House should be applied to for justice upon one of their members, but the majority of the council were afraid and only ordered a vote to be published declaring the falshood of the account in the former paper. Although this had a tendency to appease the rage of the rabble against me yet it was so dishonorable to the council to contradict such an aspersion without any further notice that with the governor's approbation I excused my self from any further attendance that session. The board after this, instead of passing upon the resolve recommended to the Justices of the superior court to determine whether they would proceed or not at their next term. This they refused to do but gave it as their opinion that if the affairs of government continued in the present state they should find themselves under a necessity of proceeding. This was not satisfactory to the house who insisted that the board should pass on their resolve but they kept altercating upon it until the court was over by a long adjournment. A majority of the superior court I imagine will find the necessity they supposed they should. I hope to excuse my self from joining with them.

The majority of the house are not disaffected or unfriendly to government, but are afraid to act their judgment this boulefeu threatning to print their names who vote against his measures. In council the valiant Brigadier Royall who has thrown up his commission is at the head of all popular measures and become a great orator. Erving Brattle Gray Otis and Bradbury and Sparhawk whose characters you well know are in the same box. Tyler is sometimes of one side and sometimes of the other.

It must be a pleasure to you sometimes to look back upon your old government, otherwise I should fear I had quite tired you with this long epistle.

I had wrote thus far the 8th. The constant intelligence every day or two of one occurrent and another which demonstrates that there is no authority subsisting in any of the colonies makes me doubt whether of our selves we shall ever return to a state of government and order. In the Jersies New York and Connecticut there is a settled plan of union of the populace of those governments who correspond by Committees and are settling a committee to represent the whole. About a fortnight ago the distracted demagogue of Boston attacked my history of the colony and censured me in his news paper for charging the government with a mistake in imagining that an act of the colony was necessary to give force to an act of Parliament for regulating trade. A few days after upon a seizure of molosses and sugar at Newbury half a dozen boats well manned went after the officer took the goods from him and the boat he was in and left him all night upon the beach. A proclamation with promise of reward upon discovery is nothing more than the shew of authority, no man will venture a discovery and I imagine a few more such instances will make it settled law that no act but those of our own legislatures can bind us.

CHAPTER VII

REPEAL

ENGLISH MERCHANTS and manufacturers, even before they received news of American non-importation agreements, mobilized to secure repeal of the Stamp Act. Led by Barlow Trecothick, a former Bostonian, the London merchants sent letters (No. 50) to their colleagues in other towns, and Parliament was deluged with petitions like the one drawn up in London (No. 51).

While the merchants and manufacturers were exerting pressure for repeal, the opposition was feeding on news of riots and resolutions from America. Though the Rockingham administration was anxious to please the merchants by repeal, its own position in Parliament was shaky and not improved by the steady hammering of Anti-Sejanus in the press (Nos. 52-55). After accepting the ministry, Lord Rockingham tried again and again to secure the support of William Pitt, then the most popular man in England. Pitt consistently refused to oblige. When Parliament opened in January, 1766, he made a speech that gained him the principal credit for repeal of the Stamp Act (No. 56). Distinguishing between legislation and taxation, he argued that "taxation is no part of the governing or legislative power." He believed that the Stamp Act had been founded on an erroneous principle and urged immediate repeal. He also suggested a formula by which repeal might be made palatable to the opposition, namely by an assertion of Parliament's authority over the colonies, extended "to every point of legislation whatsoever."

Rockingham also perceived the necessity of affirming Parliament's authority and devised a series of resolutions to embody it. When the attorney general, Charles Yorke, suggested that the formula be made to designate taxation specifically, Rockingham refused for fear of offending Pitt (No. 57). Rockingham's phrasing was purposely vague, stating Parliament's power to pass laws to bind the people of America "in all cases whatsoever." This declaratory act and repeal became part of a parliamentary package, and Rockingham's strategy was to soft-pedal, as far as possible, the Americans' denial of Parliament's authority. For that reason he suppressed the declarations and petitions of the Stamp Act Congress; instead, he brought a host of British merchants and visiting Americans before the House of Commons to testify to the evil consequences of the Stamp Act. Benjamin Franklin fell in with Rockingham's purpose in a good-humored and carefully rehearsed performance (No. 58). Henry Cruger, Jr., a Bristol merchant with colonial mercantile connections, reported on the success of these tactics (No. 60). He accurately predicted repeal, which passed the House of Commons by a vote of 275 to 167 and the House of Lords by 105 to 71 (No. 61).

Charles Garth, Member of Parliament and agent for Maryland, explained Rockingham's attitude in a letter to his constituents (No. 59A). In another letter Garth described the debate on the Declaratory Act, in which Pitt and his friends opposed the inclusion of the phrase "in all cases whatsoever" (No. 59B). The final act nevertheless included that phrase (No. 62).

On both sides of the Atlantic repeal of the Stamp Act was greeted with rejoicing. In England the merchants celebrated, and one friend of the colonies sketched a popular cartoon entitled "The Repeal, or the Funeral Procession of Miss Americ-Stamp" (see frontispiece). But the opposition remained bitter, and vitriolic ballads suggested that England had been worsted by America (No. 63). Indeed, the London merchants, fearful of antagonizing the opposition further, cautioned the colonists against "breaking out into intemperate strains of triumph and exaltation" (No. 64). In America the rejoicing was not dampened by this warning nor by the Declaratory Act. Pitt, rather than Rockingham, was generally credited with bringing about repeal, and Pitt's views on taxation were well known. Rockingham's phraseology left the issue of taxation in doubt, but this very vagueness led colonists such as George Mason to wonder whether the mother country had actually given up the attempt to tax them (No. 65). They did not, of course, have long to wait, for in 1767 Parliament passed the Townshend Acts.

The student of the American Revolution, examining the colonial reaction to these and other parliamentary measures of 1767-76, may ask himself how much the Americans and the British learned from the Stamp Act. How closely did they adhere to the ideas formulated in their first great imperial crisis? Did the colonists later demand more freedom than they did in 1765? Could peace have been restored in 1775 on the same terms as in 1766? If not, why not?

QUESTIONS

1. On what grounds did the merchants advocate repeal of the Stamp Act?
2. On what grounds did Pitt advocate repeal?
3. What did Pitt mean by his statement that "taxation is no part of the governing or legislative power?"
4. What did he mean by the words: "If the gentleman does not understand the difference between internal and external taxes, I cannot help it"?

5. Did Pitt himself differentiate between internal and external taxes?

6. Did Franklin?

7. Did either Pitt or Franklin indicate what he meant by these terms?

8. Were the words "external tax" and "duty on trade" used synonymously in this controversy?

9. How accurately did Franklin represent the American position?

10. How did Rockingham interpret the assertions of the Stamp Act Congress about Parliament's authority in the colonies?

11. Was the Declaratory Act incompatible with the resolutions of the colonial assemblies?

12. What was meant by the phrase "in all cases whatsoever"?

13. Did the Americans' resistance to collection of the tax help to bring about repeal?

The Merchants Advocate Repeal

50.   The Committee of London Merchants to the Lord Mayors in England

[The Committee of London Merchants Trading to North America, to the Lord Mayor &c. of the Seaport and Manufacturing Towns, in England &c., *Massachusetts Gazette*, March 6, 1766.]

London, December 6, 1765

The present State of the British Trade to North-America, and the Prospect of increasing Embarrassments, which threaten the loss of our depending Property there and even to annihilate the Trade itself, having occasioned a general Meeting to be called of the Merchants in this City, concerned in that Branch of Business.

As the Gentlemen of your—and of almost every other Maritime and manufacturing Part of these Kingdoms must be affected by the Distresses of North-American Commerce, we have thought it our Duty to acquaint you (as we now do by the Copy inclosed) with our Proceedings, as well as to ask your and their Concurrence and Assistance, in support of a regular Application to Parliament, or otherwise a Petition from your Body, and by all the Interest you can make with your own Members, and with the Members in your Neighbourhood, who with all other Landholders, we think greatly interested in the Prosperity of Trade and Manufactures, from which so large an additional Value is derived to their Property. We desire to unite with you in a Measure so essential to the best Interests of Great Britain, wishing to have your Sentiments on the Subject, thro' the Course of which, we mean to take for our Guide, the Interests of these Kingdoms,—it being our Opinion that conclusive Arguments for granting every Ease or Advantage the North-Americans can with Propriety desire, may be fairly deduced from that principle only.

I am, with great Respect,

Sir, your most Obedient humble Servant,

BARLOW TRECOTHICK

Chairman to the Committee of the Merchants of London, trading to North-America.

51.   The Petition of the London Merchants to the House of Commons

[*Journals of the House of Commons* (London, 1803), XXX, 462 (Jan. 17, 1766).]

A Petition of the Merchants of *London,* trading to *North America,* was presented to the House, and read; Setting forth, That the Petitioners have been long concerned in carrying on the Trade between this Country and the *British* Colonies on the Continent of *North America;* and that they have annually exported very large Quantities of *British* Manufactures, consisting of Woollen Goods of all Kinds, Cottons, Linens, Hardware, Shoes, Houshold Furniture, and almost without Exception of every other Species of Goods manufactured in these Kingdoms, besides other Articles imported from abroad, chiefly purchased with our Manufactures and with the Produce of our Colonies; by all which, many thousand Manufacturers, Seamen, and Labourers, have been employed, to the very great and increasing Benefit of this Nation; and that, in return for these Exports, the Petitioners have received from the Colonies, Rice, Indico, Tobacco, Naval Stores, Oil, Whale Fins, Furs, and lately Pot Ash, with other Commodities, besides Remittances by Bills of Exchange and Bullion, obtained by the Colonists in Payment for Articles of their Produce, not required for the *British* Market, and therefore exported to other Places; and that, from the Nature of this Trade, consisting of *British* Manufactures exported, and of the Import of raw Materials from *America,* many of them used in our Manufactures, and all of them tending to lessen our Dependence on neighbouring States, it must be deemed of the highest Importance in the Commercial System of this Nation; and that this Commerce, so beneficial to the State, and so necessary for the Support of Multitudes, now lies under such Difficulties and Discouragement, that nothing less than its utter Ruin

is apprehended, without the immediate Interposition of Parliament; and that, in consequence of the Trade between the Colonies and the Mother Country, as established and as permitted for many Years, and of the Experience which the Petitioners have had of the Readiness of the *Americans* to make their just Remittances to the utmost of their real Ability, they have been induced to make and venture such large Exportations of *British* Manufactures, as to leave the Colonies indebted to the Merchants of *Great Britain* in the Sum of several Millions Sterling; and that at this Time the Colonists, when pressed for Payment, appeal to past Experience, in Proof of their Willingness; but declare it is not in their Power, at present, to make good their Engagements, alleging, that the Taxes and Restrictions laid upon them, and the Extension of the Jurisdiction of Vice Admiralty Courts established by some late Acts of Parliament, particularly by an Act passed in the Fourth Year of His present Majesty, for granting certain Duties in the *British* Colonies and Plantations in *America,* and by an Act passed in the Fifth Year of His present Majesty, for granting and applying certain Stamp Duties, and other Duties, in the *British* Colonies and Plantations in *America,* with several Regulations and Restraints, which, if founded in Acts of Parliament for defined Purposes, are represented to have been extended in such a Manner as to disturb legal Commerce and harrass the fair Trader, have so far interrupted the usual and former most fruitful Branches of their Commerce, restrained the Sale of their Produce, thrown the State of the several Provinces into Confusion, and brought on so great a Number of actual

Bankruptcies, that the former Opportunities and Means of Remittances and Pay-
ments are utterly lost and taken from
them; and that the Petitioners are, by
these unhappy Events, reduced to the
Necessity of applying to the House, in
order to secure themselves and their
Families from impending Ruin; to prevent
a Multitude of Manufacturers from becoming a Burthen to the Community, or else
seeking their Bread in other Countries,

to the irretrievable Loss of this Kingdom;
and to preserve the Strength of this Nation
entire, its Commerce flourishing, the
Revenues increasing, our Navigation, the
Bulwark of the Kingdom, in a State of
Growth and Extension, and the Colonies,
from Inclination, Duty, and Interest, firmly
attached to the Mother Country: And
therefore praying the Consideration of the
Premises, and intreating such Relief, as to
the House shall seem expedient.

Opposition to Repeal

52.   Anti-Sejanus: Enforce the Stamp Act with Spirit and Resolution

[*London Chronicle*, XIX, 77 (Jan. 23, 1766).]

To the PRINTER.

THE only shadow of an argument, that
can be brought to support the repeal of the
Stamp Act, is that our trade with that
country will suffer, if we enforce the tax
with spirit and rigour. I grant it will—
but what then? It will suffer only for a
time; and this necessary severity will support and secure it for the future. Whereas
if the tax is repealed, it will give a blow
to our trade, that will be felt for ages—
it will open a channel to the Americans
for a free commerce with all the world:
The manufactures of this country will be
rejected, in proportion as other nations
underwork, and undersell us: In short,
America will be no longer British, but
German, French, Spanish, Russian—and
what not? Forbid it Heaven, that I should
live to see the day, when a country, which
has cost us so much blood and treasure to
defend, will be made the bubble of popularity, or the plaything of power; liable to
be blown away by vanity on one hand, or
lost, by childish weakness and timidity,
on the other.

The trade of this kingdom with America produces annually about two millions

of money; from which circumstance, I
overheard a gentleman in the coffee-house
defend a repeal of the act; because, as he
alleged, one hundred thousand pounds a
year (the greatest supposed produce of the
tax) was not an object, when two millions
were in danger. But this way of arguing
is to the last degree absurd and fallacious.
It is not for the paltry sum of one hundred
thousand pounds a year that we are contending; but for the honour of the Crown,
the dignity of P——, the credit and welfare of the nation, together with the very
essence of our excellent constitution. These
are great and inestimable treasures, which
no man, who loves his country, would be
afraid to defend with the last drop of
blood that he could drain from his heart.

But allowing the necessity of enforcing
the Stamp-act, with spirit and resolution,
it is worthy the wisdom of a British p——
to investigate, and determine on the proper
measures, that ought to be pursued. This
important affair is at present under their
consideration: And it ill becomes any
individual presumptuously to think of
advising so prudent, illustrious, and able a
body; who in all times of difficulty and

danger, have taken such wise and salutary steps, as oblige us to adore the goodness of that special providence, by whom they are influenced and directed. But I cannot help lamenting the weakness of those hands, that are to put the measures into execution.

Your's, &c.   ANTI-SEJANUS.

53.   Anti-Sejanus: The "ingratitude of the Americans"

[*London Chronicle*, XIX, 92 (Jan. 28, 1766).]

I am equally grieved and surprised at the waywardness and ingratitude of the Americans, to make such an undutiful return to the mother-country, for that parental care and tenderness with which she has fostered and protected them. What unnatural towardness is it, to repine at so light and easy an imposition, after the abundant kindness which they have experienced? An imposition that bears no proportion to those heavy burthens with which unhappy Britain is laden, and is levied besides on the ablest and most wealthy parts of their kingdom. Has not it cost us upwards of fifty millions to defend America from the assaults of foreign enemies, under whom she would have groaned with every kind of oppression and tyranny? And what? Will she refuse to pay a small share of the burden; and must the British landholders be saddled with an additional tax, upon Her account, with two shillings in the pound? Can we support so vast and enormous a grievance! Will not a tax upon the land of six shillings in the pound infallibly ruin the manufacturers of this kingdom; and so raise the price of provisions, that the poorer people must either rise up in arms, or submit to perish with hunger? I tremble to think what will be the fate of this wretched country, if for any emergency of state, it should be found necessary to raise larger supplies, than what the present duties and impositions already bring in! It is incumbent upon our Ministers to look out for some little assistance from abroad; and not to submit to the unreasonable and refractory colonists; who though they experience every indulgence, in their trade and commerce, that the mildest government can afford; though they have been supported with so much blood and treasure; and are at present protected, at the expence of between three and four hundred thousand pounds a year, notwithstanding all this, refuse to bear a light and modest part of the grievances of government, and shew a disposition to shake off all dependance and subjection.

I am, Your's, &c.
ANTI-SEJANUS.

54.   Anti-Sejanus: "frivolous pretences"

[*London Chronicle*, XIX, 100 (Jan. 30, 1766).]

HAVE the Ministerial writers proved that the Members of the present administration are men of knowlege, capacity, and experience? Have they proved that the harbour of Dunkirk is destroyed, the Manilla ransom paid, and the Canada bills discharged, to the full demand of the several claimants? Have they proved that the Public money has not been prostituted, by our lavish stewards, to private purposes? Have they proved that there have been no presents made for *former* or *future* services; no payment of arrears; no pensioning of superficial Secretaries, and importunate Exiles? Have they proved that the present state of the revenue will allow of such needless, wasteful, and scandalous profusion? Have they proved that the Cyder-act will be repealed, and the Land-tax lowered? Or have they proved that Mr. D——, and the present C—— of the E——are two distinct persons, who are neither of them responsible for what the other says and does? Have they proved that we are not in a perilous and desparate situation, and that our indolent and inactive pilots have not slumbered for six months together at the helm? One question more, and I have then done.—Have they proved that Mr. Pitt, upon whose shoulders they have endeavoured to exalt themselves, will support either them or their system? Has not he more than once hinted at some private influence which they are under, and ridiculed them in the most notorious and public manner? Have they been able by wheedling and fawning, by cringing and crouching, with supple and abject servility, to draw one single drop of comfort from that popular gentleman? Will he espouse their cause, and support them in P——t, or leave them to shuffle and scramble for themselves? Dare they adopt his idea, or dare they confront it? Will they not rather, lest they should offend the Idol, find out a middle way, and retain the shadow of power over the colonists, while they give up the substance? These are plain questions; and from the proper answers, that are due to them, the world will judge of me and my writings. It is not the impudent assertion of a nameless and shameless hireling, that there is nothing but declamation and falshood in these papers, that will draw off the attention of the Public from those arguments and facts, which I have thought it my duty to lay before them. The time is now come, when we are no longer to be imposed upon by—specious I cannot call them, but—frivolous pretences: The several predictions, that I have published, will inevitably be accomplished. . . .

I wonder that a writer for the present Ministry should be so injudicious, as to mention fulsome praise, nauseous flattery, and Mr. Pitt, in one and the same sentence. Has he forgot the mean, abject, fawning, and parasitical behaviour of his own friends, upon a late occasion? Did not they coax, bow, cringe, and compliment, in the most dastard and extravagant stile of adulation; in hopes that he would let something drop out of his mouth, for them to feed and live upon? And after this mean and unmanly conduct, did not they flock about him, ready to perform the most menial and dirty office? I have no patience to think that Gentlemen, in such exalted stations, should stoop to such amazing meanness; and shall not wonder if they become as contemptible in the opinion of the world, as they must have been in their own, before they could have acted in so unbecoming a manner.

Your's &c.
ANTI-SEJANUS.

55.   Anti-Sejanus: "the spirit of rebellion"

[*London Chronicle*, XIX, 149 (Feb. 13, 1766).]

To the PRINTER.
SIR,

Equally vain and inconclusive is the argument which a writer, who signs himself a BRITON, draws from the wisdom and prudence of the Americans. They would not, he thinks, thrive and flourish so vigorously, if they were lopt off from the parent-root, as they do in their present state, while they continue as branches, that shoot from the original stem. Far otherwise do the Colonists reason upon this reciprocal relation between the two countries. They regard it as their greatest misfortune that they are not allowed to take root themselves; and wish for nothing more than to be sever'd from the mother trunk, that is now dry, sapless, and wither'd. While they remain in their present state, they look upon the blossoms and fruit that they bear as not their own; and had rather be blighted and barren themselves, than that we should reap any advantage from their productions. This untowardly disposition in the Americans is owing in a great measure to the inconveniences, under which they are laid by the Act of Navigation; and they seem determined, at all events, to rid themselves of it. The opposition which they make to the Stamp-act, is only the beginning of troubles; it is nothing but a prelude to the game that they intend to play. Though this point should be entirely given up, they would not be a jot more pliant and tractable: They might indeed for a few months lay down their arms, but they would still be working underhand, and collecting strength daily; till at last the seditious flame would burst out afresh, and having been for a-while pent up, would rage afterwards with redoubled fury.

The Americans imbibe notions of independance and liberty with their very milk, and will some time or other shake off all subjection. If we yield to them in this particular, by repealing the Stamp-Act, it is all over; they will from that moment assert their freedom. Whereas if we enforce the Act, we may keep them in dependance for some years longer: they are not yet in a condition to resist us—they cannot live without our manufactories; and as to their hopes of procuring them from the Dutch or other nations, they may easily be blasted, by watchful and vigorous measures. But if we are supine and indolent, if we are irresolute and fearful, if we shew that we cannot, or dare not resist them, they will grow insolent by such encouragement, and rather push matters to the very last extremity, than submit to our authority. In short, the spirit of rebellion is now gone forth, and it is of too fierce and savage a nature to be subdued by kindness and indulgence: It animates the scum and refuse of the people, whose breasts are too callous to be touched by gentle and generous treatment. I am, your's, &c.

ANTI-SEJANUS.

The Campaign in Parliament

56.   The Role of William Pitt

[*Parliamentary History*, XVI, 97-108.]

Mr. *Pitt* spoke next. As he always began very low, and as every body was in agitation at his first rising, his introduction was not heard, till he said, I came to town but to-day; I was a stranger to the tenor of his Majesty's Speech, and the proposed Address, till I heard them read in this House. Unconnected and unconsulted, I have not the means of information; I am fearful of offending through mistake, and therefore beg to be indulged with a second reading of the proposed Address. [The Address being read, Mr. Pitt went on:] He commended the King's Speech, approved of the Address in answer, as it decided nothing. every gentleman being left at perfect liberty to take such a part concerning America, as he might afterwards see fit. One word only he could not approve of, an 'early,' is a word that does not belong to the notice the ministry have given to parliament of the troubles in America. In a matter of such importance, the communication ought to have been immediate: I speak not with respect to parties; I stand up in this place single and unconnected. As to the late ministry (turning himself to Mr. Grenville, who sat within one of him) every capital measure they have taken, has been entirely wrong!

As to the present gentlemen, to those at least whom I have in my eye (looking at the bench where Mr. Conway sat, with the lords of the treasury) I have no objection; I have never been made a sacrifice by any of them. Their characters are fair; and I am always glad when men of fair character engage in his Majesty's service. Some of them have done me the honour to ask my poor opinion, before they would engage. These will do me the justice to own I advised them to engage; but notwithstanding, I love to be explicit; I cannot give them my confidence; pardon me, gentlemen, (bowing to the ministry) confidence is a plant of slow growth in an aged bosom: youth is the season of credulity; by comparing events with each other, reasoning from effects to causes, methinks, I plainly discover the traces of an over-ruling influence.

There is a clause in the Act of Settlement, to oblige every minister to sign his name to the advice which he gives his sovereign. Would it were observed! I have had the honour to serve the crown, and if I could have submitted to influence, I might have still continued to serve; but I would not be responsible for others. I have no local attachments: it is indifferent to me, whether a man was rocked in his cradle on this side or that side of the Tweed. I sought for merit wherever it was to be found. It is my boast, that I was the first minister who looked for it, and I found it in the mountains of the north. I called it forth, and drew it into your service, an hardy and intrepid race of men! men, who, when left by your jealousy, became a prey to the artifices of your enemies, and had gone nigh to have overturned the state, in the war before the last. These men, in the last war, were brought to combat on your side: they served with fidelity, as they fought with valour, and conquered for you in every part of the world: detested be the national reflections against them! they are unjust, groundless, illiberal, unmanly. When I ceased to serve his Majesty as a minister, it was not the country of the man by which I was moved, but the man of that country wanted wisdom, and held principles incompatible with freedom.

It is a long time, Mr. Speaker, since I have attended in parliament. When the resolution was taken in the House to tax America, I was ill in bed. If I could have endured to have been carried in my bed, so great was the agitation of my mind for the consequences! I would have solicited some kind hand to have laid me down on this floor, to have borne my testimony against it. It is now an act that has passed; I would speak with decency of every act of this House, but I must beg the indulgence of the House to speak of it with freedom.

I hope a day may be soon appointed to consider the state of the nation with respect to America. I hope gentlemen will come to this debate with all the temper and impartiality that his Majesty recommends, and the importance of the subject requires. A subject of greater importance than ever engaged the attention of this House! that subject only excepted, when near a century ago, it was the question whether you yourselves were to be bound, or free. In the mean time, as I cannot depend upon health for any future day, such is the nature of my infirmities, I will beg to say a few words at present, leaving the justice, the equity, the policy, the expediency of the act, to another time. I will only speak to one point, a point which seems not to have been generally understood, I mean to the right. Some gentlemen (alluding to Mr. Nugent) seem to have considered it as a point of honour. If gentlemen consider it in that light, they leave all measures of right and wrong, to follow a delusion that may lead to destruction. It is my opinion, that this kingdom has no right to lay a tax upon the colonies. At the same time, I assert the authority of this kingdom over the colonies, to be sovereign and supreme, in every circumstance of government and legislation whatsoever. They are the subjects of this kingdom, equally entitled with yourselves to all the natural rights of mankind and the peculiar privileges of Englishmen. Equally bound by its laws, and equally participating of the constitution of this free country. The Americans are the sons, not the bastards, of England. Taxation is no part of the governing or legislative power. The taxes are a voluntary gift and grant of the Commons alone. In legislation the three estates of the realm are alike concerned, but the concurrence of the peers and the crown to a tax, is only necessary to close with the form of a law. The gift and grant is of the Commons alone. In ancient days, the crown, the barons, and the clergy possessed the lands. In those days, the barons and the clergy gave and granted to the crown. They gave and granted what was their own. At present, since the discovery of America, and other circumstances permitting, the Commons are become the proprietors of the land. The crown has divested itself of its great estates. The church (God bless it) has but a pittance. The property of the Lords, compared with that of the Commons, is as a drop of water in the ocean: and this House represents those Commons, the proprietors of the lands; and those proprietors virtually represent the rest of the inhabitants. When, therefore, in this House we give and grant, we give and grant what is our own. But in an American tax, what do we do? We, your Majesty's Commons of Great Britain, give and grant to your Majesty, what? Our own property? No. We give and grant to your Majesty, the property of your Majesty's commons of America. It is an absurdity in terms.

The distinction between legislation and taxation is essentially necessary to liberty. The Crown, the Peers, are equally legislative powers with the Commons. If taxation be a part of simple legislation, the Crown, the Peers, have rights in taxation as well as yourselves: rights which they will claim, which they will exercise, whenever the principle can be supported by power.

There is an idea in some, that the colonies are virtually represented in this House. I would fain know by whom an American is represented here? Is he represented by any knight of the shire, in any county in this kingdom? Would to God that respectable representation was augmented to a greater number! Or will you tell him, that he is represented by any representative of a borough—a borough, which perhaps, its own representative never saw. This is what is called, 'the rotten part of the constitution.' It cannot continue the century; if it does not drop, it must be amputated. The idea of a virtual representation of America in this House, is the most contemptible idea that ever entered into the head of a man; it does not deserve a serious refutation.

The Commons of America, represented in their several assemblies, have ever been in possession of the exercise of this, their constitutional right, of giving and granting their own money. They would have been slaves if they had not enjoyed it. At the same time, this kingdom, as the supreme governing and legislative power, has always bound the colonies by her laws, by her regulations, and restrictions in trade, in navigation, in manufactures, in every thing, except that of taking their money out of their pockets without their consent.

Here I would draw the line, 'Quam ultra citraque nequit consistere rectum.'

He concluded with a familiar voice and tone, but so low that it was not easy to distinguish what he said. A considerable pause ensued after Mr. Pitt had done speaking.

Mr. *Conway* at length got up. He said, he had been waiting to see whether any answer would be given to what had been advanced by the right hon. gentleman, reserving himself for the reply: but as none had been given, he had only to declare, that his own sentiments were entirely conformable to those of the right hon. gentleman—That they are so conformable, he said, is a circumstance that affects me with most sensible pleasure, and does me the greatest honour. But two things fell from that gentleman, which give me pain, as whatever falls from that gentleman, falls from so great a height as to make a deep impression. I must endeavour to remove it. It was objected, that the notice given to parliament of the troubles in America was not early. I can assure the House, the first accounts were too vague and imperfect to be worth the notice of parliament. It is only of late that they have been precise and full. An over-ruling influence has also been hinted at. I see nothing of it; I feel nothing of it; I disclaim it for myself, and (as far as my discernment can reach), for all the rest of his Majesty's ministers.

Mr. *Pitt* said in answer to Mr. Conway, The excuse is a valid one, if it is a just one. That must appear from the papers now before the House.

Mr. *Grenville* next stood up. He began with censuring the ministry very severely, for delaying to give earlier notice to parliament of the disturbances in America. He said, They began in July, and now we are in the middle of January; lately they were only occurrences, they are now grown to disturbances, to tumults and riots. I doubt they border on open rebellion; and if the doctrine I have heard this day be confirmed, I fear they will lose that name to take that of revolution. The government over them being dissolved, a revolution will take place in America. I cannot understand the difference between external and internal taxes. They are the same in effect, and only differ in name. That this kingdom has the sovereign, the supreme legislative power over America, is granted. It cannot be denied; and taxation is a part of that sovereign power. It is one branch of the legislation. It is, it has been exercised, over those who are not, who were never represented. It is exercised over the India Company, the merchants of London, the proprietors of the stocks, and over many great manufacturing towns. It was exercised over the palatinate of Chester, and the bishopric of Durham, before they sent any representatives to parliament. I appeal, for proof, to the preambles of the acts which gave them representatives: the one in the reign of Henry 8, the other in that of Charles 2. [Mr. Grenville then quoted the acts, and desired that they might be read; which being done, he said:] When I proposed to tax America, I asked the House, if any gentleman would object to the right; I repeatedly asked it, and no man would attempt to deny it. Protection and obedience are reciprocal. Great Britain protects America; America is bound to yield obedience. If not, tell me when the Americans were emancipated? When they want the protection of this kingdom, they are always very ready to ask it. That protection has always been afforded them in the most full and ample manner. The nation has run itself into an immense debt to give them their protection; and now they are called upon to contribute a small share towards the public expence, an expence arising from themselves, they renounce your authority, insult your officers, and break out, I might almost say, into open rebellion. The seditious spirit of the colonies owes its birth to the factions in this House. Gentlemen are careless of the consequences of what they say, provided it answers the purposes of opposition. We were told we trod on tender ground; we were bid to expect disobedience. What was this, but telling the Americans to stand out against the law, to encourage their obstinacy with the expectation of support from hence? Let us only hold out a little, they would say, our friends will soon be in power. Ungrateful people of America! Bounties have been extended to them. When I had the honour of serving the crown, while you yourselves were loaded with an enormous debt, you have given bounties on their lumber, on their iron, their hemp, and many other articles. You have relaxed, in their favour, the Act of Navigation, that palladium of the British commerce; and yet I have been abused in all the public papers as an enemy to the trade of America. I have been particularly charged with giving orders and instructions to prevent the Spanish trade, and thereby stopping the channel, by which alone North America used to be supplied with cash for remittances to this country. I defy any man to produce any such orders or instructions. I discouraged no trade but what was illicit, what was prohibited by act of parliament. I desire a West India merchant, well known in the city (Mr. Long), a gentleman of character, may be examined. He will tell you, that I offered to do every thing in my power to advance the trade of America. I was above giving an answer to anonymous calumnies; but in this place, it becomes one to wipe off the aspersion.

Here Mr. Grenville ceased. Several members got up to speak, but

Mr. *Pitt* seeming to rise, the House was so clamorous for Mr. Pitt! Mr. Pitt! that the Speaker was obliged to call to order. After obtaining a little quiet, he said, 'Mr. Pitt was up!' who began with informing the House, That he did not mean to have gone any further upon the subject that day: that he had only

designed to have thrown out a few hints, which, gentlemen who were so confident of the right of this kingdom to send taxes to America, might consider; might, perhaps, reflect in a cooler moment, that the right was at least equivocal. But since the gentleman, who spoke last, had not stopped on that ground, but had gone into the whole; into the justice, the equity, the policy, the expediency of the Stamp-Act, as well as into the right, he would follow him through the whole field, and combat his arguments on every point.

He was going on, when

Lord *Strange* got up, and called both the gentlemen, Mr. Pitt, and Mr. Grenville, to order. He said, they had both departed from the matter before the House, which was the King's Speech; and that Mr. Pitt was going to speak twice on the same debate, although the House was not in a committee.

Mr. *George Onslow* answered, That they were both in order, as nothing had been said, but what was fairly deducible from the King's Speech; and appealed to the Speaker. The Speaker decided in Mr. Onslow's favour.

Mr. *Pitt* said, I do not apprehend I am speaking twice: I did expressly reserve a part of my subject, in order to save the time of this House, but I am compelled to proceed in it. I do not speak twice; I only finish what I designedly left imperfect. But if the House is of a different opinion, far be it from me to indulge a wish of transgression, against order. I am content, if it be your pleasure, to be silent. —Here he paused—The House resounding with, 'Go on, go on;' he proceeded:

Gentlemen, Sir, (to the Speaker) I have been charged with giving birth to sedition in America. They have spoken their sentiments with freedom, against this unhappy act, and that freedom has become their crime. Sorry I am to hear the liberty of speech in this House, imputed as a crime. But the imputation shall not discourage me. It is a liberty I mean to exercise. No gentleman ought to be afraid to exercise it. It is a liberty by which the gentleman who calumniates it might have profited. He ought to have profited. He ought to have desisted from his project. The gentleman tells us, America is obstinate; America is almost in open rebellion. I rejoice that America has resisted. Three millions of people, so dead to all the feelings of liberty, as voluntarily to submit to be slaves, would have been fit instruments to make slaves of the rest. I come not here armed at all points, with law cases and acts of parliament, with the statute-book doubled down in dogs-ears, to defend the cause of liberty: if I had, I myself would have cited the two cases of Chester and Durham. I would have cited them, to have shewn, that, even under any arbitrary reigns, parliaments were ashamed of taxing a people without their consent, and allowed them representatives. Why did the gentleman confine himself to Chester and Durham? He might have taken a higher example in Wales; Wales, that never was taxed by parliament, till it was incorporated. I would not debate a particular point of law with the gentleman: I know his abilities. I have been obliged to his diligent researches. But, for the defence of liberty upon a general principle, upon a constitutional principle, it is a ground on which I stand firm; on which I dare meet any man. The gentleman tells us of many who are taxed, and are not represented—The India company, merchants, stock-holders, manufacturers. Surely many of these are represented in other capacities, as owners of land, or as freemen of boroughs. It is a misfortune that more are not actually represented. But they are all inhabitants, and, as such, are virtually represented. Many have it in their option to be actually represented. They have connexions with those that elect, and they have influence over them. The gentleman mentioned the stockholders: I hope he does not reckon the debts of the nation as a part of the national estate. Since the accession of king William, many ministers, some of great, others of more moderate abilities, have taken the lead of government.

He then went through the list of them, bringing it down till he came to himself, giving a short sketch of the characters of each of them. None of these, he said, thought, or ever dreamed, of robbing the colonies of their constitutional rights. That was reserved to mark the aera of the late administration: not that there were wanting some, when I had the honour to serve his Majesty, to propose to me to burn my fingers with an American Stamp-Act. With the enemy at their back, with our bayonets at their breasts, in the day of their distress, perhaps the Americans would have submitted to the imposition; but it would have been taking an ungenerous, and unjust advantage. The gentleman boasts of his bounties to America! Are not those bounties intended finally for the benefit of this kingdom? If they are not, he has misapplied the national treasures. I am no courtier of America, I stand up for this kingdom. I maintain, that the parliament has a right to bind, to restrain America. Our legislative power over the colonies is sovereign and supreme. When it ceases to be sovereign and supreme, I would advise every gentleman to sell his lands, if he can, and embark for that country. When two countries are connected together, like England and her colonies, without being incorporated, the one must necessarily govern; the greater must rule the less; but so rule it, as not to contradict the fundamental principles that are common to both.

If the gentleman does not understand the difference between internal and external taxes, I cannot help it; but there is a plain distinction between taxes levied for the purposes of raising a revenue, and duties imposed for the regulation of trade, for the accommodation of the subject; although, in the consequences, some revenue might incidentally arise from the latter.

The gentleman asks, when were the colonies emancipated? But I desire to know, when they were made slaves? But I dwell not upon words. When I had the honour of serving his Majesty, I availed myself of the means of information, which I derived from my office: I speak, therefore, from knowledge. My materials were good. I was at pains to collect, to digest, to consider them; and I will be bold to affirm, that the profits to Great Britain from the trade of the colonies, through all its branches, is two millions a year. This is the fund that carried you triumphantly through the last war. The estates that were rented at two thousand pounds a year, threescore years ago, are at three thousand pounds at present. Those estates sold then from fifteen to eighteen years purchase; the same may be now sold for thirty. You owe this to America. This is the price that America pays you for her protection. And shall a miserable financier come with a boast, that he can fetch a pepper-corn into the exchequer, to the loss of millions to the nation! I dare not say, how much higher these profits may be augmented. Omitting the immense increase of people, by natural population, in the northern colonies, and the migration from every part of Europe, I am convinced the whole commercial system of America may be altered to advantage. You have prohibited, where you ought to have encouraged; and you have encouraged where you ought to have prohibited. Improper restraints have been laid on the continent, in favour of the islands. You have but two nations to trade with in America. Would you had twenty! Let acts of parliament in consequence of treaties remain, but let not an English minister become a customhouse officer for Spain, or for any foreign power. Much is wrong, much may be amended for the general good of the whole.

Does the gentleman complain he has been misrepresented in the public prints? It is a common misfortune. In the Spanish affair of the last war, I was abused in all the news-papers, for having advised his Majesty to violate the law of nations with regard to Spain. The abuse was industriously circulated even in hand-bills. If administration did not propagate the abuse, administration never contradicted it. I will not say what advice I did give to the King. My advice is in writing, signed by myself, in the possession of the crown. But I will say, what advice I did not give to the King: I did not advise him to violate any of the laws of nations.

As to the report of the gentleman's preventing in some way the trade for bullion with the Spaniards, it was spoken of so confidently, that I own I am one of those who did believe it to be true.

The gentleman must not wonder he was not contradicted, when, as the minister, he asserted the right of parliament to tax America. I know not how it is, but there is a modesty in this House, which does not chuse to contradict a minister. I wish gentlemen would get the better of this modesty. Even that Chair, Sir, looks too often towards St. James's. If they do not, perhaps, the collective body may begin to abate of its respect for the representative. Lord Bacon had told me, that a great question would not fail of being agitated at one time or another. I was willing to agitate that at the proper season, the German war: my German war, they called it. Every session I called out, Has any body any objections to the German war? Nobody would object to it, one gentleman only excepted, since removed to the upper House, by succession to an ancient barony, (meaning lord le Despencer, formerly sir Francis Dashwood;) he told me, "he did not like a German war." I honoured the man for it, and was sorry when he was turned out of his post.

A great deal has been said without doors, of the power, of the strength of America. It is a topic that ought to be cautiously meddled with. In a good cause, on a sound bottom, the force of this country can crush America to atoms. I know the valour of your troops. I know the skill of your officers. There is not a company of foot that has served in America, out of which you may not pick a man of sufficient knowledge and experience, to make a governor of a colony there. But on this ground, on the Stamp Act, when so many here will think it a crying injustice, I am one who will lift up my hands against it.

In such a cause, your success would be hazardous. America, if she fell, would fall like a strong man. She would embrace the pillars of the state, and pull down the constitution along with her. Is this your boasted peace? Not to sheath the sword in its scabbard, but to sheath it in the bowels of your countrymen? Will you quarrel with yourselves, now the whole House of Bourbon is united against you? While France disturbs your fisheries in Newfoundland, embarrasses your slave trade to Africa, and withholds from your subjects in Canada, their property stipulated by treaty; while the ransom for the Manillas is denied by Spain, and its gallant conqueror basely traduced into a mean plunderer, a gentleman, (colonel Draper)

whose noble and generous spirit would do honour to the proudest grandee of the country. The Americans have not acted in all things with prudence and temper. They have been wronged. They have been driven to madness by injustice. Will you punish them for the madness you have occasioned? Rather let prudence and temper come first from this side. I will undertake for America, that she will follow the example. There are two lines in a ballad of Prior's, of a man's behaviour to his wife, so applicable to you and your colonies, that I cannot help repeating them:

'Be to her faults a little blind:

'Be to her virtues very kind.'

Upon the whole, I will beg leave to tell the House what is really my opinion. It is, that the Stamp Act be repealed absolutely, totally, and immediately. That the reason for the repeal be assigned, because it was founded on an erroneous principle. At the same time, let the sovereign authority of this country over the colonies, be asserted in as strong terms as can be devised, and be made to extend to every point of legislation whatsoever. That we may bind their trade, confine their manufactures, and exercise every power whatsoever, except that of taking their money out of their pockets without their consent.

57. Rockingham's Formula for Repeal

A. The Proposed Resolutions Preceding the Declaratory Act

[George Thomas, Earl of Albemarle, ed., *Memoirs of the Marquis of Rockingham* (London, 1852), I, 285-88.]

I.

Resolved, That it appears to this Committee that the most dangerous tumults and insurrections have been raised and carried on in several of the North American colonies, in open defiance of the powers and dignity of his Majesty's government there, and in manifest violation of the laws and

legislative authority of this kingdom.

II.

Resolved, That the said tumults have been *greatly* [unwarrantably][1] encouraged and inflamed by *sundry* [leave out] votes and resolutions passed in several assemblies of the said provinces [directly contrary to

1. The words in brackets are Charles Yorke's suggestions.

law, highly injurious to the honour of his Majesty and this House], *greatly derogatory* to the honour and dignity of his Majesty's Government, destructive of the legal and constitutional dependency of the said Colonies on the Imperial Crown and Parliament of Great Britain.

III.

Resolved, That an humble address be presented to his Majesty, to desire that his Majesty would be pleased to give directions to the *Governors of the aforesaid North American provinces* . . .[His Governors in N. America,] to take the most effectual methods for discovering and bringing to deserved punishment the authors, abettors, and perpetrators [and principal actors in] of the said riots and *insurrections*.

IV.

Resolved, That a humble address be presented to his Majesty to desire that his Majesty would be [graciously] pleased to give orders to the Governors of the several provinces where the *above-mentioned* [said] riots and insurrections have happened, that they should apply and recommend to the assemblies of the said provinces to make proper recompense to those who have suffered in their persons or properties in consequence thereof.

V.

Resolved, That the Parliament of Great Britain had, hath, and of a right ought to have, full power and authority to make laws and statutes of sufficient force and validity to bind the Colonies and people of America *in all cases whatsoever* [as well in cases of Taxation, as in all other cases whatsoever.]

B. The Marquis of Rockingham to the Hon. Charles Yorke

[Albemarle, ed., *Memoirs of Rockingham*, I, 288.]

Jan. 25, 1766, Saturday evening.
GENERAL CONWAY having sent to me the proposed Resolutions with some alterations which you have made, I cannot help troubling you with my *doubts* upon *some* of them. The Resolutions in general exceed in spirit what the generality of our friends wish, but, in expectation that coming into them will pave the way for the *actual repeal of the Stamp Act,* I think they will be agreed to. In one of your alterations I dislike the *expression* of *undoubted* rights, and am sure, upon consideration how goading that word would be to a great person in the House of Commons, it cannot be advisable to put it in.

The other alteration which I particularly object to, is the insertion of *"taxation,"* and I think I may say that it is our firm resolution in the House of Lords (I mean among ourselves) that that word must not be inserted. I see more and more the difficulties that surround us, and therefore feel the necessity of *not temporizing*. Convinced as I am that the confusion at home will be much too great (if the repeal is not obtained) for us to have withstood, either as private or public men, my opinion being entirely for repeal, I shall certainly persist in that measure; and though many in the House of Commons may be against us, and particularly some who have lately called themselves under the denomination of Lord B.'s friends; yet I am persuaded that the House will repeal the Stamp Act by a great majority. *If it does,* we shall then show *how* we stand as Administration. If it does not, I wish no man so great a curse as to desire him to be the person to take Administration, and be obliged to enforce the Act. . . . On all occasions ever your most affectionate friend,

ROCKINGHAM.

58.   The Role of Benjamin Franklin

[*The Examination of Dr. Benjamin Franklin* (London, 1766), 1, 9-10, 12-14, 22-26, 40-41, 45-47, 49.]

Q. What is your name, and place of abode?

A. Franklin, of Philadelphia. . . .

Q. What was the temper of America towards Great-Britain before the year 1763?

A. The best in the world. They submitted willingly to the government of the Crown, and paid, in all their courts, obedience to acts of parliament. Numerous as the people are in the several old provinces, they cost you nothing in forts, citadels, garrisons or armies, to keep them in subjection. They were governed by this country at the expence only of a little pen, ink and paper. They were led by a thread. They had not only a respect, but an affection, for Great Britain, for its laws, its customs and manners, and even a fondness for its fashions, that greatly increased the commerce. Natives of Britain were always treated with particular regard; to be an Old-England man was, of itself, a character of some respect, and gave a kind of rank among us.

Q. And what is their temper now?

A. O, very much altered.

Q. Did you ever hear the authority of parliament to make laws for America questioned till lately?

A. The authority of parliament was allowed to be valid in all laws, except such as should lay internal taxes. It was never disputed in laying duties to regulate commerce. . . .

Q. What is your opinion of a future tax, imposed on the same principle with that of the stamp-act; how would the Americans receive it?

A. Just as they do this. They would not pay it.

Q. Have not you heard of the resolutions of this House, and of the House of Lords, asserting the right of parliament relating to America, including a power to tax the people there?

A. Yes, I have heard of such resolutions.

Q. What will be the opinion of the Americans on those resolutions?

A. They will think them unconstitutional and unjust.

Q. Was it an opinion in America before 1763, that the parliament had no right to lay taxes and duties there?

A. I never heard any objection to the right of laying duties to regulate commerce; but a right to lay internal taxes was never supposed to be in parliament, as we are not represented there.

Q. On what do you found your opinion, that the people in America made any such distinction?

A. I know that whenever the subject has occurred in conversation where I have been present, it has appeared to be the opinion of every one, that we could not be taxed in a parliament where we were not represented. But the payment of duties laid by act of parliament, as regulations of commerce was never disputed.

Q. But can you name any act of assembly, or public act of any of your governments, that made such distinction?

A. I do not know that there was any; I think there was never an occasion to make any such act, till now that you have attempted to tax us; that has occasioned resolutions of assembly, declaring the distinction, in which I think every assembly on the continent, and every member in every assembly, have been unanimous.

Q. What then could occasion conversations on that subject before that time?

A. There was in 1754 a proposition made, (I think it came from hence) that in case of a war, which was then apprehended, the governors of the colonies should meet, and order the levying of troops, building of forts, and taking every other necessary measure for the general defence; and should draw on the treasury here for the sums expended, which were afterwards to be raised in the Colonies by a general tax, to be laid on them by act of parliament. This occasioned a good deal of conversation on the subject, and the general opinion was, that the parliament neither would nor could lay any tax on us, till we were duly represented in parliament, because it was not just, nor agreeable to the nature of an English constitution. . . .

Q. Can anything less than a military force carry the stamp-act into execution?

A. I do not see how a military force can be applied to that purpose.

Q. Why may it not?

A. Suppose a military force sent into America, they will find nobody in arms; what are they then to do? They cannot force a man to take stamps who chuses to do without them. They will not find a rebellion; they may indeed make one.

Q. If the act is not repealed, what do you think will be the consequences?

A. A total loss of the respect and affection the people of America bear to this country, and of all the commerce that depends on that respect and affection.

Q. How can the commerce be affected?

A. You will find, that if the act is not repealed, they will take very little of your manufactures in a short time.

Q. Is it in their power to do without them?

A. I think they may very well do without them.

Q. Is it in their interest not to take them?

A. The goods they take from Britain are either necessaries, mere conveniences, or superfluities. The first, as cloth, &c. with a little industry they can make at home; the second they can do without, till they are able to provide them among themselves; and the last, which are much the greatest part, they will strike off immediately. They are mere articles of fashion, purchased and consumed because the fashion in a respected country, but will now be detested and rejected. The people have already struck off, by general agreement, the use of all goods fashionable in mournings, and many thousand pounds worth are sent back as unsaleable.

Q. Is it their interest to make cloth at home?

A. I think they may at present get it cheaper from Britain, I mean of the same fineness and neatness of workmanship; but when one considers other circumstances, the restraints on their trade, and the difficulty of making remittances, it is their interest to make every thing.

Q. Suppose an act of internal regulations connected with a tax, how would they receive it?

A. I think it would be objected to.

Q. Then no regulation with a tax would be submitted to?

A. Their opinion is, that when aids to the Crown are wanted, they are to be asked of the several assemblies, according to the old established usage, who will, as they always have done, grant them freely. And that their money ought not to be given away, without their consent, by persons at a distance, unacquainted with their circumstances and abilities. The granting aids to the Crown, is the only means they have of recommending themselves to their sovereign, and they think it extremely hard and unjust, that a body of men, in which they have no representatives, should make a merit to itself of giving and granting what is not its own, but theirs, and deprive them of a right they esteem of the utmost value and importance, as it is the security of all their other rights.

Q. But is not the post-office, which they have long received, a tax as well as a regulation?

A. No; the money paid for the postage of a letter is not of the nature of a tax; it is merely a quantum meruit for a service done; no person is compellable to pay the money, if he does not chuse to receive the service. A man may still, as before the act, send his letter by a servant, a special messenger, or a friend, if he thinks it cheaper and safer.

Q. But do they not consider the regulations of the post-office, by the act of last year as a tax?

A. By the regulations of last year the rate of postage was generally abated near thirty per cent through all America; they certainly cannot consider such abatement as a tax.

Q. If an excise was laid by parliament, which they might likewise avoid paying, by not consuming the articles excised, would they then not object to it?

A. They would certainly object to it, as an excise is unconnected with any service done, and is merely an aid which they think ought to be asked of them, and granted by them, if they are to pay it, and can be granted for them by no others whatsoever, whom they have not impowered for that purpose.

Q. You say they do not object to the right of parliament, in laying duties on goods to be paid on their importation; now, is there any kind of difference between a duty on the importation of goods, and an excise on their consumption?

A. Yes, a very material one; an excise, for the reasons I have just mentioned, they think you can have no right to lay within their country. But the sea is yours; you maintain, by your fleets, the safety of navigation in it, and keep it clear of pirates; you may have therefore a natural and equitable right to some toll or duty on merchandizes carried through that part of your dominions, towards defraying the expence you are at in ships to maintain the safety of that carriage. . . .

Q. Do you think the assemblies have a right to levy money on the subject there, to grant to the Crown?

A. I certainly think so; they have always done it.

Q. Are they acquainted with the declaration of rights? And do they know, that, by that statute, money is not to be raised on the subject but by consent of parliament?

A. They are very well acquainted with it.

Q. How then can they think they have a right to levy money for the Crown, or for any other than for local purposes?

A. They understand that clause to relate to subjects only within the realm; that no money can be levied on them for the Crown, but by consent of parliament. The colonies are not supposed to be within the realm; they have assemblies of their own, which are their parliaments, and they are, in that respect, in the same situation with Ireland. When money is to be raised for the Crown upon the subject in Ireland, or in the Colonies, the consent is given in the Parliament of Ireland, or in the assemblies of the Colonies. They think the parliament of Great-Britain cannot properly give that consent till it has representatives from America; for the petition of right expressly says, it is to be by common consent in parliament, and the people of America have no representatives in parliament, to make a part of that common consent.

Q. If the stamp act should be repealed, and an act should pass, ordering the assemblies of the Colonies to indemnify the sufferers by the riots, would they obey it?

A. That is a question I cannot answer.

Q. Suppose the King should require the Colonies to grant a revenue, and the parliament should be against their doing it, do they think they can grant a revenue to the King, without the consent of the parliament of Great-Britain?

A. That is a deep question.—As to my own opinion, I should think myself at liberty to do it, and should do it, if I liked the occasion. . . .

Q. Don't you know that there is, in the Pennsylvania charter, an express reservation of the right of parliament to lay taxes there?

A. I know there is a clause in the charter, by which the King grants that he will levy no taxes on the inhabitants, unless it be with the consent of the assembly, or by act of parliament.

Q. How then could the assembly of Pennsylvania assert, that laying a tax on them by the stamp-act was an infringement of their rights?

A. They understand it thus; by the same charter, and otherwise, they are intitled to all the privileges and liberties of Englishmen; they find in the great charters, and the petition and declaration of rights, that one of the privileges of English subjects is, that they are not to be taxed but by their common consent; they have therefore relied upon it, from the first settlement of the province, that the parliament never would, nor could, by colour of that clause in the charter, assume a right of taxing them, till it had qualified itself to exercise such right, by admitting representatives from the people to be taxed, who ought to make a part of that common consent.

Q. Are there any words in the charter that justify that construction?

A. The common rights of Englishmen, as declared by Magna Charta, and the petition of right all justify it.

Q. Does the distinction between internal and external taxes exist in the words of the charter?

A. No, I believe not.

Q. Then may they not, by the same interpretation, object to the parliament's right of external taxation?

A. They never have hitherto. Many arguments have been lately used here to shew them, that there is no difference, and that if you have no right to tax them internally, you have none to tax them externally, or make any other law to bind them. At present they do not reason so, but in time they may possibly be convinced by these arguments.

Q. Do not the resolutions of the Pennsylvania assembly say all taxes?

A. If they do, they mean only internal taxes; the same words have not always the same meaning here and in the Colonies. By taxes they mean internal taxes; by duties they mean customs; these are their ideas of the language.

Q. Have you not seen the resolutions of the Massachuset's Bay assembly?

A. I have.

Q. Do they not say, that neither external nor internal taxes can be laid on them by parliament?

A. I don't know that they do; I believe not.

Q. If the same Colony should say neither tax nor imposition could be laid, does not that province hold the power of parliament can lay neither?

A. I suppose that by the word imposition, they do not intend to express duties to be laid on goods imported, as regulations of commerce.

Q. What can the Colonies mean then by imposition as distinct from taxes?

A. They may mean many things, as impressing of men, or of carriages, quartering troops on private houses, and the like; there may be great impositions that are not properly taxes. . . .

Q. If the stamp act should be repealed, would it induce the assemblies of America to acknowledge the rights of parliament to tax them, and would they erase their resolutions?

A. No, never.

Q. Are there no means of obliging them to erase those resolutions?

A. None that I know of; they will never do it, unless compelled by force of arms.

Q. Is there a power on earth that can force them to erase them?

A. No power, how great soever, can force men to change their opinions.

59.   A Colonial Agent's Report of the Debates in Parliament

A. CHARLES GARTH TO RINGGOLD, MURDOCH, AND TILGHMAN, FEBRUARY 26, 1766

[*Maryland Historical Magazine*, 6 (1911), 283-86.]

I am now to inform you that upon the 27th Janry a Petition from the Congress on the Part of the Massachusets Bay had been offer'd to the House of Commons, wch brought on a long Debate, Objections being taken to its Admission, the first to the Form, as contrary to an express Order of the House touching Petitions, Vizt. "1689 Ordered that all Petitions to be presented to this House, shall be signed by the Petitioners themselves by their own Names or Marks" that this was the Petition of the Freeholders and other Inhabitants &c but signed by a few particular Persons as Committees from several Assemblys, to which it was answered, that the Gentlemen who had sign'd it, tho' the Addition of Committee was added to each Name, might notwithstanding be very properly taken to be Freeholders of the respective Colonies petitioning, being Members of the respective Assemblys; Another Objection was that it partook too much of a federal Union assembled without any Requisition on the Part of the supreme Power, and that the House by receiving a Petition from Persons so unconstitutionally assembled without legal Warrant or Authority wou'd give Countenance to a Step, it ought in the strongest Manner to set its Face against, as pregnant with great Danger to his Majesty's Authority and Government; to this it was reply'd that the Meeting had was apparently for no ill Purpose whatsoever, but with a View to consider of the most proper Method of applying to their Sovereign and to both Houses of Parliament for a Redress of a general Grievance, for which Purpose a general Application seem'd to be the properer Mode, at the same Time that considering how little Attention was last Year given to the separate Petitions of particular Colonies, or of the Agents and others in Behalf of the People in America, it might well be imagined that a general Petition prepared and signed by able Gentlemen, in whom each Colony reposed a Confidence, might carry more Weight with it, and be entitled at least to a different Treatment; and as to the Unconstitutionality of the Meeting, it as little deserved that sort of Construction to be put upon it, as any of the Meetings of a Variety of Gentlemen from several Counties and Corporations in England to consider of proper and effectual Measures for an Application to Parliament for a Repeal of any Act that might be deemed burthensome to those Bodies, which was the Case in the Cyder Counties: When the People or any Part thereof are aggrieved, it was said there was no Law nor Constitution within any Part of the Dominion of Great Britain to hinder them from assembling in a quiet and peaceable Manner to consider of their Grievances and the Means to obtain Relief and Redress; this was declaredly the Object of that Meeting and apparently the Case and no other.

A third Objection that it tended to question not only the Right of Parliament to impose internal Taxes, but external Duties, both being blended together as necessary to be repealed, and it was said that for questioning the Right in the first Instance the Petitions last Year were refused a Reception; much more then a Petition questioning the Power in the Case of Duties necessary for the Regulation of Trade, wch went to the very Vitals of the Legislative Authority and Strongly pointed at Independency upon the Mother

Country. It was this Circumstance that prevented the Ministry from cordially Supporting it, who after much Debate on this Head expressed their Wish that the Motion, made for Leave to hear the Petition read by the Clerk and referr'd to the Committee, might be withdrawn, but this not being readily complied with, there being an Order of the Day not gone into, they moved about Eleven at Night for the Order of the Day, which was agreed to, and in that Manner the Fate of that Petition determin'd: As I could not see the Force of the Arguments urged against receiving it, being of Opinion that no Defect in Point of Form (when the Rules and Forms of the House cou'd not only not be known to the Petitioners but which if known, tho' not strictly and literally adher'd

to) ought to be urged and insisted upon in a Matter of Such Importance and Concernment, and further thinking it much better and more parliamentary that Parliament should receive the Petitions tendered, when if there was any indecent or unbecoming Expressions or Assertion therein it might be a proper Subject for a Resolution after Debate thereon, I most heartily wished the Ministry wou'd have countenanced and divided upon its Admission, and the rather as Mr. Pitt was strong in Favour of its Reception, the Petitioners expressing therein their unbounded Affection for their Mother Country and that their Subordination to the Parliament was universally acknowledged which he wish'd should remain to Posterity in the Journals of the House. . . .

B. Charles Garth to Ringgold, Murdoch, and Tilghman, March 5, 1766

[*Maryland Historical Magazine*, 6 (1911), 286-305. In the original this passage is broken into three paragraphs only.]

The 3d of Febry we went into a Debate to consider of Resolutions proper to be agreed upon, after the Information and Intelligence that had been communicated; when Mr Secretary Conway had proposed a Resolution Vizt "That the King's Majesty by and with the Consent of the Lords Spiritual and Temporal and Commons in Parliament assembled had, hath, and of Right ought to have full Power and Authority to make Laws and Statutes of sufficient Force and Validity to bind the People in America, Subjects of Great Britain, in all Cases whatsoever." Mr Conway and the Chancellor of the Exchequer said they were induced to offer the Proposition in this extensive Manner, not only as necessary to meet the Resolutions and Language of several of the Colonies, but because upon the fullest Enquiry into the Constitution of Great Britain, they were convinced that in Point of Law, the King, Lords and Commons were undoubtedly possessed of that Power, tho' in Point of

Policy, Justice or Equity, it was a Power that they ought to exercise but in the most extraordinary Cases only.

Colonel Barrie mov'd to have the Words "in all Cases whatsoever" left out, and he shou'd have no objection to the Resolution as it wou'd then stand, he was seconded by Mr Pitt. The Arguments in Support of this Motion imported among the Variety of Suggestions offer'd, that the Subjects in the Colonies, when first they emigrated from hence, went with License, carrying with them every Right the Crown could grant, and every Right of British Subjects, carrying with them the Common Law of the Land; that by the Common Law and Spirit of this Constitution no Man could be taxed without being represented, that the People of America could not with the smallest Propriety be said to be represented in the Parliament of Great Britain, and it was Representation that alone gave the Right and Power to the Commons of imposing Taxes, this was the Foundation of all Mr Locke's Arguments and Reasoning, greater Authority could not be produced: That the Principles of Taxation as distinguished from Legislation were as distinct Principles and Powers as any two Propositions under the Sun, had been considered uniformly such by our Ancestors thro' many Ages; the Counties Palatine of Chester & Durham always tax'd themselves by Writs of Requisition, and on that Account when the Grant of a Charter was made out erecting Lancaster into a County Palatine there was therein an express Reservation of the Power of Parliament to impose Taxes upon the People within that County, which wou'd have been unnecessary, if the Power of Parliament was such as contended for, but which became proper, the separate Claim of taxing within the respective Counties Palatine of Chester and Durham under their respective Charters being at that Time known, and the Inconveniences felt from the Exercise of that Power by themselves, without the Interposition of Parliament, precluded by those Charters; That the Clergy taxed themselves, and yet were no Part of the Legislature, for tho' the Abbots, Archbishops and others sat in Parliament, yet not upon the Ground of Representation, and therefore the Body of the Clergy would not suffer them to tax them, but separately and by themselves of their own free Gift granted to the Crown the Subsidies they did from Time to Time, the Lords nor Commons ever altering or attempting to vary the Taxes granted by the Clergy, a strong Authority to prove not only that Legislation is one Thing and Taxation another, but in what the true Constitution of this Country, as handed down to us by our Ancestors, consisted: The Commons granted, it was the Grant of the Commons that was the Substratum upon which King, Lords and Commons agree to give the Force of a Law, and make it an Act of Legislation to empower and enforce legal Obedience to the Grant.

Further all Bills that have pass'd both Houses remain in the Upper House for the King's Fiat, except Bills of Subsidy and Taxation, which when pass'd by the Lords are again sent down to the Commons, whose Speaker presents it to the Sovereign as the free Gift of the Commons, and it is to them only the King applies both when he asks and when he thanks for a Supply: That Powers have by express Compact been granted to and accepted by the Colonists and repeatedly recognized by Parliament, it was plain we intended them to be free as ourselves, having given them a Constitution as nearly resembling our own as we can; They have the Power given them of raising and of granting their Money, a Power which constitutes the very Essence of Parliament, if this Power is taken from them, the very Existence the very Essence of Assemblies is destroy'd. Grievances then can never be redress'd, and Grievances they have had and will in all Probability have again, which ought always to take Place of Grants of Money, otherwise very material Grievances among those distant Subjects may sometimes (at least for a long Time) remain without Redress. Upon this Principle the Stamp Act cou'd not but be deemed a Grievance, and circumstanc'd as they are calls loudly for Redress, but at the same Time that you redress the Grievance, the Violence committed calls equally for the Hand of Resentment, and it greatly imported the Dignity of Parliament to see that the principal Offenders were brought to condign Punishment; The Claim of Contribution from the Colonies none can deny to be just, but the Mode of procuring it may be quite the reverse, Great Britain and the Colonies in the Article of Taxes may have very opposite Interests, and there may be a Probability of Alleviation to the Burthens of one at the Expense of Oppression to the other: Besides that the Circumstances and Abilities of the Colonies cannot be so justly and truly known to the Commons of England as to their own immediate Representatives in their several and Respective Assemblies; there they enjoy the Exercise of that fundamental Right, of having some one in the Case of Tallages to speak for them and to represent their Condition and Abilities, in Parliament it is an almost impracticable and impossible thing, and by that Means they lose a very important Privilege belonging to the Represented. The supreme Power wheresoever lodged is undoubtedly comptroulable, for it must and it will controul itself by the Powers of Reason, always should act upon the Principles of Humanity and Justice; Circumstanc'd then as the Colonists are in Point of Distance, Situation, Abilities and Rights, the greatest Caution cannot be too great in the Exercise of this great Supreme Power, as it is to affect the Subject there: It was Lenity, Humanity and Magnanimity that did more to preserve to Rome the Roman Colonies secure and dependent than all the Legions she ever was Mistress of or cou'd at any Time command; That shou'd it be the Sense of the House after all, that Parliament is in Possession of this *Summum Jus,* it will do well to remember, the *summa Injuria* is its well known Offspring.

On the other Hand, the Attorney General York, the Chancellor of the Exchequer, all the Gentlemen of the long Robe, and others express'd themselves in favour of the Proposition, as offered by Mr Conway, after approving the Propriety of confining the Debate to the single Point of Power and the Right in the Parliament, without intermingling therewith any thing touching the Expediency of a Repeal of the Law so greatly complained of, which wou'd become a fit and proper Subject for the Consideration of another Day, they entered fully and at large into the great Question; The Heads of the most material Arguments I think were to the Effect following; That the Establishment of the Colonies was originally by License from the Crown, who by Charter gave them the *Jura regalia* and Powers of Government as necessary for their Protection, Defence, and Support, of Civil Government among them, being to be so far distant from the great executive Power of the Realm, which Powers of Government so given by the Crown were of a Nature with those granted to the East India Company and to great Cities and Corporations in England, each having a Power of raising Money for their Support, but neither of which cou'd by any Grant the King cou'd make, be exempt from the supreme Authority of King, Lords & Commons.

That the Crown was but a Part of the supreme Power of the Realm, and therefore cou'd give no more, indeed in some Instances seem'd to have granted all that he had to grant, but by no Construction cou'd be deem'd to have granted that which he had no Power to grant, that which belonged to the supreme legislative Power, which in all Ages did extend wheresoever the Sovereignty of the Crown did extend; That the Colonists carried with them all the Subjection and Allegiance they owed when resident in Great Britain, that no Time nor Distance cou'd terminate that Subjection and Allegiance, which by the Law of the Land must descend to their own immediate Heirs, and to all their Posterity; whatever Compact was stipulated between the Crown and those his Subjects upon their Emigration no Condition whatever was made or wou'd have been suffer'd between them and the supreme Sovereign Power.

That the Parliament had Power to alter and change their Property, to enact Laws for Punishment of great Offences and in particular of High Treason, by which the Property might be divested, Inheritance taken away etc. without their immediate Consent, and yet not have a Power to impose a Tax upon their Property, seem'd an extraordinary Proposition; That after the Revolution, upon an Application to have the Judgment reversed which in 1684 had adjudged the Charter of Massachusetts Bay to be null and void upon a Writ of Quo Warranto of King James the 2nd. the Agent urged Illegality in the Manner of Proceedings, upon which that arbitary Judgment was grounded, and insisted that the Judgment shou'd be revers'd, and in Consequence the Charter restor'd in toto, but Pollexfen and Holt gave their Opinions that if the Charters were restor'd because of the Illegality of the Proceedings, yet they must expect to have that Charter in due Manner repeal'd, because the Crown had not, nor cou'd have the Power to grant, as in that Charter had been granted, and accordingly it was not sent back in its first Extent but alter'd in very material Points, a Proof and Authority of the Sense and Opinion of the Kingdom upon the Revolution touching the Force and Efficiency of the Charters to the Colonies as controulable by an Authority in Great Britain short of the Supremacy of the Realm: That in the Year 1713 a Bill was brought into Parliament for the Purpose of raising a Revenue within the Province of New York, in Consequence of a Refusal there to levy for the Support of his Majesty's Government, a Bill advis'd and prepar'd by Sir Edward Northey and Lord Raymond, who were well known the ablest Lawyers and greatest Sticklers and Defenders of the Liberty and Property of the Subject wheresoever inhabiting, that this Kingdom cou'd at any Period boast of, That in 1716 a Bill was brought in by the great Secretary Stanhope for resuming Powers which had been granted in the Colony Charters: That in 1717 a Bill was brought in to take away the Charters which had been granted to the several Colonies, the Power of Parliament in any of those Cases was never questioned, that if the Parliament had the Power to take away those Charters, by Virtue of which the Colonists claim the Right and Power of imposing and levying Taxes, it cou'd not but be possessed of the Power of Taxation; Mr Dummer, than whom,

it was said, no Man better understood the Nature and Extent of the Colony Constitutions, in the able Defence he made in Behalf of the Colonies, never so much as suggested a Hint tending to question the Power of Parliament, he desir'd their Charters might be considered in the same Manner with all other Charters of Incorporation, which in Times when civil Liberty flourished, were never taken away or forfeited unless the Incorporated had done something to deserve & incur a Forfeiture.

That as to Representation, either actual or virtual, it was by no Means the sole and antient Basis of the Supreme Power and Authority of Parliament. The Clergy, it was true tax'd themselves for a considerable Length of Time, not because they were not represented in Parliament, Gentlemen conversant in the true and antient History of this Country cannot be ignorant how great the Power of the Church was in this Kingdom, amongst other Exertions of that Power at the Instance of the Clergy, the Pope issued his Mandate, exempting their Lands from being tax'd as appropriated to the Maintenance of Holy Church, but not having exempted their Chattels in subsequent Times Parliament was about to exercise the Power of Taxation thereon, which occasioned a Stipulation between the Crown and the Pope, to whom the Clergy again complained, that the Bull of Exemption shou'd be repeal'd, and the Clergy should yield Contribution to Government; provided they shou'd grant alone and for themselves, this was the Foundation of the Clergy's subsidizing their Lands and Property separate and apart, an undoubted Infraction upon the Constitution and which in after and more enlighten'd Days was restor'd to its antient pristine Power; That the supreme Power must be compleat and entire; in Legislation and Taxation coequal and coextending, and tho' by Equity from Regard to Circumstances and Situations Indulgence had been given either to come to Parliament or to raise Money in the Way of Taxation for the local Purposes of subordinate Districts and Governments, yet that Indulgence cou'd never abridge the Supremacy in any of its Powers and Authority; Upon this Principle the Parliament of Great Britain alone could and did, (Ireland having that Indulgence granted) absolve the People of Ireland from Duties due to the Crown, impos'd by Acts pass'd in their own Parliament; It was the Commons of England that directed that the Charge of the Army, kept up for the Defence and Security of that Kingdom, shou'd be provided for by the People of Ireland, leaving the Provision to be made by the Irish Parliament, which if not complied with, wou'd have been enforc'd by a Law of Great Britain, and was so understood and known at that Time in both Kingdoms: That in all the antient Subsidy Acts, the Form and Tenor thereof runs that the Subsidies laid and impos'd are to be paid by his Majesty's Subjects within the Realm and in all the King's Dominions, particular Parts and Places were sometimes expressly excepted, as Wales constantly before the Statute of H. 8. Ireland, the Counties Palatine upon whom the Charge of defending the Northern Frontiers fell by their Charters, Calais, Guienne, Gascony, and particular Corporations upon particular Accounts, which Exceptions, it was said, prove that if they had not been particularly excepted, altho' not represented, they must have been comprised under the Act and within the View thereof; This the Parliament in those Times knew, and that too as Calais, before it had Representatives, had in several Subsidy Acts not been excepted, but had been assessed and paid its Assessment: The Counties Palatine notwithstanding their Power of raising Levies within themselves, unless expressly excepted in the Acts of Parliament which was usually done in Ordinary Cases, were subject and liable to the Taxes and Impositions of Parliament, when upon particular Occasions judged necessary.

That the Strength of the Empire in America depends upon an entire and exact Obedience to the Supreme Authority in Great Britain, which if infring'd in any Instance, no Man cou'd foresee the Confusion that must inevitably follow, Cases might and undoubtedly wou'd happen to puzzle the ablest Lawyers of the Time to distinguish the Difference between Duties and Taxation, between the Right of laying one and the other; That this was settled and established to be one entire Power lodged in the Commons of England in the great Conference in William the 3d's Time, between the House of Lords and Commons, when the Lords were inclin'd to have establish'd a Difference between Duties and Impositions upon Merchandize, and the Grant of Taxes and Subsidies, with a View to confine the Power of the Commons to the latter only, the Commons said it was the Usage of Parliament the Uniformity of all Ages which limits the Power of the Crown and the Power of both Houses of Parliament; under this Sanction they claim'd the Power entire and in its full Extent. That this Power which the People of America seem'd to question at this Time it was for the Happiness and Welfare of the whole, as well as for the Honour and Dignity of Parliament, to support with Firmness and Resolution; and it was the more extraordinary to be questioned by the Americans, as so late as the year 1755 a general and universal Complaint of the People of one Province, that of Pennsylvania, against their Assembly for a Breach of Trust in the Omission of their Duty to make the necessary Provisions for the Defence, Protection and Support of that Colony was transmitted, a Complaint the more considerable not so much from the Numbers, or the Opulence of the Complaints, as from the intrinsic Weight of the Complaint: Circumstances happening prevented the Interposition of Parliament, which if not occurr'd in good Time, Parliament undoubtedly would have interfer'd.

It was said also that in Consequence of a Provincial Difference the Province of Maryland contributed little or nothing to the general Expence of the American War, the Burthen by that Means falling heavier upon the other Colonies, it was in Idea with all the Colonies to send home Representations against Maryland, for the Interposition of Parliament; With what Propriety could those Representations have been transmitted, had not the Americans at that Time thought differently of the Power which they now question? It was therefore for the sake of the Subject there the Sovereignty should not be given up in any one Point. The Parliament would in that Case never have it in its Power to give Redress in any Application or Complaint hereafter to be preferr'd by any Subject or Subjects in America. That all Government is founded in Trust, wherever the Trust is placed, that Trust is absolute and entire, the Kingdom and Colonies compose one great Mass of political Strength, and tho' the jealous Language of Liberty cou'd not but approve itself to every Lover of Liberty and Admirer of this Constitution, yet when that Jealousy was carried so far as to tell the Sovereign Power they will not trust you, unless you recede from your Power, it becomes too alarming and calls for the Exertion of Spirit & of Wisdom. Ask France what Occasion She wou'd wish for yr Destruction, she will answer, let Divisions be kept up and fomented between you and your Colonies, that a Departure from your Sovereign Power will be that Diminution and Weakening of yr Authority, she wou'd be most pleased to see as the surest Means to her of compassing the great Object of her Ambition; this Sovereignty then is so necessary to be compleat and entire for the Sake of Great Britain and America equally, so essential for the Benefit and Happiness of the whole, that if once broke into, the Dependency of the Colonies once given

Way to, your Power and Authority, as a great respected Kingdom in Europe, is blasted, no Friend will trust you, no Enemy will fear you.

The Debate ended about 4 in the Morning, when the Question was put in Consequence of Colo. Barrie's Motion, "that the Words in all Cases whatsoever stand Part of the Resolution"; I believe from the Sound there were not more than ten dissenting Voices; Learned as the Arguments were, that were offered in Support of the Antiquity of this Power in Parliament over all Parts of the King's Dominions as well Parcell of the Realm as *infra Dominium Regis* only, Yet I am free to confess I was not so sufficiently convinced as to have any other than a dissenting Voice upon that Occasion: The Arguments alledged, many of them collected from Times of Antiquity, it was then scarce known, much less defin'd what the Nature and Spirit of this Constitution was, and as to those, urged from the Propositions made at and after the Time of the Revolution touching the Charters, tho' under the Sanction of great Names yet nothing being carried into Execution, by wch the Acquiescence of the Colonies cou'd be collected seem'd to my Mind not sufficiently cogent in a Case of this Nature, a Dispute of Right upon the Principles of Reason. But indeed the Statutes of Chester and Durham, tho' offer'd as a Proof of the Power of Parliament in taxing those who had been unrepresented, are in my Mind the strongest Parliamentary Declaration of the Illegality and Injustice of that Power. The Statutes of H. 8. touching Wales and more particularly the 110th Ordinance in the 34th and 35th H. 8. Ca. 26 seems clear and plain that the Parliament in those Kingly and Prerogative Times deem'd a Representation the *sine qua non* of a Subsidy and Taxation to be impos'd by Parliamt; when for almost three Centuries Laws had been enacted from Time to Time in the Parliamt of England touching the Inhabitants of that Principality, but in no one Subsidy Act was Wales ever comprehended unless by way of Exception untill the Statutes of H. 8. had been enacted, and yet I believe it wou'd be difficult to find any Terms so expressive of the Supremacy of England over Wales, as made Use of in the Preamble to the 27th H. 8. Ca. 26.

Crompton, Ld Cooke, and other great Lawyers have in their Time denied the Power of Parliament to lay Taxes upon the People of Ireland, for Want of Representation therein, and in almost the same Breath have asserted the Legislative Authority of Parliamt to bind the Subjects and Inhabitants of that Island: This was another Reason why I was against the Extent of this Proposition, as being carried farther than in the Case of Ireland (as will appear by looking into the Act of Geo. 1st for better securing the Dependency of Ireland) for which there is not a Ground of Reason or in Justice. I had another Difficulty Vizt to bring myself to say I am in Possession of a Constitu-tion which in Point of Justice and Equity I ought not to exercise; it seem'd to my poor Understanding no Honour to the Mother Country to pride itself upon a Power neither founded in Justice or Equity: And as to the Use or Benefit she will derive from this Assertion, Time alone can elucidate, in ordinary Cases with neither Policy Justice or Equity to support such an Exertion, upon extraordinary Occurrences if any such should offer to demand an extraordinary Interposition of the Supreme Power, it wou'd not upon such Exigencies, I believe, be for searching into Precedents.

A fuller House I don't recollect to have seen, and it is to the Honour of Parliament I must add, that I believe there never was a Debate so temperate, serious, solemn, and Parliamentary, without the least Appearance of Party or Faction, (disunited and divided as we are) intermingling in the Arguments upon the Question on one Side or other.

60. An English Merchant Predicts Repeal

[Henry Cruger, Jr., to Aaron Lopez, Bristol, March 1, 1766, Massachusetts Historical Society, *Collections*, 7th ser., 9 (1914), 145-46.]

The Stamp Act is not *yet* repeal'd, but it is as good as done. a Motion was made in the House of Commons for a Bill to be brought in for a Repeal and was carried by 275 against 167; the latter were only for a Modification of the Act. the Debates pro and con have been very warm and serious. . . . there is little doubt but the affairs will be finish'd in a few days and the Act *repealed;* You'll be informed that the Parliament have settled their *Right* of taxing you. when that was done they proceeded to the *Expediency* of repealing the Act, which never wou'd have come to pass had it not been for the Merchants and Manufacturers of *England*. Trade here was totally stagnated, not one American Merchant [i.e., English merchant trading to America] gave out a *single order* for Goods, on purpose to compel all Manufacturers to engage with us in petitioning Parliament for a Repeal of the Stamp Act, by which thousands were out of employ, and in a starving condition. You, Dear Sir, shared in the common calamity I hope and persuade myself you will not murmur at this Momentary Disapointment when so much Good will come out of it. I hugg myself the Parliament will never trouble America again. . . . I congratulate you on our Success, and with redoubled Joy—as the contrary was at one time much dreaded.

61.   The Act Repealing the Stamp Act, March 18, 1766

[Pickering, ed., *Statutes at Large*, XXVII, 19. The act is designated as 6 George III, c. 11.]

WHEREAS *an act was passed in the last session of parliament, intituled,* An act for granting and applying certain stamp duties, and other duties, in the *British* colonies and plantations in *America,* towards further defraying the expences of defending, protecting, and securing the same; and for amending such parts of the several acts of parliament relating to the trade and revenues of the said colonies and plantations, as direct the manner of determining and recovering the penalties and forfeitures therein mentioned: *and whereas the continuance of the said act would be attended with many inconveniencies, and may be productive of consequences greatly* detrimental to the commercial interests of these kingdoms; may it therefore please your most excellent Majesty, that it may be enacted; and be it enacted by the King's most excellent Majesty, by and with the advice and consent of the lords spiritual and temporal, and commons, in this present parliament assembled, and by the authority of the same, that from and after the first day of *May,* one thousand seven hundred and sixty six, the above-mentioned act, and the several matters and things therein contained, shall be, and is and are hereby repealed and made void to all intents and purposes whatsoever.

62.   The Declaratory Act, March 18, 1766

[Pickering, ed., *Statutes at Large*, XXVII, 19-20. The act is designated as 6 George III, c. 12.]

An act for the better securing the dependency of his Majesty's dominions in America *upon the crown and parliament of* Great Britain.

WHEREAS *several of the houses of representatives in his Majesty's colonies and plantations in* America, *have of late, against law, claimed to themselves, or to the general assemblies of the same, the sole and exclusive right of imposing duties and taxes upon his Majesty's subjects in the said colonies and plantations; and have, in pursuance of such claim, passed certain votes, resolutions, and orders, derogatory to the legislative authority of parliament, and inconsistent with the dependency of the said colonies and plantations upon the crown of* Great Britain: may it therefore please your most excellent Majesty, that it may be declared; and be it declared by the King's most excellent majesty, by and with the advice and consent of the lords spiritual and temporal, and commons, in this present parliament assembled, and by the authority of the same, That the said colonies and plantations in *America* have been, are, and of right ought to be, subordinate unto, and dependent upon the imperial crown and parliament of *Great Britain;* and that the King's majesty, by and with the advice and consent of the lords spiritual and temporal, and commons of *Great Britain,* in parliament assembled, had, hath, and of right ought to have, full power and authority to make laws and statutes of sufficient force and validity to bind the colonies and people of *America,* subjects of the crown of *Great Britain,* in all cases whatsoever.

II. And be it further declared and enacted by the authority aforesaid, That all resolutions, votes, orders, and proceedings, in any of the said colonies or plantations, whereby the power and authority of the parliament of *Great Britain,* to make laws and statutes as aforesaid, is denied, or drawn into question, are, and are hereby declared to be, utterly null and void to all intents and purposes whatsoever.

Reactions to Repeal

63.   An English Ballad

[*The* World *turned upside down, or the* Old Woman *taught Wisdom,* March 11, 1766, *London Chronicle,* 19 (1766), 236.]

GOODY Bull and her Daughter together fell out,
Both squabbled and wrangled, and made a damn'd rout;
But the cause of their quarrel remains to be told;
Then lend both your ears, and the tale I'll unfold.
Derry down, &c.

The old Lady, it seems, took a freak in her head,
That her Daughter, grown woman, might earn her own bread:
Self-applauding her scheme, she was ready to dance,
But we're often too sanguine in what we advance.
Derry down, &c.

For mark the event: Thus by Fortune we're crost,
Nor should any one reckon without their good host;
The Daughter was sulky, and wou'dn't come to,
And pray what in this case could the Old Woman do?
Derry down, &c.

In vain did the Matron hold forth in the cause,
That the young one was able; her duty, the laws,
Ingratitude vile, disobedience far worse;
But she might e'en as well have sung psalms to a horse.
Derry down, &c.

Young, froward, and sullen, and vain of her beauty,
She tartly reply'd, that she well knew her duty,
That other folks children were kept by their friends,
And that some folks lov'd people but for their own ends.
Derry down, &c.

She sobbed and blubber'd, she bluster'd and swore,
If her Mother persisted, she'd turn common whore,
The Old Woman thus threaten'd fell down in a fit,
And who in the nick should hop in but Will. P-tt.
Derry down, &c.

Zounds! Neighbour, quoth he, what the Devil's the matter;
A man cannot rest in his house for your clatter:
Alas! cries the Daughter, here's dainty fine work,
The Old Woman's grown harder than Jew or than Turk.
Derry down, &c.

She be d—nd, cries the Farmer, and to her he goes,
First roars in her ears, and then tweaks her old nose,
Holla, Goody, what ails you? Wake woman, I say,
I am come to make peace in this desperate fray.
Derry down, &c.

Adsooks, ope thine eyes, what a pother is here,
You've no right to compel her, you have not I swear:
Be rul'd by your friends, kneel down and ask pardon;
You'd be sorry, I'm sure, should she walk Covent Garden.

Derry down, &c.

Alas! cries the Old Woman, and must I comply!
But I'd rather submit than the Hussy should die;
Pooh, prithee be quiet, be friends, and agree,
You must surely be right, if you're *guided by me.*

Derry down, &c.

Unwillingly aukward, the Mother knelt down,
While the absolute Farmer went on with a frown,
Come, kiss the poor child, then, come kiss and be friends,
There, kiss your poor Daughter, and make her amends.

Derry down, &c.

No thanks to you Mother; the Daughter replied;
But thanks to my Friend here, I've humbled your pride:
Then pray leave off this nonsense, 'tis all a meer farce,
As I've carried my point, you may now kiss my ——.

Derry down, &c.

64. The London Merchants Warn the Colonists to Behave

[Letter of the London merchants to the American merchants, Feb. 28, 1766, *Virginia Gazette* (Purdie and Dixon), May 16, 1766.]

GENTLEMEN,

After much anxiety, we have at length the pleasure to acquaint you that a bill is now in the House of Commons for repealing the Stamp Act; it has been read the second time. We also look forward to some beneficial regulations and extensions of the trade of America, which we hope may be obtained in the course of this session of Parliament, during which the most serious attention and application shall take place on our part to every point which may tend to the general good.

Permit us now, Gentlemen, to lay before you our sentiments on the present state of affairs, to submit them to your good judgment; and to request that, so far as they agree with it, you will be pleased to inculcate the propriety of the conduct we recommend.

It has been a constant argument against the repeal that in case it should take place the Parliamentary vote of right will be waste paper, and that the colonies will

understand very well that what is pretended to be adopted on mere commercial principles of expedience is really yielded through fear, and amounts to a tacit, but effectual surrender, of its right, or at least a tacit compact that it will never use it.

In this line of argument every debate, and every question from opposition, has run: How material, how necessary, therefore, is it that the event should not support, or even seem to support those arguments.

The event will justify those arguments in the strongest manner if the colonies should triumph on the repeal, and affect to seize the yielding of Parliament as a point gained over Parliamentary authority. The opposition (from whom the colonies have suffered so much) would then throw in the teeth of our friends, *See your work, it is as we said: it is but too well proved what use the colonies make of your weak and timid measures.* On the contrary, if duty, submission, and gratitude, be the returns made by the colonies, then our friends may exult. They may say, *We are in the right; is it not as we said? See the colonies regained to this country by our moderation, regained with their loyalty, their affections, and their trade.*

It is needless to say how extremely preferable the latter supposition is to the first, how much more desirable for this country, and for the colonies.

You must be sensible what friends the colonies have had in the present Ministry, and are doubtless informed what pains they have taken to serve them. It is justice likewise to them to inform you that they have had great difficulties to encounter in the cause, the principal of which was unhappily thrown in by the colonies themselves, we mean the intemperate proceedings of various ranks of people on your side the water; and the difficulties of the repeal would have been much less, if they had not by their violence, in word and action, awakened the honour of Parliament, and thereby involved every friend of the repeal in the imputation of betraying the dignity of Parliament. This is so true that the act could not certainly have been repealed, had not mens minds been in some measure satisfied with the declaration of right. If therefore you would make the proper returns to your country, if you have a mind to do credit to your friends, and strengthen the hands of your advocates, hasten, we beseech you, to express filial duty and gratitude to your parent country. Then will those who have been (and while they have the power we doubt not will be) your friends, plume themselves on the restoration of peace to the colonies, union, trade, and reciprocal advantages to them and to us: But if violent measures are continued, and triumphs on the point gained; if it is talked of as a victory; if it is said the Parliament have yielded up the right; then indeed your enemies here will have a complete triumph; your friends must certainly lose all power to serve you; your taskmasters probably be restored; and such a train of ill consequences follow as are easier for you to imagine than for us to describe; at least, such measures on your side will greatly tend to produce these effects. We have no doubt that you will adopt the contrary conduct, and inculcate it to the utmost of your influence, to which we sincerely wish the utmost extensive regard may be paid; and that uninterrupted mutual affection may continue between Great Britain and her colonies, to the latest ages. We are, with unfeigned regard,

Gentlemen, your affectionate humble servants.

(The above letter was signed by 30 principal merchants, residing in London)

65.   An American Reaction

[George Mason to the Committee of London Merchants, June 6, 1766, Kate Mason Rowland, *The Life of George Mason, 1725-1792* (New York, 1892), I, 381-89.]

Virginia, Potomack River
June 6th, 1766

GENTLEMEN:

There is a letter of yours dated the 20th of February last, lately printed in the public papers here, which, though addressed to a particular set of men, seems intended for the colonies in general; and, being upon a very interesting subject, I shall, without further preface or apology, exercise the right of a freeman in making such remarks upon it as I think proper.

The epithets of parent and child have been so long applied to Great Britain and her colonies, that individuals have adopted them, and we rarely see anything from your side of the water free from the authoritative style of a master to a schoolboy:

"We have with infinite difficulty and fatigue got you excused this one time; pray be a good boy for the future, do what your papa and mama bid you, and hasten to return them your most grateful acknowledgements for condescending to let you keep what is your own; and then all your acquaintance will love you, and praise you, and give you pretty things; and if you should at any time hereafter happen to transgress, your friends will all beg for you, and be security for your good behaviour; but if you are a naughty boy, and turn obstinate, and don't mind what your papa and mama say to you, but presume to think their commands (let them be what they will) unjust or unreasonable, or even seem to ascribe their present indulgence to any other motive than excess of moderation and tenderness, and pretend to judge for yourselves, when you are not arrived at the years of discretion, or capable of distinguishing between good and evil; then everybody will hate you, and say you are a graceless and undutiful child; your parents and masters will be obliged to whip you severely, and your friends will be ashamed to say anything in your excuse: nay, they will be blamed for your faults. See your work—see what you have brought the child to. If he had been well scourged at first for opposing our absolute will and pleasure, and daring to think he had any such thing as property of his own, he would not have had the impudence to repeat the crime."

"My dear child, we have laid the alternative fairly before you, you can't hesitate in the choice, and we doubt not you will observe such a conduct as your friends recommend."

Is not this a little ridiculous, when applied to three millions of as loyal and useful subjects as any in the British dominions, who have been only contending for their birth-right, and have now only gained, or rather kept, what could not, with common justice, or even policy, be denied them? But setting aside the manner, let me seriously consider the substance and subject of your letter.

Can the honor of parliament be maintained by persisting in a measure evidently wrong? Is it any reflection upon the honor of parliament to show itself wiser this year than the last, to have profited by experience, and to correct the errors which time and indubitable evidence have pointed out?

If the Declaratory Act, or Vote of Right, has asserted any unjust, oppressive, or unconstitutional principles, to become "waste paper" would be the most innocent use that could be made of it; by the copies we have seen here, the legislative authority of Great Britain is fully and positively asserted in all cases whatsoever. But a just and necessary distinction between legislation and taxation hath been made by the greatest and wisest men in the nation; so that if the right to the latter had been disclaimed, it would not have impeached or weakened the vote of right; on the contrary, it would have strengthened it, for nothing (except hanging the author of the Stamp Act) would have contributed more to restore that confidence which a weak or corrupt ministry had so greatly impaired.

We do not deny the supreme authority of Great Britain over her colonies; but it is a power which a wise legislature will exercise with extreme tenderness and caution, and carefully avoid the least imputation or suspicion of partiality. Would to God that this always had been, that it always may be the case! To make an odious distinction between us and our fellow-subjects residing in Great Britain, by depriving us of the ancient trial, by a jury of our equals, and substituting in its place an arbitrary civil-law court—to put it in the power of every sycophant and informer ("the most mischievous, wicked, abandoned and profligate race," says an eminent writer upon British politics, "that ever God permitted to plague mankind") to drag a freeman a thousand miles from his own country (whereby he may be deprived of the benefit of evidence) to defend his property before a judge, who, from the nature of his office, is a creature of the ministry, liable to be displaced at their pleasure, whose interest it is to encourage informers, as his income may in a great measure depend upon his condemnations, and to give such a judge a power of excluding the most innocent man, thus treated, from any remedy (even the recovery of his costs) by only certifying that *in his opinion* there was a *probable* cause of complaint; and thus to make the property of the subject, in a matter which may reduce him from opulence to indigence, depend upon a word before unknown in the language and style of laws! Are these among the instances that call for our expression of "filial gratitude to our parent-country"? These things did not altogether depend upon the stamp act, and therefore are not repealed with it.

Can the foundations of the state be sapped and the body of the people remain unaffected? Are the inhabitants of Great Britain absolutely certain that, in the ministry or parliament of a future day, such incroachments will not be urged as precedents against themselves? Is the indulgence of Great Britain manifested by prohibiting her colonies from exporting to foreign countries such commodities as she does not want, and from importing such as she does not produce or manufacture, and therefore cannot furnish but upon extravagant terms? One of your own writers (I think it is Bishop Burnet) relates a remarkable piece of tyranny of the priesthood in Italy: "They make it an article of religion," says he, "for the people to mix water with their wine in the press, by which it is soured; so that the laity cannot drink a drop of good wine, unless they buy it from the convents, at whatever price the clergy think fit to set upon it." I forbear to make the application.

Let our fellow-subjects in Great Britain reflect that we are descended from the same stock with themselves, nurtured in the same principles of freedom; which we have both sucked in with our mother's milk; that in crossing the Atlantic Ocean, we have only changed our climate, not our minds, our natures and dispositions remain unaltered; that we are still the same people with them in every respect; only not yet debauched by wealth, luxury, venality and corruption; and then they will be able to judge how the late regulations have been relished in America.

You need not, gentlemen, be afraid of our "breaking out into intemperate strains of triumph and exaltation"; there is yet no cause that our joy should exceed the bounds of moderation.

If we are ever so unfortunate [as] to be made slaves, which God avert! what matter is it to us whether our chains are forged in London or at Constantinople? Whether the oppression comes from a British parliament or a Turkish divan?

You tell us that "our task-masters will probably be restored." Do you mean the stamp officers, or the stamp ministry? If the first, the treatment they have already found here will hardly make them fond of returning. If the latter, we despise them too much to fear them. They have sufficiently exposed their own ignorance, malice and impotence. The cloven foot has been too plainly seen to be again concealed; they have rendered themselves as obnoxious to Great Britain as to America.

If the late ministerial party could have influenced the legislature to have made so cruel and dangerous an experiment as attempting to enforce the stamp-act by military power, would the nation have engaged heartily in such an execrable cause? Would there have been no difficulty in raising and transporting a body of troops sufficient to occupy a country of more than two thousand miles in extent? Would they have had no dangers to encounter in the woods and wilds of America? Three millions of people driven to desperation are not an object of contempt. America, however weak in herself, adds greatly to the strength of Great Britain; which would be diminished in proportion by her loss; with prudent management she might become an impenetrable bulwark to the British Nation, and almost enable it to stand before the stroke of time.

Say there was not a possibility of failing in the project, what then would have been the consequence? Could you have destroyed us without ruining yourselves? The trade of Great Britain is carried on and supported principally by credit. If the American merchant [i.e., London merchants trading to America] has an hundred thousand pounds due to him in the colonies, he must owe near as much to his woolen-draper, his linen-draper, his grocer, &c., and these again are indebted to the manufacturer, and so on; there is no determinate end to this commercial chain; break but one link of it and the whole is destroyed. Make a bankrupt of the merchant by stopping his remittances from America, and you strike at the credit of every man who has connections with him; there is no knowing where the contagion would stop. You would overturn one another like a set of ninepins. The value of your lands and produce would fall, your manufacturers would starve for want of employment, your funds might fail, your public credit sink, and let but the bubble once burst, where is the man who could undertake to blow it up again?

These evils are for the present removed. Praised be Almighty God! Blessed be our most gracious sovereign! Thanks to the present mild and prudent temper of parliament. Thanks to the wise and honest conduct of the present administration. Thanks to the unwearied diligence of our friends, the British merchants and manufacturers; thanks to that happy circumstance of their private interest being so interwoven with ours that they could not be separated. Thanks to the spirited and disinterested conduct of our own merchants in the northern colonies, who deserve to have their names handed down with reverence and gratitude to posterity. Thanks to the unanimity of the colonies themselves. And many thanks to our generous and able benefactor, Mr. Pitt, who has always stood forth a champion in the cause of liberty and his country. No thanks to Mr. Grenville and his party, who, without his genius or abilities, has dared to act the part that Pericles did, when he engaged his country in the Peloponnesian War, which, after a long and dreadful scene of blood, ended in the ruin of all Greece, and fitted it for the Macedonian yoke.

Some bungler in politics will soon, perhaps, be framing schemes for restraining our manufactures—vain attempt. Our land is cheap and fresh; we have more of it than we are able to employ; while we can live in ease and plenty upon our farms, tillage and not arts will engage our attention. If, by opening the channels of trade, you afford us a ready market for the produce of our lands, and an opportunity of purchasing cheap the conveniences of life, all our superfluous gain will sink into your pockets, in return for British manufactures. If the trade of this continent with the French and Spaniards, in their sugar islands, had not been restrained, Great Britain would soon have undersold them, with their own produce, in every market of the world. Until you lay us under a necessity of shifting for ourselves, you need not be afraid of the manufactures of America. The ancient poets, in their elegant manner of expression, have made a kind of being of necessity, and tell us that the gods themselves are obliged to yield to her.

It is by invitations and indulgence, not by compulsion, that the market for British manufactures is to be kept up and increased in America: without the first you will find the latter as ineffectual, as destructive of the end it aims at, as persecution in matters of religion; which serves not to extinguish but to confirm the heresy. There is a passion natural to the mind of man, especially a free man, which renders him impatient of restraint. Do you, does any sensible man think that three or four millions of people, not naturally defective in genius, or in courage, who have tasted the sweets of liberty, in a country that doubles its inhabitants every twenty years, in a country abounding in such variety of soil and climate, capable of producing, not only the necessaries, but the conveniences and delicacies of life, will long submit to oppression; if unhappily for yourselves oppression should be offered them? Such another experiment as the stamp-act would produce a general revolt in America.

Do you think that all your rival powers in Europe would sit still and see you crush your once flourishing and thriving colonies, unconcerned spectators of such a quarrel? Recollect what happened in the Low Countries a century or two ago. Call to mind the cause of the revolt. Call to mind, too, the part that England herself then acted. The same causes will generally produce the same effects; and it requires no great degree of penetration to foretell that what has happened may happen again.

—"If I could find example
Of thousands that by bare submission had
Preserv'd their freedom, I'd not do 't; but since
Nor brass, nor stone, nor parchment bears not one;
Let cowardice itself forswear it."

God forbid there should be occasion, and grant that the union, liberty and mutual happiness of Great Britain and her colonies may continue uninterrupted to the latest ages!

America has always acknowledged her dependence upon Great Britain. It is her interest, it is her inclination to depend upon Great Britain. We readily own that these colonies were first settled, not at the expence but under the protection of the English government; which protection it has continued to afford them; and we own, too, that protection and allegiance are reciprocal duties. If it is asked at whose expence they were settled, the answer is obvious—at the expence of the private adventurers, our ancestors; the fruit of whose toil and danger we now enjoy. We claim nothing but the liberty and privileges of Englishmen, in the same degree, as if we had still continued among our brethren in Great Britain; these rights have not been forfeited by any act of ours; we cannot be deprived of them, without our consent, but by violence and injustice; we have received them from our ancestors, and, with God's leave, we will transmit them, unimpaired, to our posterity. Can those who have hitherto acted as our friends, endeavour now, insidiously to draw from us concessions destructive to what we hold far dearer than life?

Our laws, our language, our principles of government, our intermarriages, and other connections, our constant intercourse, and above all our interest, are so many bands which hold us to Great Britain, not to be broken but by tyranny and oppression. Strange that among the late ministry there should not be found a man of common sense and common honesty, to improve and strengthen these natural ties by a mild and just government, instead of weakening and almost dissolving them by partiality and injustice! But I will not open the wounds which have been so lately bound up, and which still require a skilful and a gentle hand to heal them.

These are the sentiments of a man who spends most of his time in retirement, and has seldom meddled in public affairs, who enjoys a moderate but independent fortune, and, content with the blessings of a private station, equally disregards the smiles and frowns of the great; who, though not born within the verge of the British Isle, is an Englishman in his principles, a zealous assertor of the Act of Settlement, firmly attached to the present royal family upon the throne, unalienably affected to his Majesty's sacred person and government, in the defence of which he would shed the last drop of his blood; who looks upon Jacobitism as the most absurd infatuation, the wildest chimera that ever entered into the head of man; who adores the wisdom and happiness of the British Constitution; and if he had his election now to make, would prefer it to any that does or ever did exist. I am not singular in this my political creed; these are the general principles of his Majesty's subjects in America; they are the principles of more than nine-tenths of the people who have been so basely misrepresented to you, and whom you would lately have treated as rebels and outlaws, a people to whom you can never grant too much, because you can hardly give them anything which will not redound to the benefit of the giver.

If any person should think it worth his while to animadvert upon what I have written, I shall make no reply. I have neither ability nor inclination to turn author. If the maxims I have asserted and the reflections I have made are in themselves just, they will need no vindication; if they are erroneous, I shall esteem it a favour to have my errors pointed out, and will, in modest silence, kiss the rod that corrects me.

I am, Gentlemen, your most obedient servant,

A VIRGINIA PLANTER.